COLLECTING
OLD
PHOTOGRAPHS

COLLECTING OLD PHOTOGRAPHS

Margaret Haller

ARCO PUBLISHING COMPANY, INC.
NEW YORK

Published by Arco Publishing Company, Inc.
219 Park Avenue South, New York, N.Y. 10003

Library of Congress Cataloging in Publication Data

Haller, Margaret.
  Collecting old photographs.

  Bibliography: p. 259
  Includes index.
  1. Photographs—Collectors and collecting.
I. Title.

TR6.5.H34   779'.075   77-3328
ISBN 0-668-04244-3 (Library Edition)

Printed in the United States of America

Preface

There are plenty of books on photography, especially on its technology. There are also numerous books on the history of photography. Since almost all of these books are not only filled with useful facts but handsomely produced as well, and often lavishly illustrated, why, then, this particular book? In brief, it is designed to answer some of the questions about old photographs and old-fashioned methods of photography not generally covered, and to do so in such a concise manner that it may serve as a handy reference work. It is addressed to the photographer who is curious about the outmoded methods which have produced images we still admire, to the social historian who has recently been discovering that old photographs can be a fascinating source of new information, and, most of all, to the individual who may own a collection of old photographs —or is interested in collecting them—and would like more information on present-day values. Our handbook has been arranged so that the reader may, we hope, fairly readily find the information he needs about a wide range of subjects, all related to old photographs and their history.

Photography is a way of seeing. There are, of course, much more technical definitions, but for those of us interested in the result more than the technique, photography constitutes a form of picture-language, important because of the insights it can communicate. What has been called by Charles Swedlund the "candor of photography" is capable of revealing us to ourselves, of telling us something we perhaps never knew before, and of doing so either with "straight" photography or the altered print, the documentary or a fanciful allegorical composition made up from five, six, or even thirty negatives. This "trap of images," in Lartigue's phrase, is capable not only of freeing the photographer himself for new achievements in self-realization, but produces a kind of mirror, a mirror in which each man can, if he will, see himself in a new light.

Photography is also a means of conveying information. The information may be factual—that is, intended to convey the truth of some situation—or it may be slanted for a purpose, as indeed a news story may be slanted, or the advertisement for a product. One of its most exciting uses as a means of conveying information is in producing sight beyond that possible for the unassisted human eye, as in photographing the progression of the universe in outer space, or the minute world of the photo-micrograph.

Photography permits us to see ourselves as we once were, as well. Historic photographs, particularly those of the nineteenth century, reveal the customs, dress, idiosyncrasies, manners, housing, social organization, equipment, and tools of everyday use, and other, sometimes surprising social facets of days now gone by. There, before us, is the evidence of how our grandfathers, great-grand-fathers, and even, in some instances, their grandparents actually lived, back to around 1840. Photographic images are sometimes divided into those which serve a utilitarian purpose, the documentary, and the creative. However, the collector of old photographs who is interested in them as social documents prob-ably finds these distinctions arbitrary and meaningless.

Collectors of old photographs soon learn that they would be wise to define their collecting interests and confine them within certain boundaries, concen-trating perhaps on the photographs produced just within one historical period, or on those, possibly, made in one locality or by some one photographer or one studio, or those produced by just one process, possibly the daguerreotype, ambrotype, or tintype. The collector may find he wishes to limit himself to the portraits of children, or actresses, or the deceased, or to pictures of fire engines, Niagara Falls, or Florida before 1890. On the way to any such close definition of interests, however, there may be many decisions to be made and a great many facts to be learned. It is hoped that this handbook, not written for the tech-nician and therefore not overloaded with technical terms, will be of some assistance along the line.

There are three major parts to this handbook, on the images, the photog-raphers, and on the literature of photography, with a major concentration on photography during its first hundred years, to 1940.

Information about types of outmoded techniques and the old-fashioned terms for various processes is contained in a glossary which draws its definitions in good part from nineteenth-century manuals of instruction and old dictionaries of photography, but also from the standard histories of photography. Some of the definitions will be too short to satisfy all purposes, and it is hoped that, combined with the bibliography which has also been furnished, they may at least provide the necessary clues for further research.

The section on important names in photography is divided between the nineteenth and twentieth centuries. Photographers whose working lifetimes bracketed the turn of the century have for the most part been placed, admit-tedly somewhat abritrarily, in one century or the other according to their major achievements. Some of the members of the Photo-Secessionist group, for exam-ple, are placed in the nineteenth century though it might be argued that their work was at least as important an influence on later photographers as signifi-cantly related to work which had been done before them. Any categorizing by date obviously has its problems.

The literature of photography has been given a separate section. There are many "photographic treasures" still to be rounded up in old books—books by photographers, about photographers, about the various processes of photog-raphy, and books which are among the earliest to have been illustrated with photographs. This is an area of collecting interest for both the collector of old photographic material and the collector of books. Since books have been col-lected a good deal longer than have old photographs, it is an area in which value may possibly be more standardized than it is for photographic images.

In addition, there is a separate section on current values, which has been based on the published evidence of current auction prices or in a few cases prices set by dealers, for the most part in the American market. Since the prices for old photographic images have been rising rapidly, particularly so in the last few years, and most dramatically for the so-called classics—the most familiar images by well-known photographers—it is possible that many of the prices quoted here will seem, within a short time, fairly low. A word of caution on prices generally: It is difficult to evaluate an image, and thus the propriety of the price asked or paid for it, without actually seeing it. As with paintings, reproductions in catalogues or books rarely do justice to the original. Even photogravures such as those which were published in *Camera Work* are more lovely in the original, since they were often produced under the direct supervision of the photographer.

Furthermore, there is, on the one hand, the market value which can be noted and to some extent analyzed, and on the other the value of any photograph for the individual viewer, whose immediate critical reaction is based on the photograph's meaningfulness to *him*. Obviously some photographs speak to us more directly than do others. The true collector is said to be the one with his own strong inner sense of fitness which enables him to build his collection around his own personal tastes without too much regard for what may be popularly collected at the moment.

In a plea that photographs be treated as works of art and judged as such which appeared in a discussion of photographic criticism in *The Criticism of Photography as Art/The Photographs of Jerry Uelsmann*, John L. Ward says that what is significant about art is its ability to produce a "sense of heightened reality . . . this sense is not a quality which is built into the work of art, but . . . produced by the interaction between the work and a viewer who is looking at the work as art. Art cannot function without a responsive viewer. Perhaps we must simply say that a work of art is anything which is separated from nature and which is contemplated for that portion of its meaning which may be intuitively experienced apart from its practical value."

For each of us, a great photograph can be simply one to which we cannot help responding. Or, as Arnold H. Crane, who has a collection of some 55,000 vintage prints, has been quoted, a photograph has to hit him first "in the gut" and then in the eye. Perhaps there can be no formula for the visual aesthetic. Whether or not a photograph is the work of an outstanding and well-known photographer, the image must be able to stand alone, by itself. "The result is the only fair basis for judgment," according to Alfred Stieglitz, one of the ultimate masters of technique.

The illustrations which have been included in this book have been chosen as examples of the interesting or beautiful photographs of the type which the collector might be wildly lucky to find, in a valuable family collection, antiquarian shop, gallery specializing in the sale of old photographs, or even in the unexpected place such as a flea market. Because they are excellent photographs, they may set a standard against which some new finds might be compared.

To find out what he likes and might possibly be interested in collecting, the novice collector can turn for more information to any number of beautiful modern books, from the histories of photography to the handsomely printed works of a single photographer, to the authoritative catalogues of the works of one photographer or of images representative of some period in photography, such as are issued frequently these days by museums which display photographs. If he lives close enough, he can visit those museums, or if fortunate enough to live in a large city or perhaps near an art center or colony, one of those modern galleries fairly recently established for the sale of photographic images. As *Photography: Source & Resource* (1973) points out, "there are more museums with collections of photographs than there are galleries showing photographs. Nevertheless, photography is often more accessible at the gallery. This is because few museums have a permanent exhibit of photographs, while a single gallery will mount ten or twelve different shows in a year's time." Fortunately for the collector, the photographic gallery is in business to sell photographs, not simply exhibit them, and usually the atmosphere there is informal and images may be examined at leisure. Frequently there is the opportunity to discuss prospective purchases with other persons similarly interested in old photographs.

A quick rundown of the gallery shows listed in the first issues of the magazine *Photograph* (Summer, 1976) finds 21 states represented along with the District of Columbia, with, however, an impressive concentration of the galleries within New York City. Exhibits range from shows of students' work to that of the leading modern American and European photographers, to "vintage prints," and exhibits clustered about themes of place (Victorian India), event (a jazz funeral), attitude ("fun in photography"), the photographer as artist (Curtis' photogravures of Indian life), and method (the carbon-gelatin Woodbury process, of particular interest because of its permanency). The collector of old photographs might wish that the galleries would devote more of their space to the nineteenth-century masters and some of the recently discovered talent of a hundred years ago rather than so consistently featuring, as some do, that modern view of reality which, as one reviewer has put it, includes an element of boredom. Quite possibly we shall see more new galleries devoted specifically to exploring the many fascinating aspects of historic photographs.

Many of the most familiar images have, however, already disappeared into the museums or, if still available, will be priced extravagantly high, out of the reach of most collectors. But collectors are, on the whole, an optimistic breed and cannot resist the hope that they may, sometime, somewhere, make a lucky find. "One story we ran across told of a traveling photographer who always browsed for photographic items. One day he bought what appeared to be a very out-of-date, unopened box of paper for twenty-five cents. It contained twenty signed prints by Edward Weston. The moral, besides looking more carefully at old paper boxes in the future, is that there are photographs of real artistic merit floating around in the world though they aren't easy to find. Searching requires capital like anything else, though it may be in the form of the time to travel as much as the actual money needed." This quote is, again, from *Photography: Source & Resource* and occurs in a discussion of the operations of photographic galleries located in the United States.

Often the so-called lucky find is not so much the result of luck, however, as of perseverance and good detective work. For example, if the collector has a particular interest in one photographer, he may find it profitable to visit the place where that photographer lived and search around in the old book stores, antique shops, and curio shops in the locality. Sometimes images turn up in fairly unlikely places, and sometimes just talking to people will provide new leads. The descendant of a nineteenth-century photographer may either own examples of his work or know where they might be found. If there were plates made from the original negatives, sometimes the engraver, or his descendant, has the treasures you are seeking stored away in some loft. Old glass plates have even turned up in such an unlikely place as in use in a greenhouse, from which they have been rescued, to be printed with satisfactory results!

Leads to old photographs are sometimes provided in the roster of a nineteenth-century organization of amateur photographers, many of whom were possibly themselves collectors of the works of others. There is an extensive listing of the names and addresses of late nineteenth-century photographic societies, in many cases with the names of the founding members, provided in William Welling's *Collector's Guide to Nineteenth Century Photographs* (1976). His list of American societies, originally published in 1889, is arranged by city as an aid to the modern collector seeking to trace lost records or missing photographic items.

The important subject of the care and preservation of old photographs must regrettably be omitted from this book. There are a few basic rules, however, which should be mentioned. A valuable photograph or photographic image should not be placed in contact with any acidic paper or boards, since the acid will, in time, break down into compounds which will eventually destroy the photograph. One source for photographic archival storage products is TALAS, a division of the Technical Library Service, 104 Fifth Avenue, New York, New York 10011.

Many experienced collectors feel it is vastly better to store an old photograph exactly as it is found rather than attempt to repair, mount, or otherwise frame it. Most agree that, in any case, it is inappropriate to use the process of dry-mounting, which may present a chemical danger to the print and, in any event, seems inappropriate since the process of dry-mounting is relatively modern.

There are available at least two inexpensive brochures on the preservation and care of old photographs. The first of these is a pamphlet published by the auction house of Sotheby Parke Bernet in 1976. By Doris Bry, it may be obtained by writing to the auction house, Dept. AH, 1425 York Avenue, New York, New York 10021 and sending a stamped self-addressed envelope. Noting that a photograph on paper is both chemically and physically fragile, Bry cites the following chief enemies of the photograph: strong light, air pollution, heat and humidity, insects, and careless handling in general—including any unskilled attempts at restoration. Photographs most vulnerable to damage are those which were not processed properly in the first place, she says. The second work costs 75¢ and is available from the International Museum of Photography, George Eastman House, Rochester, New York 14607. "Preservation, Deterioration, Restoration of Photographic Images" is an offprint from *The Library Quarterly* of January, 1970.

A full-length book on this subject is *Restoration and Photographic Copying* by Alexander Shafran, published in 1967. Shafran states that his book may be the first basic text on the subject, exclusive of works specifically on retouching or airbrushing. He prefers the term "copy-restoration" since rather than subject an original photograph to the process of restoration he advocates its being copied, restoring the copy, and finally re-photographing after the manner of the original. In his experience the only photographs which should be subjected to restoration are those from a family collection with chiefly sentimental value. Shafran firmly believes that any copy-restoration needs an expert hand, requiring skills in photography, retouching, and drawing. He covers the entire procedure, from the initial preparation and cleaning of the photograph, to the copying, retouching and art work on the copy negative, positive retouching, and final restoration work, then the re-copying.

Highly regarded for its thorough coverage and helpful photographs is the Time-Life book *Caring for Photographs*, published in 1972 and now a standard work. This book points out that original photographs, even when considerably less than perfect, have unique qualities which no copy can match, even though copying is capable of providing a sturdy duplicate of an old and possibly fragile picture and of minimizing any damage which may have already altered the image by employing a variety of optical tricks.

The collecting of antique cameras and other items of photographic equipment similarly is beyond the scope of this book. There is, however, a considerable body of literature available on this subject, including the descriptions of the contents of some of the outstanding collections. Books include the *Illustrated History of the Camera* (1975) by Michael Auer, containing a glossary, and *Century of Cameras* (1973) by Eaton S. Lothrop, describing the comprehensive collection of cameras at the George Eastman House of the International Museum of Photography, and this work is, like the first, profusely illustrated. The dryplate camera is discussed in *Age of Cameras* by John Edward Holmes, published in London in 1974. Many kinds of antique cameras are discussed and illustrated in *Collecting Photographica* (1976) by George Gilbert, who also provides information on some of the major collections of cameras and camera equipment, as well as stories about the collectors of antique cameras, how they began and have built their collections. There is also the 1972 reprint of the 1937 edition of *A Catalogue of the Epstean Collection on the History and Science of Photography*. Furthermore, the old catalogues describing cameras and equipment issued by the manufacturers of photographic materials are sometimes to be found in reprint. A number of such reprints have been issued by Classic Photographic Apparatus, P.O. Box 161, Simsbury, Connecticut 06070.

Two other subjects only scantily covered here are motion pictures and color photography. Many of the major developments in both of these areas occurred well past the period principally covered in our book.

The purpose of this present book is limited to the already considerable task of helping the reader find his way around the world of old photographs by providing some understanding of the importance of various photographers and photographic trends and by offering clues to the meaning of the unfamiliar terms which may be encountered. This guide book can be no substitute for the study in depth of the history of photography such as can be found in the recognized texts on this subject. The three most venerable histories are those by Gernsheim, Taft, and Newhall. Each, from a different point of view, provides the narrative and detailed account essential to a full understanding of the nineteenth-century achievements and, in the histories by Gernsheim and Newhall, early twentieth-century achievements.

The History of Photography (1955) by Helmut Gernsheim covers the earliest use of the camera obscura in the eleventh century to photography in the year 1914. Written in collaboration with Alison Gernsheim, it is particularly valuable for its information on the science and mechanics of photography, offering the most complete guide in this respect to be found in the three histories. *Photography and the American Scene*, originally published in 1938, is by Robert Taft, professor of chemistry at the University of Kansas. A work based on extensive, and impressive, original research, this book covers the years 1839 to 1889, the first fifty years of photography. *The History of Photography* by Beaumont Newhall has appeared in numerous editions following its first publication as the illustrated catalogue for an exhibition titled "Photography 1839–1937" which Newhall organized in 1937 for the Museum of Modern Art in New York City. A modern edition contains a bibliography of individual photographers which readers may find very helpful.

Each of these three histories has been invaluable in the preparation of this book. They are recommended as the nucleus of a library on photographic history, supplemented by whatever other basic works relate to the particular field of one's specialty, such as: *American Daguerreian Art* by Floyd and Marion Rinhart (1967); *Mirror Image* by Richard Rudisill (1971); Beaumont Newhall's *The Daguerreotype in America* (revised edition, 1968); *Stereo Views* by William Culp Darrah (1964); *Era of Exploration: The Rise of Landscape Photography in the American West, 1860–1885*, which originated with the Metropolitan Museum of Art in New York City as the catalogue for an exhibit held in 1975.

In addition to the histories, there are numerous books recently published dealing with various aspects of history and collecting images, many of them in hardcover and lavishly illustrated. *Collector's Guide to Nineteenth Century Photographs* (1976) by William Welling, a director of the Photographic Historical Society of New York, is particularly valuable for its numerous illustrations, many drawn from the Arnold H. Crane collection of daguerreotypes and the George R. Rinhart collection of card stereographs, many of the images now first published. Among the paperbacks there are two books which, although quite different, might each prove valuable to the new collector. The first is *Photographers on Photography* (1966), a critical anthology edited by Nathan Lyons, presenting various points of view which have contributed to the development of contemporary photographic expression, but with reference to past trends. The second is *Photography: Source & Resource* (1973) prepared collaboratively by Steven Lewis, James McQuaid, and David Tait and distributed by Light Impressions, Box 3012, Rochester, New York 14614. This "source book for creative photography" contains seven major sections, on teaching, work-shops, publishing, criticism, the galleries, the major collections, and a bibliog-raphy. The collection index can be useful in locating material which is accessible to the public, even though there is an emphasis on "artistic photography" rather than on images primarily of historic interest. There is also a listing of the theses written by scholars on a variety of photographic subjects.

There are so few periodicals devoted exclusively to the history of photog-raphy or to photography as art, rather than its technique or science, that those which are published deserve the collector's support. Those in the brief listing which follows offer dependable and helpful information on new discoveries and current showings.

Image, the journal of photography and motion pictures published by the International Museum of Photography located in the George Eastman House in Rochester, New York, is issued four times a year. Each issue contains sev-eral articles which cover a subject authoritatively and in considerable depth, with handsome illustrations. Its original material provides information which is often new to scholars and to collectors and certainly not easily found elsewhere.

Another periodical is *Photographica*, published ten times a year by the Photographic Historical Society of New York and available with a membership in the Society, which may be reached by writing Box 1839, Radio City Station, New York, New York 10019. This is a journal published specifically for collec-tors. It contains information of exhibits, of new publications of interest, and of new finds, as well as articles of interest to the collectors of old images and col-lectors of antique cameras and equipment.

The first issue of the magazine *Photograph* (210 Fifth Avenue, New York, New York 10010) appeared in the summer of 1976. Published ten times a year, its purpose is to meet "serious non-technical interests" in photography. The magazine's staff represents "a wide portion of the photographic community" sufficiently committed to establishing "a publication which speaks to us and for us." *The Photo Reporter* is published monthly by Modernage of New York (319 East 44th Street, New York, New York 10017). This journal, packed with current news of photographers, workshops, and exhibits, also contains some news of interest to collectors. A feature of an international newsletter called *Printletter* (Postfach 250, CH-8046 Zurich, Switzerland) is the listing of the prices paid for photographic prints as reported by galleries in both the United States and in Europe. An international quarterly journal which began publica-tion in 1976 is *History of Photography*, addressed to scholars in the field as well as to serious collectors, art historians, librarians and archivists, social historians, and scientists. This journal is published by Taylor and Francis at 10-14 Mack-lin Street, London, WC 2B 5NF. In addition, *Artforum* magazine (667 Madison Avenue, New York, New York 10021) claiming to be the "first art magazine to recognize the importance of photography," publishes major articles on this subject from time to time.

I am deeply grateful to my husband Ben for his understanding and support during the preparation of this manuscript, and I wish also to thank the members of the various library and museum staffs who responded generously to my requests, and also the dealers and collectors who so patiently answered my questions. Although they all helped make this book more "meaty" than it could otherwise have been, the responsibility for any errors which may have crept in, or any omissions, must be entirely my own.

Acknowledgments

The author gratefully acknowledges the following permissions to quote: on page vii, John L. Ward in *The Criticism of Photography As Art/The Photographs of Jerry Uelsmann*, The University Presses of Florida; page viii, *Photography: Source & Resource*, permissions granted by editor David B. Tait, affiliated with the Institute for Research, State College, Pennsylvania; page 55, Pete Daniel and Raymond Smock in *A Talent for Detail*, Harmony Books; pages 79 and 114, Arthur Siegel writing in "Fifty Years of Documentary" (1951) which appeared in *Photographers on Photography*, the Foundations of Modern Photography Series edited by Nathan Lyons (1966), Prentice-Hall, Inc. in collaboration with the George Eastman House, Rochester, New York; page 145, Andrew H. Eskind, "Mutoscopes Old and New," appearing in the March, 1976, issue of *Image* (IMP/GEH, Rochester, New York); page 6, George Gilbert in *Collecting Photographica*, reprinted by permission of Hawthorn Books, Inc.; page 216, Gail Buckland in *Reality Recorded*, by permission of David & Charles, in the U.K.

Contents

COLLECTING
OLD
PHOTOGRAPHS

Introduction

New Interest in Old Photographs

That box of old photographs the family has been saving for years, or at least not throwing out, may today prove to contain treasures of interest to the collectors of old photographs. Some of the photographs, and not just the daguerreotypes, might even have considerable monetary value in today's runaway market.

Is this old photograph valuable? Yes, if it is a daguerreotype made before 1845. Yes, if it is a photograph made west of the Rocky Mountains before 1858. Yes, if it is a portrait by Brady, or a Civil War print by Gardner, or an American calotype, one of the earliest of the stereographs—on thin board—a Stanhope, or a lovely photogravure from a copy of *Camera Work*. The answer is a *strong* yes in all these instances and in many more as well.

As more people have become interested in collecting photographs—quite a different matter from simply saving them—more dealers and more art galleries are undertaking to meet the growing interest in old photographs. As more museums establish separate departments of photography to preserve, catalogue, and display photographs as works of art, the value of many kinds of photographs has been rising dramatically within the last ten years, but most swiftly in the last two. Bundles of photographs handed down in the family, once treasured simply for sentimental reasons, should perhaps now be re-examined for the photograph which may have importance for others outside the family.

It may turn out that a collector will be enormously impressed by your studio portrait of your great-aunt Lydia, not because it is of the venerable Lydia, who led a blameless but, alas, uneventful life, but because it is a fine example of the early work of the firm of Southworth and Hawes, a mid-nineteenth-century Boston firm noted both for its meticulous work and the easy grace of the poses in which its two proprietors arranged the men and women who came to sit for their camera. The George Eastman House in Rochester, New York, in 1976 staged a major exhibition of the work of Southworth and Hawes.

Perhaps there is a photograph brought back from California by Cousin Edward, a legendary character in the family, who sailed from Boston in 1849 with other young men to make his fortune in the western gold fields but who stayed on instead in San Francisco to mine the wealth to be made in importing flour.

1

Cousin Edward, on a visit back east in 1870, brought photographs showing the docks, the Bay, and one large photograph which reveals a magnificent panoramic view of the craggy slopes of the Rocky Mountains. Not only may the pictures of San Francisco in the 1850s be of considerable value in today's market, but almost certainly if the Rocky Mountain photograph should prove to be an example of the early work of Muybridge, for example, it will be of interest to a museum. In 1975 the Metropolitan Museum of Art staged a major exhibit of photography from the "era of exploration" producing a new surge of interest in the work of all photographers associated with the opening of the West, and particularly in photographs made in connection with government surveys or the building of the transcontinental railroad.

There may be in the family collection a wedding portrait in its heavily embossed miniature case, the case carefully wrapped in a linen handkerchief. The portrait is of a handsome young man, seated with his bride, dressed in coat and bonnet standing at his side. It may not be, as you had supposed, a pretty hopelessly tarnished daguerreotype, but an ambrotype, which might be more easily restored. The spotting in the lower part of the picture is not, as you had thought, a defect wrought by time in the image itself, but the appearance caused by the rotting away of the piece of black velvet which was used as a backing, for the ambrotype is a photograph made directly on glass which appears as a positive when it is backed by a dark material. Simply replacing the velvet can make the ambrotype lovely once more.

Among the portraits in the family collection which actually are daguerreotypes, there are several of elderly men of severe expression. Their hats are on their heads, their hands stiffly on their knees, and they look sternly and unblinkingly straight into the lens. Why were these pictures of such a forbidding appearance saved? If your ancestors included a judge, the founder of a business, an inventor, editor, radical, or Civil War general, then one could possibly be his portrait. The same reason that made the family save the portrait could make it of some interest to the social historians today.

Among the kinds of pictures most particularly sought after now are the daguerreotypes which are larger than those that fit into the standard miniature case, as well as any daguerreotype showing an outdoor scene. Often, as a matter of fact, the larger plate was used to record the outdoor scene. Few daguerreotype operators, however, cared to attempt the difficult task of setting up their relatively slow cameras outside the studio, where it would not be easy to control each part of the picture they wished to take. Scenes with people in them were especially difficult, since the people might move about and thus blur the image. Scenes in snow were considered next to impossible.

In 1972, when a set of daguerreotypes made in 1846 showing various scenes in Washington, D.C., including the White House and other government buildings, turned up in a flea market in California, their discovery was promptly hailed as a major find. The daguerreotypes were acquired by the Library of Congress which, according to report, paid about $2000 apiece for them.

Most ambrotypes and tintypes, similarly, were made indoors in the studio. It was a daring photographer who would venture outside the studio with his camera. Thus, any direct photograph on glass or on metal made by the wet-collodion process showing a village street, perhaps, or a stagecoach, peddlar's cart or, most especially, photographer's van, may be of considerable interest not only to the social historian but to the student of the history of photography as well. Such images made between 1855 and 1870 have brought $100 and more at auction in New York.

The usual family collection of photographs, even though extensive, is more likely to contain nineteenth-century images of interest than important images from the twentieth century. The exception might lie in the collection of photographs accumulated by a person who was in the arts himself and specifically interested in photography, or was possibly himself a photographer or a friend of some photographers. The chance of a collection's yielding the work of one of the early twentieth-century photographers usually is in some member of the family's having had some specific reason to collect these photographs close to the time at which they were originally made.

There is the possibility that a household collection of what has been called "wayside" photographs, up to and including snapshots, taken by some amateur camera buff, may include pictures of newsworthy events, possibly of happenings for which there is no other visual record: the first flight of an experimental plane, or some disaster not previously known to have been photographed, or a series of pictures showing a way of life which has now departed—on the plantation, among the Indians of Alaska, or among recent immigrants to city streets. Such documentation made before the date 1870 has a special interest.

The 1880s separated an earlier era of photography from the later period to come. During this decade the dry plate came into general use, replacing the cumbersome wet plate, which had required both considerable dexterity and speed in its use. The dry plate came ready to use in the camera. The hand-held camera which was then made practical, of lighter weight and using a shutter rather than the simple lens cap, took photography out of the solemn studio. "Detective" cameras became popular. These hidden cameras made it possible to sneak a picture by secretly pressing a button to open the shutter. Such a camera might be hidden in one's vest, the eye of the camera looking like a button, hidden in the hat, or made to look like a book. In 1888 Kodak marketed the first of its compact cameras to use film, the Kodak No. 1, which came loaded with film for 100 exposures and had to be returned to the factory to be reloaded. Successive Kodaks offered improvements—though a reduction in the number of exposures—and the "snapshot era" was under way. The introduction of film, outmoding photography both on glass and on metal, placed the means of photography quickly in the hands of millions of people. The idea that "you press the button, we do the rest" proved irresistible. Photography on film gave rise to a huge new international complex of commercial endeavor, including the new occupation of developing and printing the pictures for the customer-photographer as well as the business of selling him an ever-increasing complexity of darkroom equipment and a wide variety of cameras. It also produced as a spinoff, perhaps inevitably, family albums which would rapidly fill with out-of-focus shots of self-conscious adults smirking at the camera. The snapshot would quickly begin to perform a social function quite distinctly apart from the artistry inherent in the medium. Much as we love them as keepsakes, these snapshots are not what interest collectors these days—not yet, but the history of photography so far has certainly been full of surprises.

Most collectors of old photographs might be fairly perplexed if asked by someone new to collecting for help in deciding what kinds of photographs one should be looking for these days. Many collectors seemed to have started in their area of specialty almost by accident. Their collecting experience began, they will tell you, when they just happened to acquire that first photograph they felt they could not do without. Perhaps they inherited a box of family pictures and became interested in identifying some of them. This may have lead on to an interest in the photographs themselves, aside from their subjects. Sometimes it is a particular kind of photograph, often the daguerreotype, with its elusive silvered picture and pre-Civil War costumes and poses, which caught their fancy and sparked an interest in finding other examples. Sometimes it has been the pictures from the Spanish-American War, a young Teddy Roosevelt surrounded by his stalwarts in their puttees, and the moving photograph of the superstructure of the sunken *Maine* still rising from the waters of the harbor at Havana. Then, somehow, these future collectors of old and sometimes rare images came across the opportunity to acquire several more of their favorite kind of photograph, and then, finally, they became interested in going out to look for more.

Collecting the works of just one known photographer fascinates a good many people. Usually this can offer several advantages. There may be several published works which can serve as references and guides for the beginning collector. It may be possible, for example, to start an in-depth study of the work of this one photographer by collecting copies of the catalogues for the exhibits which have included his or her works, those held at museums or in galleries. If the photographer is sufficiently well-known, there is probably a record of the sale of his photographs. Sales made at the galleries and auction houses may have set a price scale for other similar examples of his work. There are undoubtedly photographic dealers who know and appreciate this photographer's style and will welcome the assignment of helping to find more examples of his work.

To be able to recognize value in a photographer's work, there may be a great deal we will have to know. The questions to be answered may include the following: How many prints of this image were originally made? How likely is the possibility that more of these prints will turn up at some future time? Is there any record to show what the photographer himself felt about the quality of this particular photograph or print? Did he customarily sign those of which he most approved? If so, is this his genuine signature, or perhaps the logo he consistently used for this type of print? What interior signs are there within the picture to tell us that this is indeed the work of the master? What evidence is there that this one print is a vintage copy made from the original negative? To answer, we must certainly know the dates within which this photographer worked, and the places where he worked at various times. Although most of these questions can be answered with a fair degree of accuracy for the acknowledged masters—Lewis Carroll, Alfred Stieglitz, Edward Weston for example—the challenge may lie in answering these same questions for the relatively unknown photographer or for the photographer of talent but hitherto unacknowledged merit.

One of the best ways of learning more about old photographs of all kinds is to visit the museums and galleries where they are to be seen. Yet since there is a concentration, to date, of such institutions on the east coast, particularly in New York City, and on the west coast, this may not always be possible. Many museums and galleries, however, offer illustrated catalogues to accompany their exhibits, and frequently these are still available for past shows. The price is minimal in almost all instances, and by also following the announcements of new shows, the collector can start to build his own personal reference shelf. There are, as well, the catalogues offered by some dealers who handle their business exclusively through the mails. A charge is made for almost all of these, but often the illustrations alone make them worthwhile. Subscribing to dealers' catalogues and to those offered by the great auction houses—particularly Sotheby Parke Bernet and the Swann Galleries, both in New York City—has the advantage of providing up-to-the-minute information on prices, not to mention the opportunity to participate in the market by buying and adding to one's collection.

Obviously, when we are talking about gallery showings, sales at auction, and buying from dealers, we are discussing the kinds of photographs that are already highly valued in the market and in which there is already the kind of commerce similar to that for the products of other types of artistic efforts, such as paintings, ceramics, etchings. To enter this market with satisfaction it may be necessary not only to have a good eye for a photograph but also a nose for value—as well as the money to allow one to indulge one's taste. However, since so much photographic material is believed to be still hidden away and not yet discovered—or to date neglected and unappreciated—it can pay the amateur very well indeed to become sufficiently knowledgeable as to be able to recognize a photograph of considerable merit, whether the work of one of the great photographers or the work of someone lacking in critical acclaim. According to Richard Blodgett, reporting in *The New York Times* in 1975, prices for many photographic works have gone up 1000 percent or more in two years. (Blodgett has written a book titled *How to Make Money on the Art Market.*)

Unfortunately, as of this writing there is no annually compiled and published index for the prices paid for photographic materials as there is for the old book market. However, sufficiently large amounts are, upon occasion, paid for photographs so that the transaction is treated by the press as a newsworthy event. We therefore learn that an 1848 daguerreotype portrait of Edgar Allan Poe has sold for $9,250 and then reportedly been resold by a dealer for $35,000. Original prints by Julia Margaret Cameron, who has been called one of the leading artists of the nineteenth century in any medium, usually bring about $1,500. Her most celebrated album, one which she presented to her sister in 1963, was sold at auction for close to $100,000. The photogravures by the members of the Photo-Secessionist group published in *Camera Work* usually sell in the hundreds, and the issue of *Camera Work* for October 11, 1911, with its 16 photogravures by Alfred Stieglitz and a half-tone engraving by Picasso, has commanded $4,750 at auction, an auction where a second copy brought almost as much. Other single issues of *Camera Work*, if complete, may be worth well over $1,000.

We must be impressed by the fact that it was only a scant 25 years ago that the Swann Galleries of New York held the first American auction—perhaps the first auction in the world—devoted entirely to the sale of photographs and books with photographs or about photography. The prices then paid are astonishing by today's standards. A copy of Fox Talbot's *The Pencil of Nature* (1845), one of the most important books in the history of photography, of which there are now no more than a dozen copies, brought a meager $200. In 1971 a copy sold at auction for $6,500. Talbot's *Sun Pictures of Scotland* (1845) was worth no more than $35 in 1952. Twenty years later a copy was sold in London for $3,000. The first translation into English of the manual prepared by L. J. M. Daguerre himself to explain the process of making a daguerreotype, published in London in 1839, the year of the original announcement, sold in 1952 for $25. Recently a copy went for $700. It is not simply the photographic "incunabula" which have risen a great deal in value, however. William Bradford's illustrated chronicle of a trip along the coast of Greenland made in 1869, *The Arctic Regions* (1873), sold 25 years ago for $40, recently for $4,500. In the 1952 auction, a single lot containing three issues of *Camera Work* was handed over for a bid of $11.

Collecting photographic material need not, however, be an expensive undertaking. The big news may be the prices paid for the most outstanding items, but the news for most of us is that so much material is still available and at little cost. Although we may have to limit our acquaintance with the acknowledged masterpieces to seeing them in a museum, there are still vast areas of interest awaiting the astute collector. We may decide that we shall collect only those images which personally appeal to us as lovely. Or, finding what we know to be scarce may have its particular appeal. We may decide that we will collect strange and unusual effects, the unusual type of photograph, or storytelling pictures. We may decide that our own personal collection of photographs will be built around one period in the history of photography, or one type of photographic style associated with a time or place. The type of people photographed may determine what we collect: images of the American Indian, missionaries, children at play, actresses in costume, women wearing hats, construction workers, miners, explorers, even photographers. We could decide to concentrate on one kind of photograph used for book illustration, or the photographs which have appeared in advertisements or posters. Just precisely what it may be makes little difference as long as it provides enjoyment and is at least fairly accessible.

There are many kinds of photographs which were only lightly valued at the time they were made yet may have a special kind of charm for us today. Street photographs could be of this kind. In his book *Collecting Photographica* (1976), George Gilbert paints a picture of the street photographer who walked the city streets "with a pony to attract children to the thrill of a seated moment on the saddled back of a pavement-weary pinto. His product was any of a range of photo products from a tintype to a paper print, from a photo button to an instant bit of photographic jewelry. . . . The street photographer with his bucket of water for a quick rinse of the hyposaturated print was a familiar sight in parks and playgrounds and on boardwalks where a Sunday crowd often gathered round to see the photographer's hand emerge from the magic black box with a print to be dropped for a minute or two into the wash-water bucket at his feet."

In addition to the collectors of the humble street photograph, there are the collectors of the circular images produced by the Kodak Nos. 1 and 2, and the simple Brownie, a camera which was not capable of being focused, but only aimed at the subject. There are collectors of campaign photo-buttons and of photographic jewelry, of the posters which advertised early camera equipment or the work of various photographic studios, of photographic stamps, or coins, and even of the *backs* of cabinet cards, with their fancifully embellished ads for the studios. It's all collecting for fun.

If, however, we are also interested in building a collection of some monetary value, we shall have to look, as well, at the following criteria which must be met by any print of outstanding worth:

—It must be at least scarce, and if possible even rare, which by one definition means that a truly active dealer in photographic images might encounter it perhaps only once in ten years.

—It must be of undeniable artistic quality, and, if possible, have received critical acclaim or been published in some work on excellence in photography.

—It must be technically excellent, whatever the medium.

—Finally, it should be of some historic significance.

A nineteenth-century photograph, to have value, need be in good condition only within the limits of the condition in which other, similar, prints are customarily found.

Two of the most outstanding and comprehensive collections of old photographs in the country are located in the nation's capital. The first is at the Library of Congress (Washington, D.C. 20540). Fortunately for the researcher there is a *Guide to Special Collections of Prints and Photographs in the Library of Congress*, issued by the U.S. Government Printing Office in 1955. Among the Brady items alone there are 4,500 Civil War prints and duplicates and over 10,000 glass negatives. The "Master Photograph Collection," organized under the name of the photographer, includes the work of Jackson, O'Sullivan, members of Photo Secession, and twentieth-century photographers Genthe, Ulmann, Weston, Evans, and Lange. The topics covered include the Powell Survey (photographs by Hillers), Crimean War (265 unmounted salt prints by Fenton), yachting in the 1890s (1,500 photographs by C. E. Bolles), and many western views, including Indian scenes. The second extensive collection is housed at the Smithsonian Institution (Washington, D.C. 20560) and consists of many thousands of plates, negatives, slides, and stereograms. This collection includes a significant number of photographs made by Fox Talbot as well as a treasury of material illustrating the history of American photography.

Two of the greatest collections ever made by private individuals are now lodged in institutions. The Gernsheim Collection, at one time "the largest set of photographic antiquities in private hands," is now housed at the Humanities Research Center of the University of Texas (Austin, Texas 78712). The entire augmented collection of photographica at the Research Center includes well over 150,000 images as well as about 6,000 books and journals on photography. The Floyd and Marion Rinhart Collection, consisting of more than 1,000 daguerreotypes, 500 ambrotypes, and about 100 photographs on sheet metal, is now lodged at Ohio State University (Columbus, Ohio 43210).

Until recently the only museum in the United States devoted exclusively to photography was the International Museum of Photography, more popularly known as the George Eastman House (Rochester, New York 14607). Its collection of about 60,000 photographs covers all historical periods. There is a special collection of materials relating to the history of the motion pictures, and another special collection of antique cameras and other outmoded equipment. In the last few years there has been a movement for the establishment of more centers of photography, both for exhibition and study, and much more attention paid to the photographs among the diverse holdings of historical societies, photographs which, in many cases, had until recently never been catalogued or shown.

In New York City, there is an extensive and highly varied collection of photographs illustrating the history of the city located at the Museum of the City of New York (New York, New York 10029). The museum's holdings include well over 100,000 glass negatives showing architectural subjects, lantern slides of archaeological excavations in New York and elsewhere, Civil War views, 4,000 of the photographs made by Genthe, and 750 documentary photographs by Jacob Riis and Robert Bracklow.

The Metropolitan Museum of Art (New York, New York 10028) has estimated that its photographic collection includes as many as 10,000 plates and negatives; however, the museum restricts access to this collection, except for its exhibits, to scholars in the field of photography. The Museum of Modern Art (New York, New York 10019) has a collection of twentieth-century photographs selected on the basis of their artistic excellence. The Museum maintains an Edward Steichen Archive which includes material on Steichen's life, and photographs both by him and of him. The picture collection of the New York Public Library includes photographs and is designed to assist in pictorial research.

The collection of the New York State Historical Association (Cooperstown, New York 13326) spans a hundred years of photography in that part of New York State and includes 55,000 glass plate negatives, most of which are catalogued. Another example of a museum collection, in a different part of the country, is the Museum of New Mexico (Santa Fe, New Mexico 87501). This museum's photographic archives include thousands of early photographs, a great many of them from the nineteenth century, showing Indians and the Indian way of life.

The person interested in photographs of western pioneer life will find that there are outstanding collections of this material housed in a number of institutions. The photographic collection of the State Historical Society of Colorado, located in the Colorado State Museum (Denver, Colorado 80203), contains about 250,000 prints and negatives and includes the work of William Henry Jackson, Henry H. Buckwalter, and the Garrison brothers. The Aultman Collection there holds about 35,000 glass plates of portraits made by a local gallery beginning in the 1880s. The Western Historical Collection of the University of Colorado Libraries (Boulder, Colorado 80302) contain negatives and prints, many by as yet unidentified photographers, covering the development of that state in the early part of the twentieth century. The Bancroft Library, for research, of the University of California (Berkeley, California 94720) owns over a million "picture units," not all catalogued. The photographers include Muybridge, O'Sullivan, Jackson, Vroman, and, for Alaska, Nowell, Lase & Duclos, and Hegg. At the University of Washington (Seattle, Washington 98195) there is a collection of about 200,000 prints and negatives covering the period from 1860 to about 1930, mostly photographs taken in Washington Territory, and also the State of Washington, Alaska, and Canada. The Library of the University of Oregon (Eugene, Oregon 97403) has an outstanding collection, including many glass negatives, showing the development of Oregon and of Alaska, including those of pioneer and Indian life.

Many of the small local art and historical museums have growing collections of photographs. In addition to those collections simply based on local or regional interests, there are numerous collections which show a wide scattering of interest among individual photographers, each of whom may, however, be represented by only one or two prints. A listing of many of these museums, with their holdings, is to be found in *Photography: Source & Resource* published by Turnip Press in 1973. This work is also indexed by the names of the photographers represented in these collections, most of them active in the twentieth century.

Although not generally showing, to date, any particular strength in nineteenth-century material, there are the collections of photographs to be found in the holdings of college and university art museums. These collections, such as at Harvard and the universities of Minnesota, Nebraska, and Michigan, to name only a few, tend to be more eclectic rather than concentrating on a particular historical period or other specific category of photograph. One of the outstanding collections is held by Yale University's Beinecke Rare Book and Manuscript Library (New Haven, Connecticut 06520), where the photographic archives include many prints by twentieth-century photographers including Stieglitz, along with collections of photographs made of Walt Whitman and of Mark Twain.

As there is today a growing number of collectors who have assumed the responsibility for saving and preserving great masses of photographic material, it is hoped that eventually they will see their way clear to handing this material, as their predecessors did, over to the institutions with the capacity to care for it adequately and the facilities to make it available to the public both through exhibitions and new publications.

Among the organizations open to membership for anyone interested in photography there are two museums, or centers, which deserve special mention. The first is the International Museum of Photography at the George Eastman

Commercial prints which once seemed trite have now become precious as a record of everyday life in the past. These four prints are from the Byron Collection of more than 10,000 prints and uncounted negatives housed in the Museum of the City of New York. The Byron family's business included taking interiors by natural light highlighted by the use of exploding magnesium powder. Drifting clouds of smoke followed, and there was always some danger of fire. During the 1890s the Byron Company pioneered in stage photography, developing a special rig to photograph the stage from the auditorium.

Museums, historical societies, and libraries are today showing an increasing interest in such photographic documentation. Undoubtedly there are many family collections, yet to surface, which contain material of equal interest for other communities. (Photographs by Bryon, the Bryon Collection, Courtesy of the Museum of the City of New York.)

1. The kitchen of a wealthy New York City home in 1899. We see the white tile walls, coal-burning stove, gleaming hot-water tank, and tiny sink. The pipes on the ceiling probably indicated there were several bathrooms upstairs. The kitchen was in the home of a German-American lawyer whose wife, also interested in the law, and an active clubwoman, undoubtedly left the preparation of meals to her servants.

2. Soda fountain in a Hegeman and Company drugstore, in 1907. This elegant stand is decorated with marble and onyx, has a canopy of beveled glass and lighting fixtures shaped like bunches of grapes.

3. The study in the 1904 home of someone of rather Bohemian tastes. Interior decorators and antique dealers find a mine of information in square furniture, pictures on the wall, objets d'art.

4. Interior of the publishing office of Success magazine. This has the ring of truth: no one seems to have tidied up for the picture.

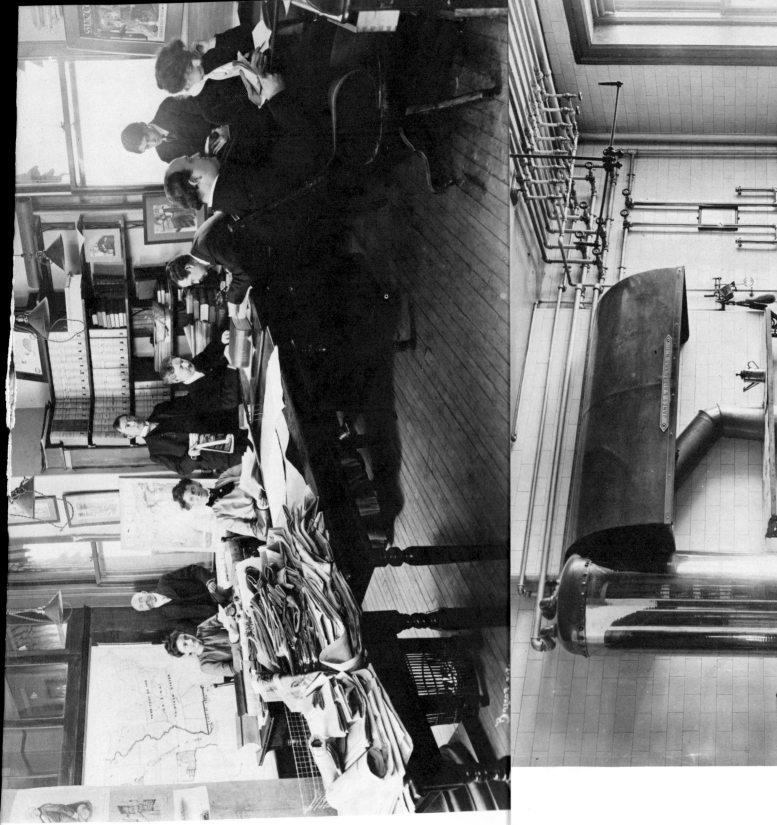

4

I

House (IMP/GEH) (Rochester, New York 14607), founded in 1949, containing a collection of pictures, films, and apparatus showing the development of the art and technology of photography. The museum collections are made available for study, and the staff of the museum appear to welcome the opportunity to be of assistance to the student or scholar with questions about the museum's holdings. The permanent exhibits include daguerreotypes, cartes de visite, tintypes, stereoviews, cameras, mutoscopes, and a great deal more. IMP/GEH publishes *Image*, a museum quarterly made available to associate members of the museum. The second center for the study of photography is the relatively new International Center of Photography (1130 Fifth Avenue, New York, New York 10028). The center is "dedicated to the appreciation of photography as the most important art/communication form of the twentieth century with the capacity to provide images of man and his world that are both works of art and moments in history. It offers to those who share this recognition a unique program of education, exhibitions, information, publications and archival facilities." Membership in the center is made available to the public.

Valuable as all these resources may be, it is still true today that the study of photographic history is in its infancy. Major photographers have been identified, major trends to some extent analyzed, but for each Julia Margaret Cameron or Lewis Carroll about whom a book has been written there are dozens upon dozens of other photographers of considerable accomplishment, about whom little is known and about whom scarcely anything at all has been written. An index of just how far we still have to go is supplied in the bibliography of theses and dissertations furnished in 1973 by *Photography: Source & Resource*. A questionnaire turned up the fact that between 1942 and 1972 there were just 139 scholarly studies completed in the United States in the field of photography as fine art. Among those reported, a good number, judging from the titles, seem to have dealt less with art and more with the technical or commercial aspects of photography. Of the 104 institutions reporting, 71 percent stated that there had never been a paper completed at their school with photography as a main subject. It would seem that photography is only just beginning to enter the mainstream of scholarly pursuit and that we have far to go.

Landmark Dates in the History of Photography

1558   Giovanni Battista della Porta described the camera obscura in his book *Natural Magic*, with the effect of encouraging the use of this rudimentary camera as well as producing a greater interest in the general study of optics.

1727   Johann Heinrich Schulze published the results of his observation that it was light rather than heat which would darken a solution of silver nitrate. This discovery would prove fundamental to the photographic process.

1802   Thomas Wedgwood and Sir Humphry Davy announced the results of experiments to produce an image by laying objects on the prepared surface of paper or leather and exposing this arrangement to the sun. The resulting pictures produced in silhouette were, however, extremely unstable.

1826   After about ten years of experimentation, the Frenchman Nicephore Niepce succeeded in taking the world's first photograph, on a polished pewter plate which he had coated with bitumen of Judea and exposed to the sun for eight hours.

1829   Niepce, failing to interest the Royal Society (of England) in his discovery of "heliographie," or sun drawing, entered into partnership with L. J. N. Daguerre in an effort to discover the practical applications of his invention; Niepce's death soon ended the partnership, however.

1835   During this summer, the Englishman William Henry Fox Talbot produced the first of his images on paper showing actual views, paper negatives only one inch square made with a tiny camera and an exposure of half an hour.

1837   Daguerre, working on the material furnished by his partnership with Niepce, produced the first of the daguerreotypes which have survived to this day. The length of the exposure time required, Daguerre found, might be as short as three hours, as long as seven or eight.

1838   Sir Charles Wheatstone invented the stereoscope, to recreate binocular vision in the viewing of pictures.

1839   Fox Talbot presented the results of several years of experiments with "photogenic drawing" to the Royal Society of London, just a few months ahead of Daguerre's announcement, through the French Government, of his own process. Fox Talbot called his photographs, made on paper, calotypes. Another Englishman, Sir John Herschel discovered that hyposulphite of soda ("hypo") would "fix" his photographs —render them stable. Also in this same year, Talbot privately printed *Some Account* *of the Art of Photogenic Drawing*, the world's first separate publication on the subject of photography.

In August, 1839, the French Government released information on Daguerre's process for making pictures from life by exposing a metal plate coated with silver and then developing a positive image with mercury vapor. The French Government announced that it intended to make the new process free to the world. Also in 1839, Daguerre succeeded in producing the first photograph containing the image of a man, in a picture taken of a Paris boulevard. In September, news of how to make a daguerreotype reached the United States and within weeks several persons with some knowledge of chemistry had succeeded in producing adequate images. The first daguerrean portrait was made by Professor John W. Draper of New York University, who one year later would become the first, as well, to take a successful photograph of the surface of the moon.

1840   The first daguerrean studio in America was established, in New York City, by the partners Alexander Wolcott and John Johnson. For more than fourteen years the daguerreotype would be overwhelmingly the type of photographic process best known and most employed in the United States.

1841   Friderich Voightlander began producing a camera containing the first good portrait lens, one designed by Joseph Max Petzval of Vienna. This same year, Fox Talbot patented his process for making the calotype. Later also called the Talbotype, this was a positive print produced from a negative, made on specially prepared writing paper. By making possible the production of a number of prints from the single negative, Talbot had laid the groundwork for modern photography. However, for the duration of its patent, Fox Talbot severely restricted the use of the calotype, thereby effectively hindering immediate further progress.

1843–48   During this period two Scotsmen, the painter David Octavius Hill and the chemist Robert Adamson, collaborated to produce over 1500 calotypes. The main body of their work constitutes one of the finest collections of portraits ever made.

1844–46   Fox Talbot's book *The Pencil of Nature* was issued in six parts, to become the first book ever published containing original photographs—one of the great milestones in the history of photographic literature.

1847   Niepce de St. Victor announced the first practical procedures for producing a photograph on glass, by coating the plate with albumen and potassium iodine, then allowing it to dry before it was sensitized. His plate was, however, too slow to permit portraits.

1850   A year that marked a major turning point in the history of photography, in which the following events took place:

L. D. Blanquart-Evrard introduced the use of albumen paper for printing; the albumen print would be standard for at least the next forty years.

F. Scott Archer introduced his wet-collodion process for making photographic negatives on glass. The new process quickly began to supplant previous methods for making photographs and would remain the leading method for the next thirty years. It would make possible a new kind of news reporting, open up new vistas for photography on the American western frontier, and generate a fad for collecting photographs, notably the carte de visite, then cabinet cards, and finally also the stereograph. During this year manufacture was commenced of a stereoscope invented the previous year by Sir David Brewster for the viewing of a pair of photographs for three-dimensional effect.

1851   The showing of photographs at the Great Exhibition held at the Crystal Palace in London spurred interest in the techniques of photography and created new enthusiasm for its progress as an art.

1852   An adaptation of the wet-collodion process, called the ambrotype, was announced by F. Scott Archer and Peter W. Fry. When introduced into the United States, the ambrotype, between 1854 and 1860, would replace the daguerreotype as the popular means of portraiture.

During this same year, Fox Talbot relaxed the patent restrictions on the calotype, retaining only the licensing of the making of portraits by professional photographers. This was followed by a brief flowering of the calotype but it was soon entirely eclipsed by the wet-collodion method of producing a negative on glass.

1853   In England, manufacture was commenced for a two-lens stereopticon camera.

1854   John C. Warren published the first American book to be illustrated with a photograph, in this case a single salt print.

Also in 1854, the carte de visite form of photograph was patented in France by Andre A. E. Disderi. By 1859–60 the collection and exchange of these cards would have become an international fad.

This year also saw at least the beginnings of a number of experiments in an attempt to develop a dry-collodion process, by which a photographic plate might be prepared in advance and then stored rather than used at once as was necessary with the wet plate.

1855   Alphonse Louis Poitevin introduced the collotype and the carbon print, thus leading the way to the popular illustration of books with photographs.

In photographing the events of the Crimean War, the Englishman Roger Fenton became the world's first accredited wartime photographer.

1856   The ferrotype, more popularly known as the tintype, was patented in the United States, becoming a cheap means of photography popular through the Civil War years and later.

In Paris, the photographer Nadar claimed to have become the world's first aerial photographer, taking his pictures while aloft in a balloon.

1859   The stereographs made by photographer C. L. Weed became the first photographs made of the Yosemite region. These and other magnificent photographs of the American West would help build the great popularity of stereoscopic viewing, a popularity which would last until around 1910.

In Edinburgh, Scotland, George Washington Wilson produced some of the first action photographs, showing pedestrians in a city street. In New York, Edward Anthony made his own "instantaneous" photographs, of traffic in that city.

1861   Sir James Clerk Maxwell demonstrated his process for color photography.

1864   B. J. Sayce and W. B. Bolton published information on their invention of a process using a collodion emulsion to coat a glass plate which could then be dried and used later; Sir Joseph Wilson Swan perfected the carbon print process; and Walter Bentley Woodbury introduced his Woodburytype process, suitable for copying photographs for book illustration.

1866   A year which marked the beginning of a series of government surveys of the American West which would, over the next decade, produce photographs important to the history of outdoor photography.

1869   Louis Ducos du Haron published the results of his experiments with the subtractive method of three-color photography.

1871   Dr. Richard Leach Maddox invented a gelatin-bromide dry plate. This plate, improved upon by others over the next few years, would come into general use in 1878.

1872   Eadweard Muybridge undertook the first of his photographic investigations of animal motion.

1878   As photographers began to shift from the wet to the dry plate, William Henry Jackson photographed scenes in Yellowstone using only the dry plate; Charles Harper Bennett refined the process of making the gelatin plate to speed the exposure time to 1/25th of a second; and, in 1879, George Eastman applied for a patent on his improved dry plate and went into production the following year.

1880   On March 4, the first newspaper photograph was published in the *New York Daily Graphic*.

1884   The Eastman Dry Plate Company of Rochester began marketing a new, improved negative paper, and the following year the basic process was modified so that now the paper provided support only and the gelatin layer could be removed—as photographic film.

1885   Peter Henry Emerson of England led a movement back to naturalism in photography, opposing the current style of "art" photography, with its sentimental poses and contrived prints.

1886   Nadar, father and son, invented the technique of the photo-interview with their combination of a series of pictures with quotations from a conversation with the aged French chemist Chevreul.
   In 1886, the use of bromide paper for printing was introduced.
   George Eastman invented and patented a simple box camera.

1887   Eadweard Muybridge published his monumental *Animal Locomotion* demonstrating conclusively that the eye of the camera could convey a truth which was capable of dispelling myth.

1888   George Eastman marketed the first Kodak. Within a few years the introduction of rollfilm within a camera which was simple to use would revolutionize photography and make it a hobby within the reach of practically anyone; also, in 1888 John Carbutt invented celluloid cut film.

1889   A patent was granted for the Eastman transparent film, and the Eastman Company at once went into the production of its nitro-cellulose rollfilm. Also, within the next ten years, through the work of Gabriel Lippmann and Frederic Eugene Ives, several processes would be successfully developed for color photography.

1892   An association of photographers called the Linked Ring Brotherhood was formed in England for the encouragement of a more creative kind of photography.

1895   The first cinema was presented before a paying audience, a show produced by the brothers Auguste and Louis Lumiere in Paris. During the same year they patented an apparatus for taking and projecting motion pictures.

1896   The first salon-type exhibition of photographs was held in the United States, in Washington, D.C.

1902 Under the leadership of Alfred Stieglitz an informal New York-based group known as Photo Secession was launched; it was to influence styles in photography profoundly, not only through exhibitions but by publication of the journal *Camera Work*.

In Brief—Clues to the Recognition of Various Types of Old Photographs

The following is a simplified guide to the recognition of those major types of photographs a person interested in old photographs might be most likely to encounter. Often, of course, the positive, final identification of a particularly unusual print can be made only by someone who has studied past styles in photography and the work of the photographers associated with different techniques. In many cases, there is a constellation of minute but important signs which would be apparent only to the highly-trained eye. However, the following brief hints should prove useful by providing leads toward identifying newly discovered images that may possibly have historical as well as artistic merit. These hints should also be of some help in guiding the novice collector through the maze of terms to be found not only in photographic literature generally but in the catalogues of dealers and auction houses now specializing in photographic materials.

Albertype   The reproduction of a photograph such as was often used for book illustration during the 1870s and 1880s but which was outmoded soon thereafter. The Albertype, invented in 1868, closely resembles the Woodburytype of approximately the same period and has the same smoothly continuous intermediate tone. Often the title page will identify the illustrations as either Albertypes or Woodburytypes.

Albumen print   Any print made on albumen paper, a thinly coated paper with a characteristically high gloss and thus a lustrous appearance. This paper was made from the whites of chicken eggs. The image on such paper is usually of a brownish cast, and the photograph is customarily mounted, although sometimes the paper is so thin that this cannot be told without running a fingernail over the edge. Cartes de visite and cabinet cards are two of the most outstanding examples of its use. Most of the photographs made from wet-collodion negatives were printed on this paper. Albumen paper came into popular use in the early 1850s and remained the most popular printing paper until around 1890, when it was replaced by bromide paper.

Ambrotype   On glass, this is a direct image produced by the wet-collodion method of photography, and it was viewed as a positive when placed against a dark background. Most of the ambrotypes made were portraits and, like the daguerreotype it is almost always found enclosed in a miniature case. However, unlike the daguerreotype, the ambrotype may be viewed at any angle. It lacks the brilliance and detail characteristic of the daguerreotype, and its appearance has been described as a creamy gray, with highlights. It is relatively easy to identify because it is on glass and because its appearance is altered with the removal of the background. The ambrotype, invented in the early 1850s, was very popular in the United States for the brief period of about six years, beginning in 1854. Few ambrotypes were made after that period.

Bromide print   Any print made on a bromide paper, though the term more often specifically refers to those prints made on bromide rather than albumen paper when the bromide paper first came into use, around 1887. It was then favored by some photographers because of its delicate grays and whites, considered more pure than the brownish (toned) albumen paper which up until that time had been standard. Many of the earliest portraits made on bromide paper have, over the years, silvered—that is, faded, especially around the edges.

Calotype   Rarely produced in the United States, the calotype is a paper print made from a paper negative by a process patented in England in 1841 by W. H. Fox Talbot. The printing paper is uncoated, usually actually a high grade of writing paper which the photographer himself has prepared; the negative may be waxed or oiled. The image, which was highly subject to fading, is of a pleasing softness, brownish in tone, but frequently lacking in detail. In England calotypes were being made, in spite of the numerous patent restrictions, until around 1855 when the process was outmoded by the wet-collodion method of photography. In 1849 the firm of Langenheim Brothers in Philadelphia secured the American rights to Fox Talbot's patent, but it was already too late for much use to be made of it.

Carbon print   A type of print that could be produced in a variety of colors: the image is composed of a gelatinous pigment and required washing in water to produce the print rather than development in the more usual sense. The carbon print was popular for "art" photographs from the time of its introduction in 1864, when it might be used for copying the old masters, to around the turn of the century. More use was made of it in Europe than in the United States, however. The paper, coated with a layer of carbon suspended in the gelatin, is heavy and usually smooth. Carbon prints are not particularly subject to fading and thus have been called "permanent."

Collodion negative   A negative on a thick piece of glass on which the edges have usually been ground down, and with a collodion coating which the photographer himself applied. The collodion is generally of a grayish and uneven appearance, unlike the smoothness of the dry plate. The wet-collodion process was invented in 1851 and by 1860 had come into universal use. The wet plate was finally outmoded with the introduction of a commercially satisfactory dry plate, around 1880.

Collotype   A reproduction of a photograph, usually for book illustration, by any one of a number of methods using an inked gelatin printing surface. Examples of the collotype include the Albertype, heliotype, and Artotype, all popular toward the end of the nineteenth century.

Cyanotype   Popularly known as the blueprint, an image on an uncoated paper realized as a bright white against a brilliant blue. Although invented very early in the history of photography, around 1840, it did not, however, come into general use until after 1880, when it began to be employed in the reproduction of line drawings such as charts and maps. However, in the late nineteenth century, there was also a brief fad for the cyanotype among amateur photographers who enjoyed the simplicity of its process for printing.

Daguerreotype   A direct image on silver-plated copper, highly recognizable not only because of its brilliance but because it cannot be viewed satisfactorily from every angle. The daguerreotype, unless corrected, is also reversed left and right, as may be observed in any writing on signs which appear in outdoor scenes. In addition to the portraits usually found housed in miniature cases, there are also some daguerreotypes of a larger size, which were made of outdoor scenes. From the announcement of its invention by J. L. M. Daguerre in 1839 and its introduction into the United States in September of that same year, the daguerreotype reigned in this country as practically the only known method of photography until around 1854, when the ambrotype came in as its competition. By 1860 the daguerreotype had been entirely outmoded by the wet-plate method of photography, which produced the collodion print on paper.

Dry plate negative   Historically speaking, the dry plate was sandwiched in between the wet-collodion method of photography, on a heavy glass plate, and the early production of film for the camera. The dry plate became commercially available around 1880, and even long after the introduction of film and its close-to-universal use, the dry plate still had its advocates, until around 1920. The dry plate glass negative can be recognized by its relative thinness and its lightness, its sharp edges, and the relative smoothness of its coating.

Film   The familiar modern medium for photography. According to information published by the International Museum of Photography/George Eastman House at Rochester, New York, negatives on film may be dated as follows:

1889 to 1903:   A rollfilm which is extremely thin and curls. It may also wrinkle fairly easily.

1903 to 1939:   A somewhat thicker rollfilm, which has been coated on both sides with a gelatin to prevent its curling.

1913 to 1939:   This period marks the introduction of rectangular machine-cut sheet film. The edges are stamped "Eastman."

From 1939:   From this date the Eastman sheet film has been made of cellulose acetate and is marked "Safety."

Gaslight print   A print made on the gelatin-chloride paper found suitable at the end of the nineteenth century for printing directly from a negative under relatively weak artificial light rather than relying upon sunlight. Such a gaslight print often had a bronzed appearance or a metallic silvery sheen. The term may, however, also refer to any print made on bromide, rather than albumen, paper. It may also be used derisively to indicate a weak print.

Gum print   Often this is a print in color, frequently one altered to resemble a drawing, a print produced by a technique that permitted a high degree of control, on an uncoated paper—often regular drawing paper. The "art" prints, mostly of nudes, made by the Frenchman Robert Demachy around the turn of the century provide fine examples of the gum print. (See also **Pigment print.**)

Halftone   A reproduction from a photograph in which the image is broken into fine dots by a screening process and then transferred to a metal plate by a process that became generally available after 1890.

This portrait of Asher B. Durand, by an unknown daguerreotypist, has the brilliance and brisk detail of the best portrait work in this medium. Durand (1796-1886), in his late forties when this picture was taken, later achieved fame as the painter of sweeping landscapes and co-founder, with Thomas Cole, of an American school of landscape painting. (Courtesy of The New York Historical Society, New York City.)

Heliograph   The name bestowed by J. N. Niepce around 1825 upon his invention of the world's first permanent photographic image, which was secured on a pewter plate.

Oil print   An oil image produced on a gelatin base, frequently to give the effect of a painting, by a method devised in 1904 and popular for a brief while for "art" photography.

Palladium print   A print on paper which has been rendered photographically sensitive with salts of palladium. The result closely resembles the silvery tones of the platinum print. Palladium was introduced as a substitute for platinum when the latter became scarce during World War I. Few palladium prints were made after 1930.

Permanent print   This is a purely descriptive term that may be applied to any print which is relatively little subject to fading, such as the carbon print or platinum print or a photomechanical print such as the Woodburytype.

Photogravure   A soft, glowing reproduction of a photograph which, when printed under the supervision of the photographer himself—as in the images published in *Camera Work*—may be valued as a true example of the photographer's art. The photogravure is the reproduction of a photograph by a graphic arts process using printer's ink and an intaglio copper plate. The process was invented around 1880 and by the 1890s had come into use for book illustration, although limited by the relatively high cost of preparing the plates.

Pigment print   Any print made on a paper rendered sensitive by using a mixture of a colloid which hardens on exposure to light and a pigment and potassium bichromate. The image appears when the print is simply washed, rather than "developed." In gum printing, the colloid is gum arabic. A pigment print is often one which has been altered by being sensitized for a second time and then exposed once more under the negative. The pigment print, which began to be popular for "art" photography around 1895, continued to have some use until around 1915.

Platinotype   Or, the platinum print, a print achieved with platinum rather than silver as the sensitizing agent. It is characterized by a long tonal scale. Its delicate gray image is sometimes admiringly described as a blue-black, sometimes called cold. The platinotype has a high degree of permanency. This kind of print is customarily made on an uncoated paper which may have a slightly pebbly surface. Platinum paper began to be offered commercially around 1879, and this type of print was a favorite with the members of the pictorial school of photography. Its use dropped off during World War I when it began to be difficult to obtain platinum. Some of this paper was still produced, however, up until around 1930.

Platinum and ferroprussiate print   Easy to identify by its color—blue-green or blue—this is a platinum print which has been exposed a second time after having been re-sensitized with iron salts. It is then washed in water to bring out the final, altered image, rather than developed in the conventional manner.

Salt print   Also called salt- or salted-paper print, or silver print—a photographic print made on a plain, uncoated writing paper which has been prepared to receive the image by the photographer himself. The resulting image is of a fairly yellow or brownish tone. Silver prints were made by Talbot in his early experiments with photography on paper, around 1840. A calotype may be hard to distinguish from a print of later date made from a collodion negative if both were made on this kind of salted paper. Since salt prints absorb colors nicely, they are often tinted. Although by 1860 albumen paper had outmoded the softer and less-sharp silver print, there was a brief revival of it in the 1880s, according to William Welling in *Collector's Guide to Nineteenth Century Photographs*, who informs us that it was at the time favored by the American portrait studio of Bachrach.

Stereograph A double photograph, two images which have been photographed so that they may be viewed as one when seen through a special optical device known as the stereoscope. The result can be a startling impression of space and depth. The pictures were mounted side by side and had almost always been produced with a camera equipped with a double lens. Introduced in the 1850s and extremely popular by 1860, the stereograph, also known sometimes as stereogram, provided popular entertainment in the parlor for the Victorians.

Tintype Ferrotype or malainotype, a direct image made on a sheet of iron which has been japanned black or brown, usually a deep chocolate color. First produced in 1854, the tintype was made generally available as an inexpensive form of portraiture and became especially popular during the Civil War years, when a tintype might be worn as an ornament, carried about in the pocket or bag, or sent through the mail. Tintypes continued to be a cheap form of popular photography into the twentieth century.

Woodburytype A slightly purplish reproduction of a photograph, characterized by its continuous tones and capable of great detail, often used for book illustration because of its fidelity to the original. The Woodburytype was invented in 1864 and the American rights secured in 1870. It remained in popular use until the 1890s. With other methods of reproduction then available, its beauty could not compensate for the fact that each Woodburytype had to be separately mounted, and attempts to overcome this handicap did not prove successful.

Historic Names in Photography

It should be an easy task to compile a list of the worthwhile and eminent photographers of the nineteenth century. Yet even among those names best known to photographic historians, final critical judgments have not been rendered, to judge by swings of opinion in the recent past; and, fortunately for all of us, the situation is complicated by the continuing discovery of new talent which has been hitherto completely unknown or, more likely, quite unappreciated. We can only add these new names as they surface in the continuing process of evaluating and re-evaluating the achievements of the past. Since the collecting of old photographs is still a relatively new field, there will certainly be other, exciting discoveries, new names to be added to our roster, and new photographers whose techniques and approaches to photography we can study and learn more about. Exploring in the field of old photographs has some of the hopeful excitement of an archeological dig where we know that what we are looking for cannot be buried very deep. Any one of us may be fortunate enough to discover the work of some nineteenth century loner who, pursuing his own private vision, produced images which we will, today, find irresistible. It has happened before. We need only think of the Parisian photographer Atget, long obscure, finally discovered and acclaimed through the efforts of Berenice Abbott.

In looking over the following list of prominent photographers and other persons in the history of photography worthy of further study, we may be tempted to speculate on what the qualities are that even the most diverse photographers must bring to their work. One brief answer was supplied by Frederick S. Dellenbaugh. When Dellenbaugh was with the Second Powell Exploratory Expedition and camping out at the head of the Colorado River, he was approached by a young man who had been engaged simply as an oarsman, by name of John K. Hillers. Hillers had been watching Dellenbaugh slosh the chemicals on the glass plate, count down as he exposed it in the camera, snatch it out and retreat inside his portable darkroom, where the still wet plate had to be developed at once.

Hillers admired the photographer's skill and wanted to know if he could possibly become a photographer too. Dellenbaugh replied that he did not see why not, since Hillers appeared to be a "careful, cleanly man." Later when he himself had become a frontier cameraman, Hillers of course discovered that in addition to the carefulness and the tidiness required in handling the chemicals and the wet plate, he must possess the fortitude, perseverance, and the simple strength needed to haul about the cumbersome and heavy equipment needed for the wet-collodion process—but, more important, he needed the perceptive eye of the photographer, capable of transforming the actuality before him into a significant photographic image.

And what else is required? Marcus A. Root, in his book *The Camera and the Pencil; or the Heliographic Art* (1864), had this to say: "In the heliographic, as in other arts, are found two classes of persons—the artists, and the mere mechanics," adding that there were also certain "specific moral qualities which may be seen at first glance to be exceedingly important to the heliographer" especially if he is engaged in portraiture: in brief, first "amenity, cordiality, grace, and ease of manners"—or, in other words, politeness—and then "a bright sunshiney face," and, finally, vast patience.

Certainly the photographer of great accomplishment also needs the spirit of dedication. It can be the kind of dedication demonstrated by Alexander Wolcott of New York City, a manufacturer of dental supplies by trade. Wolcott patiently experimented with the daguerreotype process, shortly after it first became known in this country, to get a likeness of his future partner in the photography business, John Johnson, though the portrait could be no larger than the stone in a ring. Or, it could be the dedication of Edward Steichen in setting up a still life within a tent which has been shrouded to admit only one tiny shaft of light and then making an exposure over a period of time as long as 36 hours, to achieve in his picture an unusual sense of volume.

And then there is that quality called genius, which can be instantly apparent to us but can never be explained.

The following list contains a few names of persons other than photographers: innovators, inventors, leaders of movements, some sponsors of photographic enterprises, and a few proprietors of photographic parlors.

Dates have been included where possible. One of the peculiarities of research into the history of photography is that by and large the photog-

raphers themselves have rarely been included in the biographical dictionaries, the nineteenth century equivalent of *Who's Who*. The statesmen,
the editors, the eminent divines are all respectfully catalogued with their
accomplishments, but it is apparent that photography and thus photographers had not yet made the climb into full respectability. Some names,
therefore, have been included in spite of the fact that to date very little
information is available. Perhaps their inclusion here will inspire more
research into the stories of some of these pioneer photographers about
whom we now know so little.

For the collector who may need to know if a particular stereographer
or perhaps calotypist is known to the historians, there are a number of
other sources to which he may turn. There is a compilation of names in
William Welling's *Collectors' Guide to Nineteenth Century Photographs*.
Welling lists, by name only, the English and Scottish photographers of
the Daguerrean era, photographers of the 1840s and 1850s by region
(Boston, New England, New York State, etc.), and, separately, the stereo-
photographers of the 1850s and 1860s, by their country of operation.

Adam-Salomon   Antoine Samuel Adam-Salomon (1811–1881), a French sculptor
who, turning to portrait photography around 1855, became especially well-known for
his use of light in modeling portraits after the manner of the seventeenth century
Dutch paintings.

Adamson   Robert Adamson (1821–1848), Scottish collaborator of David O. Hill in
the production of about 1500 calotypes, mostly portraits, between 1843 and 1848.
Adamson, trained as a chemist, worked with Hill to produce portraits of all the several
hundred signers to the Scottish Act of Demission, for a picture which Hill intended
to paint from the assembled photographs. Hill's "Disruption painting" is now considered little more than a mediocre work, whereas the photographs made by Hill and
Adamson remain very likely the most magnificent examples of the beauty and sensitivity of characterization possible with the calotype process. The partnership ended
with the death of Adamson at the early age of 27. (See also **Hill.**)

Albert   Josepf Albert (1825–1886), a German portrait photographer whose achievements include an improvement on the basic collotype process, early work with color,
and the production of many cartes de visite. His Albertype process, named after him
and available as a means of photographic reproduction after 1868 and extensively
used for book illustrations, was admired for its fine tone and its fidelity to the original
photograph.

Anderson   James Anderson, pseudonym of Atkinson (q.v.).

Annan   James Craig Annan (1864–1946), a pictorial photographer and a member
of the Linked Ring Brotherhood. An exponent of "pure" photography, Craig Annan
was the first president of the International Society of Pictorial Photographers, founded
in 1904. Annan is also important for his re-discovery of the work of Hill and Adamson,
reassembling their calotype negatives and making new prints and five photogravures
which were shown by the Royal Photographic Society in 1898 and, in 1905, at the

Photo-Secessionist gallery known popularly as "291," in New York City. Craig Annan's photogravures on tissue from various issues of the journal *Camera Work* have recently sold at auction for $175, $225, and $400. Aside from the photography, the quality of the gravures themselves makes his appearances in *Camera Work* important.

Annan   Thomas Annan (1829–1886) of Glasgow, copperplate engraver who in 1855 took up photography, initially photographing landscapes and works of art. His portraits, which he made later, are admired for their natural posing and freedom from the props at the time generally thought appropriate to a portrait photograph. In 1868 Annan began to take the documentary photographs for which he is especially remembered, turning to the slums of Glasgow for his subjects. A Thomas Annan portrait described as "straightforward" and initialled "T.A." in the mount recently sold at auction for $250. A single carbon print from the Annan album published in 1877 titled *Old Glasgow* is probably worth at least $300 to $400. In 1866 Thomas Annan introduced the carbon process into Scotland.

Anschutz   Ottomar Anschutz (1846–1907), a German photographer who, in the 1880s, like Eadweard Muybridge in the United States, experimented with photographing animals in motion. Anschutz invented the electrotachyscope, a device for viewing a rapid succession of photographs for the purpose of studying motion.

Anthony   Edward Anthony (1818–1888), proprietor, with his brother, of one of the largest nineteenth-century photographic enterprises in the United States. As a recent graduate from Columbia College, with a degree in engineering, Edward Anthony was one of the first Americans to experiment with the daguerreotype process. Thereafter he was to pioneer in other kinds of photography as well. In 1841 he was the first photographer to assist in a government survey, one made of the disputed boundary between Maine and Canada. In the following year, 1842, he established a portrait studio in Washington, D.C., in partnership with J. M. Edwards. His studio work is notable for a complete set of the portraits of all the members of Congress. A collection of these portraits, called the National Daguerrean Gallery (not the only collection so called), was exhibited in New York, but all too soon, in 1852, it was destroyed by fire. The only known surviving portrait is the very familiar one of John Quincy Adams. After 1847 he entered into business as an importer of photographic supplies, and then as a manufacturer of them. He later entered into a partnership with an older brother to form the firm of E. and Henry T. Anthony. In 1859 Edward Anthony took a series of "instantaneous" stereographs of people walking about the streets of New York, thus producing some of the first successful action photographs, paralleling the efforts of George Washington Wilson in Edinburgh of that same year.

Anthony   Henry T. Anthony (1814–1884), who was in the photography business with his brother Edward after 1852, in charge of the manufacturing division of the business. He discovered an instantaneous process for the wet plate in 1858 and after that the brothers' firm specialized in making stereoscopic plates.

Archer   Frederick Scott Archer (1813–1857), English inventor of the wet-collodion process of photography, possibly as early as 1848. He published the first details of his new procedures in *The Chemist* in March, 1851, and a *Manual of the Collodion Photographic Process* in 1852. His invention revolutionized photography, displacing both the daguerreotype, which at the time was just about the only form of photography known in the United States, and the calotype, or Talbotype as it was later known, at the time the characteristically English form of photography. Archer never sought a patent for his invention, and he died a poor man. A sculptor, he had taken up the calotype process in order to make portraits of his sitters as an aid to his work.

Portrait of F. Scott Archer, by an unidentified British photographer. This picture was taken some time between 1851 and 1857. Scott Archer has just introduced his procedure for flowing wet collodion onto a glass plate to obtain a sensitive photographic emulsion, a procedure which would in turn make possible other long leaps forward in technique. His discovery had the immediate effect of sending amateur enthusiasts out into the country with their heavy plates, bottles of chemicals, cumbersome cameras, and portable darkrooms. One of its most significant long-term results was to make possible the use of photographs for book illustration. (Courtesy of the International Museum of Photography/George Eastman House.)

Not happy, however, with the quality of the paper used for the calotype, he began to experiment with spreading different substances on paper, then hit on the idea of using collodion on glass to make a negative, abandoning the paper negative altogether. In his process, collodion containing a soluble iodide was flowed onto a glass plate, the plate was tilted to distribute the collodion evenly and then sensitized by being dipped into a bath of silver nitrate solution. The wet plate then had to be exposed in the camera immediately, before the collodion could dry. Then the image had to be just as quickly developed and fixed, if possible within fifteen minutes. Although the equipment was cumbersome and the procedures certainly required a quick and clever hand, Archer's method was, nonetheless, a great leap forward. Perhaps most important, from a single collodion negative a number of prints could be obtained. In a testimonial to Archer after his death, *Punch* commented: "To the Sons of the Sun. . . . Now, one expects a photographer to be almost as sensitive as the collodion to which Mr. Scott Archer helped him. A deposit of silver is wanted (gold will do), and certain faces now in the dark chamber will light up wonderfully, with an effect never before equalled in photography. . . . Now, answers must not be negatives."

Atkinson Isaac Atkinson, an Englishman who assumed the pseudonym "James Anderson" and became known for photographs made in Rome around 1850. Atkinson specialized in photographing Italian architecture and the ruins of antiquities.

Babbitt Platt D. Babbitt, the American daguerreotypist who, in 1853, was granted the sole right to photograph on the American side of Niagara Falls, an important concession since the Falls were one of the most popular backgrounds for outdoor photography. Babbitt maintained a little pavilion at Prospect Point, on the American side, which functioned as his studio. His specialty was photographing tourists against a background of the foaming waters. Most of Babbitt's photographs of the Falls were made between 1854 and 1870. A glass stereo view of his "dark tent set up" clearly dated 1860, in near-mint condition, has sold at auction for $45, other examples of his work for slightly less.

Baldry Alfred Lys Baldry, an English photographer and printer best known for his work in the 1890s with W. J. Day in photographing nudes.

Baldus A naturalized French photographer, Edouard Denis Baldus was active after 1850 photographing architecture and sculpture, and in 1865 he photographed the effects of a flood in France. His work was mostly large wax-paper negatives, with which he was able to achieve unusually fine results. A group of just ten albumen prints presumably from an album titled *Vues de Paris en Photographie* (c. 1860) has been priced at $2,500 by a dealer. An albumen print of around 1855 and signed in the negative might be worth $500–$700.

Barker George Barker, an American commercial photographer noted both for his fine work and the romantic nature of his subject material. Barker achieved national fame with his photographs of Niagara Falls, with its sometimes bizarre effects of ice and snow. He also photographed scenes in Florida before the land boom of the 1890s and thus helped to promote that state as a winter playground. In addition, he photographed Indian and Negro life there, as well as the early village life of communities which later became cities.

Barnard George N. Barnard (1819–1902), best known for his Civil War pictures. During the War, Barnard served as official photographer for the Chief Engineer's Office, Division of Mississippi, and accompanied Sherman on his historic march to the sea. Earlier, Barnard had pioneered in taking photographs out of doors rather than in the studio and had also served as an assistant to Mathew B. Brady. A single albumen print from Barnard's *Photographic Views of Sherman's Campaign* (1866) on the original card mount with the printed title and the photographer's credit may be worth from $150 to $350. The complete series of 61 prints, each 10 by 14 inches, in contemporary full morocco, brought $9,000 at auction in 1976. Original, single photographs, such as those showing Civil War gravesites, Southern cities, or ruined mansions, sell for $160 to $200, to over $1,000.

Barnardo A man known simply to us as "Dr. Barnardo" was probably the first to use photography in public relations. In Victorian England, Dr. Barnardo was a humanitarian who not only rescued homeless children from destitution and a hopeless future, but realized that their sad faces could be used to help raise money for their food and clothing. Beginning in 1870 he sold packets of photographs of the children, some showing the contrast between their former state and their spruced-up condition after residence in a home for waifs.

Barnett H. Walter Barnett (1862-1934), a portrait photographer who in 1897 emigrated from Australia to London, where his sepia-tone platinotypes of celebrities helped elevate the general level of portraiture of the time.

Barraud William Barraud, an English portrait photographer with studios in London and Liverpool during the last half of the nineteenth century. Barraud published four volumes of his photographs of celebrities, *Men and Women of the Day* (1888–91).

Barry D. F. Barry, in the mid-1870s a photographer at Bismarck in Dakota Territory, who became known for his portraits of the Indians there.

Bassano Alexander Bassano, a well-known portrait photographer in London around the turn of the century. Bassano also did fashion photography.

Bayard Hippolyte Bayard (1801–1887), a French inventor who was at work on a process to make photographs on paper when Daguerre announced his own, different process in 1839. Although Bayard was one of the first, along with Fox Talbot, to succeed in making a paper negative, he believed that the daguerreotype was superior and permitted himself therefore to be bought out by the French Government, which had acquired the rights to the daguerrotype also. Some of Bayard's direct positives on paper remain, however, an important early photographic record of life in Paris at the time.

Beaman E. O. Beaman, who in 1871 served as photographer with Major John Wesley Powell's second expedition for the United States Topographical and Geological Survey of the Colorado River.

Beard Richard Beard (c. 1801–1885), the first in Great Britain and possibly in all Europe to open a studio for taking daguerreotype portraits (in March, 1841). Beard was also the first photographer in England to apply for the permission, necessary under British patent restrictions, to make daguerreotypes. In 1842 he himself patented a method for coloring the daguerreotype. Richard Beard supplied the daguerreotypes from which the wood-engravings were made for the three-volume *London Labour and London Poor*, published between 1851 and 1864, a pioneer and influential social study by Mayhew and others.

Beato Felice A. Beato, known for his pioneer work in war photography and views made abroad. A naturalized British subject, Beato met James Robertson in Malta in 1850 and the two began a long collaboration. After photographing Malta in calotype, they switched to the wet-plate process and took pictures in Egypt, Athens, and then in India where they documented the bloody and violent Indian Mutiny. From there, Beato joined the Anglo-French campaign against China and in 1860 photographed events in the Chinese Opium War. His most memorable pictures included those of the Mandarins signing a peace treaty. In 1862 Beato traveled on to Japan and subsequently published his *Photographic Views of Japan* in 1868. A small collection of 20 albumen prints of scenes in Egypt, half of them by Beato, brought $400 at auction in 1976.

Bedford Francis Bedford (1816–1894), an outstanding English photographer of architecture and ruins who worked chiefly in the 1850s and 1860s. His activities included touring and photographing the Holy Land; his book *The Holy Land . . .* (1866) contained 48 of his photographs. Some Bedford prints may still be found reasonably priced at $35 or even less.

Bell William Bell, an early experimenter with the use of the dry plate, who accompanied Lt. George M. Wheeler's expedition into Utah and Arizona in 1872, replacing Timothy O'Sullivan. His own original dry-plate process anticipated the general adoption of the dry plate by about ten years. An auction record of $650 was set in 1976 for a single 1872 albumen print, mounted and with the War Department emblem.

Bennett Charles Harper Bennett (1840–1927), a British amateur photographer who in 1878 developed a process for refining production of the gelatin plate to permit taking successful negatives at 1/25th of a second. His process required ripening a dry-plate emulsion by using heat.

Bertsch Adolphe Bertsch (? –1871), a French photographer who in the 1850s experimented with taking photomicrographs (albumen prints from wet-collodion negatives) of insects and other small life, producing images which were later hailed for their scientific value. In 1860 Bertsch invented a new miniature automatic camera.

Bierstadt Albert Bierstadt (1830– ?), a landscape painter with a specialty in mountain scenery, who accompanied Col. F. W. Lander's expedition west in 1858–59 taking stereoscopic photographs which were subsequently published by his family firm at Bedford, Massachusetts. With his painter's vision, Albert Bierstadt became an important influence on other photographers who later ventured west also to photograph mountain scenery.

Bingham Robert J. Bingham, a photographer who worked in the 1840s both in England and in Paris and is especially known for his daguerreotypes along with his copy photographs of the paintings of Delaroche. A chemical assistant to Professor Faraday at the Royal Institution, Bingham invented a method for improving the sensitivity of the daguerreotype plate, and he published a photographic manual—instruction book—in 1848.

Biow Herman Biow (1810–1850), a noted German photographer who is credited with having made one of the earliest news photographs. Biow made his historic daguerreotype showing the devastation wreaked by a fire in Hamburg in 1842.

Bisson Freres The brothers Louis Auguste (1814– ?) and Auguste Rosalie Bisson (1826– ?), French daguerreotypists in the 1840s who later changed over to the wet plate and are best known for their dazzling views of the Alps made in the early 1860s. In 1860 the brothers attempted to climb to the summit of Mont Blanc and, although they did not succeed, brought back many photographs. In the following year August Bisson reached the summit. He was accompanied by 25 porters, needed to carry his mammoth load of photographic equipment. His photographs taken from the summit are still today some of the best pictures ever made there. A single Bisson Freres (wet-collodion) albumen print of the transept of a cathedral has been offered by a dealer for $150.

Black   Alexander Black (?–1940), an American lecturer on photography who in 1893 anticipated motion pictures with his series of lantern slides telling the serialized story of a "Miss Jerry, lady reporter." Black had a long career in photography as author, editor, and educator.

Black   James Wallace Black learned the daguerreotype process in 1845 and in 1856 became a partner of John A. Whipple, in Boston. Black is credited with having made the first aerial photograph in the United States, from a balloon in 1860.

Blanquart-Evrard   Louis Desire Blanquart-Evrard (1802–1872), a French inventor who in 1850 developed a new kind of sensitive photographic paper made with albumen. This paper immediately came into popular use and for several decades remained the standard paper for prints. Before that, in 1847, he had announced his own modification of the calotype. The house of Blanquart-Evrard was the first photographic publishing house in France. Blanquart-Evrard published his own first *Album Photographie* in the summer of 1851. One of his original calotypes—characteristically not faded as calotypes generally are—might be worth more than $400.

Boak   M. Boak, an English photographer who, in the second half of the nineteenth century, operated the firm of Boak and Sons, a chain of photographic studios for cartes de visite and then cabinet photographs. Boak is personally known for his photographs of the interiors of churches.

Bolton   W. B. Bolton (1848–1889) who, with B. J. Sayce in 1864 invented the collodion emulsion dry-plate process which successfully freed the photographer from having to prepare his own photographic plates immediately before using.

Bogardus   Abraham Bogardus (1822–1908), who opened a daguerreotype parlor in New York City in 1846 and many years later, from 1868 to 1873, served as the first president of the National Photographic Association. Bogardus' last photographs were made around 1887.

Bourne   Samuel Bourne (1834–1912), an English photographer who accomplished some of his best work in India, where he maintained a studio in Calcutta. He made several expeditions into the Himalayas and is perhaps best known for his prints, from wet-plate negatives, of the mountain scenery there, made in the 1860s.

Bradley   Henry W. Bradley, a San Francisco daguerreotypist of the 1850s. Later the firm of Bradley and Rulofson, in San Francisco, specialized in mammoth-plate photographs of western views. (There was also a Bradley's Gallery, a daguerreotype studio, in Philadelphia around the same period.)

Brady   Mathew B. Brady (c.1823–1896), photographer, photographic entrepreneur, and possibly the best-known name in American photography. Brady was an enormously successful professional photographer who made a fortune, only to lose it as an amateur directing the work of his Civil War corps of photographers. In 1844 Brady opened his first daguerreotype studio, at the corner of Broadway and Fulton Street in New York City, where he was possibly the first to use a skylight for illumination. He eventually had galleries both in New York and Washington, D. C. The Washington gallery was opened in 1847. To have your portrait made by a Brady establishment became a mark of prestige; however, "daguerreotype by Brady" was a trademark rather than a personal signature, for Brady employed many technicians, "operators" as they were known. Brady's accomplishments include making the portraits of hundreds of the most important men of his day, including among the Presidents, Andrew Jackson in 1845, the year in which Jackson died. In 1850 Brady published his *Gallery of Illustrious Americans,* a collection of 12 lithographs after daguerreotypes—collected, now, as an example of photographic ephemera. In 1860 Brady had the honor of photographing the Prince of Wales during his visit to America. His memorable portrait of Abraham Lincoln on the day he made his famous speech at Cooper Union in New York was widely circulated and, by helping to establish Lincoln as a man of both character and greater poise than he had been given credit for, helped elect him president. Robert Taft, author of *Photography and the American Scene* (1938), considers Brady one of the foremost historians of his day, but more particularly for his early daguerrean portraits than for his later accomplishments during the Civil War. Beaumont Newhall's *Masters of Photography* (1958) omitted Brady, with the explanation that the evidence pointed to him more as a pictorial historian, collector, and publisher than as photographer. As early as 1851 the *Photographic and Fine Art Journal* had noted that Mathew Brady could no longer be considered an "operator"—of the camera—because of badly fading eyesight. However, a second major phase of his career, as the organizer of other photographers, was still to come. The staff of wartime photographers under Brady numbered at times 20 men. This team produced over 7,000 negatives, for pictures which provided the first entirely realistic record of activity in war, even though many of the "battle scenes" were taken after the event. Among the photographers who served under Brady were T. H. O'Sullivan, Alexander and James Gardner, T. C. Roche, Louis H. Landy, David Knox, and others who successfully pursued independent careers later. During the 1870s Brady had to give up ownership of the Civil War negatives, and in 1874 the U.S. War Department acquired a Brady collection. Another full set of negatives held by E. and H. T. Anthony was later re-discovered by John C. Taylor of Hartford (who sold some prints in the 1880s), and was finally established as the Ordway-Rand Collection. A single Brady print of the war may be worth from around $100 up, depending both on the historic importance of the print and its rarity. The "Imperial" group photograph, taken of the Prince of Wales and his party in New York on October 16, 1860, has been offered by a dealer for $3,000. Many of the Brady Civil War photographs are in the $600 to $950 range.

Braun   Adolph Braun (1811–1877), nineteenth-century French photographer known for his copy photographs as well as portraits and large panoramas constructed from several negatives.

Brewster   Sir David Brewster (1781–1868), an English inventor who, in 1849, suggested the use of a special binocular camera for stereographic photography. However, his double camera was not enthusiastically received at first, and for a few years more it was still more usual to employ two cameras set side by side.

Brinckerhoff   J. de Witt Brinckerhoff, a New York photographer who devised a method for producing a photographic image directly on a wood block as a guide for the engraver. The first example of his work to appear in any publication was a portrait in the February, 1855 issue of the *Photographic and Fine Art Journal.*

Britt   Peter Britt (1819–1909?), an ardent daguerreotypist, who is believed to have been the first to carry his photographic equipment across the Rocky Mountains, emigrating to Oregon around 1852. However, none of the daguerreotypes made on this trip seem to have survived.

Brown Eliphat M. Brown, Jr. (1816–1886), the first photographer to be assigned to an official United States Government mission abroad. Brown's daguerreotypes made when he was attached to Commodore Perry's expedition to Japan in 1852–54 helped establish the use of photography in documentation.

Brown Among the many other Browns, there is W. Henry Brown, photographer of the West in the late nineteenth century who specialized in scenes of Indian life and of the remnants of Spanish culture in the Southwest.

Brugiere Francis Brugiere (1880–1945), member of Photo Secession, at first in San Francisco and then later, after 1919, in New York City, where he became known for his photographs of stage productions. In 1926 he began a series of light abstractions, and in his later life followed a multiple career, as stage designer, sculptor, painter, and film maker.

Buckwalter Henry H. Buckwalter, the first newspaper photographer in Colorado, whose exploits included being the first in that state to ascend in a balloon, in 1893.

Bullock John G. Bullock, late nineteenth-century Philadelphia photographer and then Photo-Secessionist, whose albumen, platinum, or sepia prints are now generally valued at more than $100 each, possibly to $400. However, a c. 1905 portrait of a fashionable woman, featured on the cover of a Sotheby Parke Bernet auction catalogue, brought $650.

Burgess John Burgess, who in 1873 marketed the first gelatin dry plates, an important step toward the outmoding of the wet plate entirely and in the direction of ease of camera use.

Camarsac Lafon de Camarsac (1821–1905), a highly skilled and prolific producer of photographic enamel miniatures.

Cameron Henry H. H. Cameron, the son of Julia Margaret Cameron, who operated his own photographic studio in London from the 1880s to 1900.

Cameron The Englishwoman Julia Margaret Cameron (1815–1879), a master of the soft focus and the romantic style, portraitist, and photographer of allegorical subjects. Active in photography only briefly, from 1863 to 1875, she had taken up photography at the age of 48. Her portrait subjects included many notables— Tennyson, Carlyle, Darwin, Browning, Longfellow—who reportedly submitted to the "torture" of sitting for the demanding Mrs. Cameron only because of the compelling image her skill could capture on the glass plate. She also drafted the humble people of her immediate community to pose for her series of allegorical studies in the costumes she devised for them. It is generally agreed that Julia Margaret Cameron was a consummate portraitist. The adjective "Dickensian" has been applied to her to describe her bouncy, domineering personality. Mrs. Cameron dared to do things entirely her own way, ignoring the current rules for focus, exposure, and lighting. Her large prints, which were never retouched, were frequently marred by dust, cracks, and even fingerprints in the negative. This is not surprising if it is true that she did her own developing in what had been the coal bin and washed her prints in the well. Her draped allegorical figures seem extravagantly romantic by today's standards, seemingly endowed with haloes even in those instances where she did not actually supply them. It has been said that Mrs. Cameron "blundered her way through technique" to succeed in faithfully recording the truth of the inner man. She has been hailed as one of the greatest of the visual artists of the nineteenth century in any medium. And, incidentally, she may have been the first to have special lenses made specifically for poor definition and soft focus. Although single Cameron portraits, with the blind stamp of her agent Colnaghi and on their original mounts, have sold for as low as $150 on occasions past, others today bring as much as $1,700. An informal portrait of Tennyson, looking as the subject himself commented like a "dirty monk," has sold for $400, a more formal portrait for $850. Her most celebrated album, called the "Mia" album, presented to her sister in 1863, and containing works by both Cameron and others including Lewis Carroll, sold at auction in London for almost $100,000.

Carbutt In 1866 John Carbutt served as the official photographer to the 100th Meridian Excursion sponsored by the Union Pacific Railroad to celebrate the building of the railroad some 250 miles west of Omaha into Indian country. Many prints from his pictures were sold at that time, and in the next few years Carbutt continued to photograph western scenes, making about 300 stereoscopic views of the plains. Later he became a manufacturer of a nitrocellulose plate for use in photography.

Carjat Etienne Carjat (1828–1906), French photographer and journalist, particularly admired for his lively portrait style. An 1863 portrait of Baudelaire has sold for $775 at auction.

Carroll, Lewis Charles L. Dodgson (1832–1898), mathematician and creator of *Alice in Wonderland*, but also well-known and admired for his photographs, mostly of little girls. Carroll was passionately interested in photography and active as an amateur photographer himself between 1856 and 1880. His portraits include many of the literary notables of his day, including Tennyson and Millais. He also frequently photographed the children of his subjects. A genuine Lewis Carroll print may be identified by writing in the plate in Dodgson's own hand. In November, 1976, an auction record of $2,800 was set for the familiar 1860 albumen print showing Alice and Lorina Liddell as Chinamen.

Carvalho Solomon N. Carvalho (1815–1899), first a painter and then a daguerreotypist, employed as a photographer by Colonel J. C. Fremont in 1853 on an exploring expedition into the West as far as Utah, at which time he is reported to have made some unusual photographs of the peaks of the Rocky Mountains in ice and snow. The paper prints made by Mathew B. Brady from these original pictures in 1855-56 were apparently destroyed in a fire. In 1860 Carvalho published a book on his western adventures titled *Incidents of Travel and Adventure* . . . Carvalho also, in 1852, invented a process for making enameled daguerreotypes.

Chapman Levi Chapman, a New York leather merchant who took up the manufacture of miniature cases around 1847 at the same time conducting a prosperous business in other photographic supplies.

Charnay Desire Charnay, in the late 1850s a photographer from France who journeyed to America and photographed the Mayan ruins.

Chilton Dr. James Chilton, a New York physician and chemist who was one of the first Americans to try making a daguerreotype; Dr. Chilton also sponsored events to acquaint the public with this new science of photography.

Civiale   Aime Civiale (1821–1893), a French photographer who specialized in mountain photography during the second half of the nineteenth century.

Clark   Lewis Gaylord Clark, author of one of the earliest articles published in the United States on the subject of the daguerreotype which appeared in the December, 1839 issue of *The Knickerbocker*. Clark's account added greatly to the public interest in what he enthusiastically called an art of "exquisite perfection."

Claudet   Antoine F. J. Claudet (1797-1867), a French artist, scientist, and inventor, who settled in London where, in 1841, he opened the second photographic gallery to be established in England, the Adelaide Gallery. Claudet later extended his operations to a number of other cities. After bankruptcy in 1850, he re-established himself in London with a "Temple of Photography." Initially a daguerreotypist, he later specialized in the carte de visite. An all-around innovator, in 1841 he invented a process for shortening the exposure time for the daguerreotype and later pioneered in devising ways to color the daguerreotype. He was also one of the first to introduce the use of the backdrop in his studio. Although daguerreotype portraits by Claudet have sold at auction for $150 to $250, a single stereoscopic daguerreotype portrait in fine condition may be worth in the neighborhood of $1,500.

Collen   Henry Collen, the first to take out a license to make use of the calotype process invented by Fox Talbot. Collen opened a photographic studio in London in 1841. He used his calotypes, however, simply as the base for paintings which he executed right over the photograph.

Constable   William Constable, English daguerreotypist of the 1840s, known for his portraits; few Englishmen employed the daguerreotype method.

Cook   George S. Cook (1819–1902), a painter who turned to daguerreotypy, establishing studios successively in several Southern cities, including New Orleans and Charleston, South Carolina, where he settled down in 1851. He is especially known for his photographs of the Civil War behind the Southern lines.

Cooke   Josiah Parsons Cooke (1827– ?), an early American experimenter with the calotype when he was only fifteen years old. His negatives are among the earliest American ones which still exist. Cooke was long associated with Harvard College, where he had a distinguished career in chemistry.

Corbett   J. Corbett, a portrait photographer with a studio in Auckland, New Zealand, in the late nineteenth century. Corbett is known for his studies of the Maori people.

Cornelius   Robert Cornelius (1809–1893), an American daguerreotypist who succeeded in making portraits as early as April, 1840.

Critchlow   Alfred P. Critchlow of Massachusetts, inventor in 1854 of a plastic substance used for miniature cases. This substance, named the Florence Compound from the place of its manufacture, was composed of shellac and wood resin rendered dark with lampblack.

Cros   Charles Cros, inventor in 1869 of the subtractive process of color photography. Both Cros and Louis Ducos du Hauron, working independently, submitted the results of their experiments to the Societe Francaise de Photographie, but Cros did not continue with his research, being more interested, it appears, in the problems of color in painting.

Croucher J. H. Croucher, author of the *Daguerreotypist and Photographer's Companion*, first published in 1852 and then in later editions, covering a great many technical aspects of photography.

Cutting James A. Cutting (1814–1867) of Boston, who in 1854 secured three patents for modifications in the wet-collodion process to produce the ambrotype, a negative on glass viewed as positive against a dark background.

Dagron P. R. P. Dagron, a French photographer of the nineteenth century who produced some of the earliest microphotographs, playing a part in the siege of Paris in 1870 by helping set up a pigeon post for conveying messages.

Daguerre Louis J. M. Daguerre (1789–1851)—pronounced "Da-ger" with a hard "g" and accented second syllable—inventor of the daguerreotype, named after him. His 1839 invention, introduced into the United States that same year, was to set the course of photography in the United States for the next fifteen years. Daguerre became interested in light images because he was a designer of scenic and lighting effects. Daguerre's contribution was to take the heliographic asphalt process, the invention of his partner Joseph Nicephor Niepce, and, following Niepce's death, to develop a method of using the vapor of mercury to bring out a latent image. The daguerreotype employs silver iodide as the light-sensitive substance: a positive is made to appear on a thin sheet of silver which is over a thicker plate of copper. Daguerre used a photographic plate which measured almost exactly 6½ by 8½ inches, and it is from this size that other daguerreotype plate sizes are derived. The first announcement of the process for making a daguerreotype was made in August, 1839, at a meeting of the French Academie des Sciences, a date usually considered to mark the beginnings of photography. The French Government, in taking over the process from Daguerre, announced that it intended to make it free to the world, and, indeed, it was always free of patent restrictions in the United States. Having sold the rights to his invention, Daguerre's great contribution to photography was accomplished.

Dancer John B. Dancer (1812–1887), an English daguerreotypist and the manufacturer of photographic supplies. Dancer is known as the father of microphotography: to Dancer goes the possibly dubious distinction of having been able to reproduce the Ten Commandments in a photograph the size of the head of a pin. Dancer was also a pioneer in stereophotography and a manufacturer of one of the first binocular (stereoscopic) cameras, in 1853.

Darwin Charles Darwin (1809-1882) whose book *The Expressions of the Emotions in Man and Animal*, published in 1872, contained a series of photographs by O. G. Rejlander pioneering "instantaneous" photography which caught various fleeting expressions.

Davie D. D. T. Davie, operator of a daguerrean parlor in Utica, New York. The careful records which he kept of his business have assisted scholars in their study of such early photographic studios.

Davison George Davison (1857–1931), British photographer credited with having taken the first Impressionist photograph, titled "The Onion Field," in 1890. In 1892 he became one of the founders of the Linked Ring Brotherhood.

Davy Sir Humphry Davy (1778–1829), who reported the early experiments of Thomas Wedgwood in 1802 in the *Journal* of the Royal Institution. Both Sir Humphry and Wedgwood had succeeded in making simple sun pictures.

Daguerreotypists were hesitant to attempt to portray more than two, or possibly three, people in one picture because of the difficulty in getting them all to hold still long enough for the exposure. This appears to have been a remarkably steady group. It includes Horace Greeley, editor of the New York Tribune, Charles A. Dana, who became owner and editor of the Sun, and Bayard Taylor, another noted journalist and later Ambassador to Germany. This daguerreotype is thus doubly important, for the importance of the men in the group, as well as because of the fine picture. (Courtesy of the Library of Congress USZ62-8777.)

Day Frederick Holland Day (1864–1933), in the 1890s, was known for his bizarre photographic exploits—such as staging a mock crucifixion outside Boston in order to photograph it—but he was also famous for his nudes. A Photo-Secessionist, he preferred the platinotype as his medium and customarily signed and dated his prints in red.

Deane James Deane produced one of the earliest books illustrated with photographs for scientific purposes, *Ichnographs . . . Connecticut River*, published in Boston in 1861.

Degas Edgar Degas (1834–1917), not only a painter but an amateur photographer as well, and an enthusiastic user of panchromatic plates in 1895 when they were still new and relatively untried. He liked making truly big photographs, but few of them seem to have survived.

Delamotte Philip Henry Delamotte (1820–1889), a leading British calotypist before 1853 when he switched to the wet plate. He was the official photographer for the Crystal Palace Company, documenting the razing of the Palace at Hyde Park, London, in 1851 and the removal of the continuing Great Exhibition to Sydenham for its new opening in 1854. A Delamotte calotype is probably worth $150, but the later Crystal Palace series may command more. In 1854 Delamotte organized, in Manchester, the first exhibit at which photographs were shown along with other forms of art. He is also the author of a manual on photography and has many books illustrated with his photographs.

Diamond Dr. Hugh Diamond (1809–1886), the English photographer who has been called the father of medical photography. Dr. Diamond made a series of sympathetic portraits of the inmates of the Surrey County (mental) Asylum where he served as superintendent between 1848 and 1858. In pointing out the value of his portraits for the patients themselves, he said that his images were "examined with much pleasure and interest, but more particularly when they mark the progress and cure of a severe attack of mental aberration." Thus, he was one of the first to point the way to the social uses of photography both in providing medical evidence and in healing. Dr. Diamond also served for a number of years as the editor of the British *Photographic Journal*.

Disderi Andre Adolphe-Eugene Disderi (1819–c.1890), the French photographer who probably invented the carte de visite, who patented it in 1854, and certainly helped to make it popular. He was the photographer for whom Emperor Napoleon III halted a parade so that the great man might step into the studio to have his portrait made on a carte de visite. Contributing to Disderi's success as the operator of a photographic studio was his rapid system for affixing the photograph to the card and his original idea of printing his name and the address of the studio on the backs of the cards. In 1857 he patented a special camera with four lenses for making eight small photographs for the cards at one sitting. Disderi maintained studios not only in Paris but also in London and several other European cities, producing great amounts of work, all of which was, however, of consistently high merit.

Dixon Henry Dixon, an English photographer especially known for his work in recording threatened London landmark buildings and other handsome old structures, for the Society for Photographing Relics of Old London. An original carbon print from the 1879 series by Dixon and A. J. Boole might be worth $400.

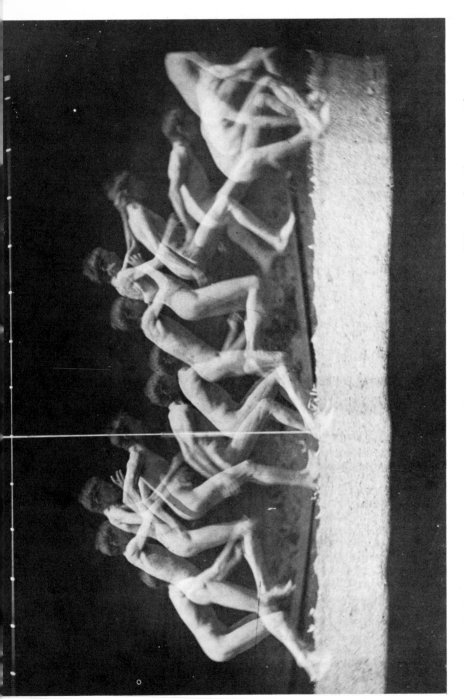

Muybridge's early experiments with the photography of motion are well known, but the painter Thomas Eakins also conducted experiments at the same time. Eakins is thought to have been responsible for the University of Pennsylvania's inviting Eadweard Muybridge to work there. One of Eakin's own contributions was suggesting to Muybridge the idea of imposing scales of measurement over the images in a print. (Courtesy of the Franklin Institute, Philadelphia.)

gravure from *Pictures of East Anglian Life,* still mounted on the original album leaf, may be worth at least $100, and sometimes two or three times that amount. Emerson was one of the most influential figures in the history of nineteenth-century photography.

England William England (? –1896), the inventor in 1861 of the focal plane shutter, and a photographer who specialized in alpine views. England served as chief photographer to the London Stereoscopic and Photographic Company in the 1850s but after 1863 conducted an independent operation.

Evans Frederick K. Evans (1852–1943), an English photographer active between 1895 and 1925, known especially for his sensitive work in architectural photography, including his pictures of cathedrals. He may be most famous, however, for his portrait of Aubrey Beardsley in profile. An adherent of platinotype printing, he gave up photography when platinum became hard to obtain after World War I. All of Evans' negatives were, it has been said, destroyed after his death. A single platinum print, with Evans' blind monogram on the mount, may be valued anywhere from $150 up. For example, a portrait of George Bernard Shaw, signed by Evans, has brought $650 at auction; one other print sold for $1,300.

Fardon G. I. Fardon, an early advocate of the plate-glass (wet-collodion) method of photography, whose work includes scenes in San Francisco photographed on glass as early as 1856.

Faris Thomas Faris, who took up photography in 1841 and, according to Marcus A. Root, a contemporary, introduced the daguerreotype into the state of Ohio and subsequently became a leading daguerreotypist in the City of Cincinnati.

Fenton Roger Fenton (1819–1869), one of the great landscape photographers, an Englishman who in March, 1855, became the first wartime accredited photographer, serving in the Crimea. He was also the first photographer to record the sight of a battlefield, as well as the behind-the-lines scenes. For the production of 360 photographs of the Crimean War, his equipment included five cameras and 700 thick glass plates, and its transportation to the front required the use of four horses. Wood-engravings made from his photographs were published in *The Illustrated London News.* Prior to this Fenton had toured Russia taking photographs and, in 1853, had been instrumental in founding the Photographic Society of London. At auction, his photographs of the Crimean War, mounted on a folio card and with the T. Agnew blindstamp and printed title, have brought from $300 to $900; also at auction, his salt prints—landscapes and portraits made in the 1850s—have been worth $200 to more than $600.

Ferrier Claude-Marie Ferrier, who with A. Ferrier and Charles Soulier in 1860 made memorable glass stereoscopic transparencies showing the traffic on a Paris street arrested in mid-action—a triumph for the day.

Fitz Henry Fitz, Jr. (1808–1863), an American daguerreotypist who, in December, 1839, became one of the first to make a daguerreotype portrait. His subject was himself, and the length of the exposure time meant that he had to keep his eyes closed. Although possibly not the first portrait to be made, it is apparently the first self-portrait. Fitz was a locksmith early in life and later a manufacturer of telescopes and lenses; he also operated a daguerrean parlor in Baltimore. Fitz was among the first photographers to try taking scenes out of doors.

Fizeau   Hippolyte Louis Fizeau (1819–1896), inventor in 1840 of a process for gilding the daguerreotype plate to increase the contrast, as well as to protect the plate. A solution containing gold chloride was flowed over the plate after it had been bathed in hypo and then heated.

Foucault   Jean Bernard Leon Foucault, a French photographer who around 1844 may have been the first to take a successful picture of the sun.

Fredricks   Charles deForest Fredricks (1823– ?), the proprietor of a New York City portrait gallery which specialized in the carte de visite. Fredricks may have been responsible for introducing the carte de visite into this country. In the middle of the nineteenth century his "Photographic Temple of Art" produced portraits of great competence, work now considered the epitome of the style of the day.

Fremont   Col. John C. Fremont (1813–1890), organizer of an expedition in 1853 to explore the West and employer in this capacity of the daguerreotypist S. N. Carvalho (q.v.), thus one of the first to see the uses of photography in exploration and scientific mapping.

Frith   Francis Frith (1822–1898), landscape photographer, some of whose most impressive photographs were taken on trips to Egypt, Palestine, and Syria between 1856 and 1860. He visited Egypt and the Holy Land year after year, customarily using three cameras, the largest producing 16 by 20 inch plates (enlargers were not in use at this time), sometimes working in the desert under conditions which would be declared impossible by most photographers. Beginning in the late 1850s his photographs were published in a number of books. Photographs by Frith are also to be found in albums, in specially large folio editions, on stereoscopic slides, or mounted separately. Since the company which he established, the Francis Frith & Co., published so many pictures, it is thought that only those with his name signed in the plate are individually his. The firm he established became one of the largest photographic publishers in the world; early in the twentieth century Frith of Reigate sold picture postcards as well. An original Frith photograph of the Pool of Hezekiah with the city of Jerusalem in the background, signed and numbered by Frith in the negative, has sold for $65.

Fry   Peter W. Fry (? –1860), a collaborator with F. Scott Archer in the development of the ambrotype in 1852.

Gardner   Alexander Gardner (1821–1882), a Scottish scientist and journalist who migrated to America in 1856, where he subsequently became famous for his photography. In that year he joined the staff of Mathew B. Brady as the manager of Brady's Washington studio, and in 1863 opened his own gallery in the same city. He served as a member of Brady's staff during the Civil War, then became official photographer to the Army of the Potomac, along with others who had previously worked with him under Brady, including O'Sullivan, Barnard, Woodbury, and his own brother James. Gardner's *Photographic Sketch Book of the War*, containing 100 actual photographs in two volumes, was published in 1866. In publishing his own war views in competition with Brady, he gave his photographers credit for each picture, which Brady did not do. In 1867 Gardner journeyed to Kansas as the official photographer for the Union Pacific Railroad, Eastern Division, making stereographs of prairie scenes, Indian life, and frontier dwellings. In 1868 he photographed a government conference with the Arapahoes and Cheyennes, at Fort Laramie in Wyoming. A single albumen print from the *Photographic Sketch Book*, on the original mount with the full printed identification—the photograph by Gardner or some other—brings from

$150 to over $300 at auction. A fine late-nineteenth century photogravure of a Lincoln portrait by Gardner may be worth as much as $150.

Gaudin A. Gaudin (1804–1880), the first to claim that he was able to make "instantaneous" views, in 1841. He was also the inventor of a number of improvements in the photographic process.

Gell R. E. Gell, a South African photographer who recorded events in the Boer War between 1899 and 1902.

Genthe Arnold Genthe (1869–1942), some of whose most notable photographs were made in 1894 in San Francisco's Chinatown and following the San Francisco earthquake of 1906. Genthe was one of the first photographers to make use of the dry-plate process to take street scenes which were unposed, and one of the first to use natural-color plates. Later, he adopted a rather different, soft-focus technique: the "Genthe style" consists of a soft focus with velvety blacks but brilliant whites. The early San Francisco prints or the later silver prints of nudes or theatrical personalities have sold at between $110 and $625 ("Study of Hands").

Girault J. P. de Frangey Girault, a Parisian daguerreotypist of the early 1840s and later a photographer of the Near East.

Glover Ridgeway Glover, a martyr to photography who was scalped by Indians when he was on assignment for *Leslie's Illustrated Weekly Magazine* to photograph scenes in the West. He was killed by a Sioux raiding party near Fort Kearney in 1866.

Goddard John Frederick Goddard (1795–1866), who in 1840 announced a practical method for increasing the light sensitivity of the daguerreotype plate by fuming it with chlorine as well as iodine. His discovery facilitated the opening of the first portrait studio in Europe, operated by Richard Beard in London.

Goodwin Hannibal Goodwin (1822–1900), inventor of the first transparent photographic film, a pellicle made by flowing a solution of nitrocellulose over a smooth surface such as glass. In 1887 he filed for a patent, but because of the many problems produced by the filing of rival patent claims, Goodwin's patent was not granted until 1898. However, the principle he had discovered became pivotal in the development of photography into a popular pastime. Goodwin was a clergyman by profession.

Gouraud Francois Gouraud, a Frenchman who arrived in New York City at the end of November, 1839, and traveled about the United States during the following year, demonstrating the newly-announced method for making a daguerreotype. Acting as an agent for Daguerre, and exhibiting a number of the daguerreotypes made by Daguerre himself, Gouraud was photography's first promoter. He provided demonstrations in New York, Boston, Providence, and other eastern cities, at an early time in photographic history when a man ambitious to become a photographer had to build his own camera and assemble his own materials and chemicals. To a certain extent Gouraud was responsible for the fact that for more than a decade the daguerreotype would be the popular American form of photography, rather than the calotype. In response to popular demand, Gouraud edited a condensed version of Daguerre's manual explaining his process. This manual, published in Boston in 1840, can thus be considered the first American—though not native—book on photography.

Griswold Victor Moreau Griswold (1819–1872), a painter and an inventor also known as a daguerrean artist. A manufacturer of sheet iron, Griswold originated the name "ferrotype" for the metal he sold for making what became known as tintypes. His rival in the manufacture of the metal plates was Peter Neff, who advertised his plates as "melainotypes," and the contest between the two came to be dubbed "The War of the Roses" after the fact that Griswold's plant was located in Lancaster, Ohio. In 1851 Griswold moved his plant to Peekskill, New York, where he continued in business for the next six years.

Gros   Baron Jean Baptiste Louis Gros (1793–1870), who in 1842 became the first to take photographs of Bogota, Colombia, where he was at that time serving as charge d'affaires.

Gurney   Jeremiah Gurney, a well-known New York daguerreotypist of the mid-nineteenth century, and a recipient of many awards. His reputation, in his own day, rivalled that of Mathew B. Brady. A partnership with C. D. Fredricks was dissolved in 1856, but Gurney's son Benjamin continued in his father's business for about fifty years. The Gurney company motto: "I have chained the sun to serve me."

Hale   Edward Everett Hale (1822–1909), as a very young man an early experimenter with the calotype process, at Cambridge, Massachusetts, as well as one of the first to make daguerreotypes in the United States. His first successful daguerreotype was apparently that of the Boston church in which he would later, coincidentally, be assigned to serve as pastor.

Harrison   C. C. Harrison, American pioneer manufacturer of photographic lenses and cameras. Harrison's portrait in the February, 1855, issue of the *Photographic and Fine Art Journal* was the first example of the transfer of a photographic image to a wood block for engraving and publication.

Hart   A. A. Hart, a Sacramento, California, photographer who photographed the development of the Central Pacific Railroad built east from California to connect with the Union Pacific in 1869. In his pictures the tracks themselves often provided a dramatic focus for the scenery. After Hart's death, in that same year, C. E. Watkins acquired his stereograph negatives, from which he sold prints.

Du Hauron   See **Ducos.**

Hawarden   Clementina Elphinstone, Lady Hawarden (1822–1865), a Victorian English photographer noted for her thought-provoking images. She often employed mirrors, windows, and costumed models to evoke the contradictions she found in upper-class life.

Hawes   Josiah Johnson Hawes (1808–1901) of Boston, who claimed to have been the first to open a daguerrean parlor there and who became one of the great portrait artists in this medium. About 1845 he formed a partnership with A. S. Southworth and their firm became well-known both for the extent of its business and the charming informality of its portraits. Hawes and Southworth owed much of their success to the personal care they gave to the details of making their portrait studies. This firm, unlike most of the other daguerreotypists of the day, made several exposures and offered the sitter his choice of whichever he considered the best. As a result, there may still be found what appear to be duplicates of just one pose, all equally authentic. Some of the most important men in art and politics came to the Boston studio to pose for Southworth and Hawes.

Hayden   Dr. Ferdinand Vandiveer Hayden, explorer and scientist, who in 1870 published *Sun Pictures of Rocky Mountain Scenery* containing photographs by Capt. Andrew J. Russell showing the building of the transcontinental railway.

Haynes F. Jay Haynes, photographer of the Yellowstone area following the initial era of exploration. In 1876 Haynes was designated the official photographer for the Yellowstone National Park, a post he held until 1916, when his son succeeded him. His portfolio of just 12 large photographs, each 17 by 22 inches, published by the photographer himself in 1874, has brought $3,000 at auction. Other publications, however, may be worth only $100 to $225, and individual views may bring between $65 and $75. Boudoir (large card) views by Haynes have sold at $20.

Heath Vernon Heath, an English calotypist who operated a London studio called the Royal Photographic Studio; Heath published his autobiographical *Recollections* in 1891.

Hedderly James Hedderly, an English photographer who specialized in making positives on ceramics or porcelain plates.

Henneman Nicholas Henneman (1813– ?), an English photographer in the 1840s and supervisor of four different publications which furnished publicity for Fox Talbot's newly-invented calotype. Henneman was instrumental in the publication of Talbot's *The Pencil of Nature* (1844–46), containing 24 mounted calotypes. Henneman also supervised the publication of the June, 1846, issue of the journal *Art Union*, each copy of which contained a whole-plate calotype—an incredible find for any collector today.

Herschel Sir John F. W. Herschel (1792–1871), who in 1839 followed Fox Talbot in reading a paper before the Royal Society of London, at which time he announced his discovery of a method of using hyposulphite of soda ("hypo") to fix the photographic image. Among his other many contributions to photography—he was an inveterate experimenter—was the introduction of the terms "photography," "negative," "positive," and "snapshot." In 1842 he invented the cyanotype process, known as the modern blueprint today. In spite of his copious and varied service to photography, he is best remembered as an astronomer.

Hesler Alexander Hesler (1823–1895), a native of Canada who became active as a daguerreotypist in Wisconsin and Illinois. His 1860 portrait of Lincoln helped to make his name well-known. A copy, a platinum print by George B. Ayers made in 1881, was recently valued by a dealer in photographica at $500. His series of photographs made in 1851 along the upper Mississippi River is supposed to have been Longfellow's inspiration for "Hiawatha."

Heyl Henry R. Heyl, who in 1870 anticipated the work of Eadweard Muybridge to some extent by inventing a wheel for rotating photographs projected upon a screen, to produce the sensation of motion.

Hill David Octavius Hill (1802–1870), of Edinburgh, who with Robert Adamson produced some of the most effective calotypes ever made. Hill was by profession a painter, chiefly of romantic landscapes, and one of the founders of the Scottish Academy of Arts. He had tried making calotypes as early as 1840, one year after the calotype process was introduced, and subsequently became one of the first artists to envision photography as a tool. In 1843, with the assistance of Adamson, who was a chemist, he undertook to make the calotype portraits of all 450 delegates to the convention at which the Free Church of Scotland was founded. His intention was to eventually paint a single huge group portrait. The photographic portraits were made in full sunlight for an exposure of about 40 seconds, the subject generally standing against the darkness of an open door or with the background of a wall, often holding a symbol of his interests or profession. These portraits have remained for us a vastly more important record of the society of Hill and Adamson's Scotland than the crowded canvas which Hill later painted. The team of Hill and Adamson took other portraits, as well, about 1500 in all, usually in their outdoor studio or in the local cemetery. In their pictures of the fishing village of Newhaven, where the pastor was seeking to develop a safer design for fishing boats, they provided one of the earliest examples of the use of photography as documentary. The collaboration ended in 1848 with the early death of Adamson. As Beaumont Newhall has stated, we remember Hill and Adamson for "the dignity and depth of their perception" and their "awareness of individual character" as much as for their technical achievements, great as those were. Hill and Adamson calotypes rarely come into the market; the collector would probably have to pay anywhere from $300 up for a single vintage print, possibly more. As long ago as 1972 an album containing 32 Hill-Adamson prints brought over $11,000 at auction.

Hill   Levi L. Hill (1816–1865), inventor and daguerreotypist, also artist and Baptist preacher, who claimed in 1850 that he had discovered the secret of taking photographs in natural colors, a claim which has been recently verified by the research of Floyd and Marion Rinhart. Hill called his process the Hillotype. He is the author of *A Treatise on Daguerreotypes* published in 1850 and *A Treatise on Heliochromy*, 1856.

Hillers   John K. Hillers learned the art of photography during the course of Major John Wesley Powell's exploratory trip into the Grand Canyon in 1871, for which he had originally been hired as an oarsman. He subsequently became the official photographer, for the years 1872–76 and 1878, and also took hundreds of stereographs of the Indians. His work became better known through the publication of *Canyon Voyage* by Frederick S. Dellenbaugh, his instructor on the first expedition. An albumen print by Hillers on the original mount, might be worth as much as $400.

Hillyer   H. B. Hillyer, early daguerreotypist in Texas, who was appointed official photographer for the State of Texas during the Civil War.

Hime   Humphrey Lloyd Hime (1833–1903), a naturalized Canadian, one of Canada's earliest documentary photographers. In 1858 Hime was associated as photographer with the Assiniboine & Saskatchewan Exploring Expedition headed by H. Y. Hind, and in 1860 he published a portfolio showing the different peoples of Canada.

Hine   For Lewis W. Hine, see page 83.

Hines   T. J. Hines, a Chicago photographer who in 1871 joined Capt. J. W. Barlow's reconnaissance of Wyoming and Montana Territories, but most of whose negatives from that trip were, unfortunately, destroyed in the Great Chicago Fire.

Hinton   Alfred Horsely Hinton (1863–1908), head of the Linked Ring Brotherhood, a British group formed in 1892 to encourage naturalistic, even Impressionist, work in photography.

Hoffman   John D. Hoffman, in 1865 a photographer attached to Major R. S. Williamson's expedition to California and Idaho.

Hollyer   English photographer Frederick H. Hollyer (1837–1933), associated in the late nineteenth century with carbon printing and, later, the platinotype. Hollyer is best known for his photographs of the leading personalities of his day, authors and artists particularly, taken either in their homes or studios.

Holmes Oliver Wendell Holmes (1809–1894), poet and essayist, eminent in photography as well as in his profession of medicine, and in literary circles. Holmes was an enthusiastic collector of stereoscopic views and the inventor, around 1863, of a viewer to duplicate binocular vision. Among his many varied accomplishments, Holmes employed photographs to study the act of walking in order to design artificial limbs for wounded veterans of the Civil War. In a series of articles for the *Atlantic Monthly*, Holmes recommended the establishment of special stereographic libraries, reported on a "stereoscopic trip" across the Atlantic, and proposed his simplified form of stereoscope for parlor viewing.

Holtermann Bernard Otto Holtermann (1838–1885), a German settler in Australia who worked with photographers H. B. Merlin and Charles Bayliss to extol the wonders of his adopted country. They produced a negative of Sydney Harbor five feet long, the largest wet-plate negative in the world. This had required the construction of a 74-foot tower topped with a 10-foot camera with a 100-inch lens. Holtermann exhibited the negative along with a 30-foot panoramic view of Sydney at the 1876 Centennial Exhibition in Philadelphia.

Hooper Captain W. W. Hooper, an English photographer especially known for his pictures made in 1876–77 of the results of a famine in Madras.

Hoppe Emil Otto Hoppe (1878–1972), a photographer who traveled in Africa and other foreign places, the operator of portrait studios in England, and the author of numerous books on photography.

Houseworth Thomas Houseworth, San Francisco photographer, publisher in 1869 of a *Catalogue of Photographic Views of Scenery on the Pacific Coast and Views in China and Japan.* Houseworth catalogues generally provide information on the works of various western photographers.

Howlett Robert Howlett (? –1858), an English portraitist active in the middle of the nineteenth century, photographer for the painter W. P. Firth in preparation for his work titled "Derby Day."

Huffman Laton Alton Huffman (? –1931), American frontier photographer with a studio at Miles City in Montana, well-known for his views of Yellowstone and documentary work on the destruction of the wild buffalo herds. In the 1880s Huffman made several trips through the Yellowstone National Park; his 1883 series of views became especially popular. Huffman rather engagingly labelled 1878 Fort Keogh, Montana, workshop, built of cottonwood with an earthen roof, "Ye Studio— La Atelier." He is the subject of a biography by Mark Brown published in 1955, *The Frontier Years.* A single Huffman print, matted and framed, may be worth between $100 and $350.

Hull A. C. Hull, western photographer who in 1869 traveled with W. H. Jackson along the route of the Union Pacific.

Hull S. Wager Hull, a mid-nineteenth century photographer, a correspondent of Oliver Wendell Holmes.

Humphrey Samuel Dwight Humphrey, American author of a series of handbooks on photography published in the 1850s which went into numerous later editions. In 1849 Humphrey made a memorable photograph of the moon and in the following year established himself as a daguerreotypist in New York City. He became the editor and publisher of the world's first magazine devoted exclusively to photography, the *Daguerreian Journal.*

Hurter   Ferdinand Hurter (1844–1898), who in 1890, along with V. C. Driffield, published the results of experiments on the properties of light-sensitive materials.

Illingworth   W. H. Illingworth, a photographer from St. Paul, Minnesota, who specialized in landscapes and who accompanied Fisk's expedition into Montana in 1866, photographing the plains. Illingworth also served as photographer with General George A. Custer's expedition to the Black Hills of the Dakotas in 1874.

Insley   Henry Insley, inventor of the method of daguerreotype processing patented in the United States in 1852 which bears his name.

Isenring   Johann Baptist Isenring (1796–1860), of St. Gallen, Switzerland, the first, according to the Gernsheims, to hold a public exhibition of photographs, in 1840.

Ives   Frederic Eugene Ives (1856–1937), an American inventor who developed the first successful and entirely practical process of orthochromatic photography and also invented the first successful process for halftone photoengraving. His "photochromo-scope camera" produced a single image in color from three transparent positives.

Jackson   William Henry Jackson (1843–1942), the first to photograph the western regions that were later designated as national parks. Jackson was instrumental, through his pictures, in having Congress set aside the Yellowstone area as a national park. Jackson is probably the best known of the photographers who explored and photographed the West, primarily from his photographs made while employed in 1870–78 by the U. S. Geological Survey of the Territories headed by Ferdinand V. Hayden. However, Jackson returned year after year to the West and new explorations. The first book of photographs to emerge from the government surveys was Jackson's album titled *Yellowstone's Scenic Wonders,* published in 1871. Jackson started his career in partnership with his brother in Omaha in 1867, doing mostly portraits, but in 1868 he toured the Territory taking pictures of Indian life. The next year he followed the route of the Union Pacific Railroad with his camera, along with A. C. Hull, but his stereoscopic views were not especially successful. In 1879, when the Hayden Survey ended, Jackson established the Jackson Photographic Company with a studio located in Denver and subsequently became a specialist photographer for the railroads. He also produced photographs for the postcards marketed by the Detroit Publishing Company. In 1892 he visited the Grand Canyon and became the first to produce a substantial series of landscapes of that region. His autobiography *Time Exposure,* published in 1940, is particularly interesting for his account of the difficulties involved in packing his mammoth-plate camera and heavy load of equipment into mountainous regions. A portfolio of 41 photographs of Yellowstone by Jackson has brought $5,750 at auction. Albumen prints by Jackson, with the caption printed in the negative and mounted on the original board, may be worth anywhere from $100 to over $300; although, in 1976, an auction record of $1,700 was set for a single albumen print. A dealer has asked $250 for just six cabinet cards, all with Jackson's imprint on the reverse. A contemporary published work, such as an accordian folder of Jackson's pictures, has sold at around $80.

Johnson   George H. Johnson, an amateur photographer of Bridgeport, Connecticut, with whom George Eastman corresponded extensively in the process of working out his emulsion for the gelatin dry plate.

Johnson   John Johnson, who in March, 1840, with his partner Alexander Wolcott, opened the first daguerrean parlor in the United States, in New York City.

Johnson   Walter R. Johnson (? –1852), a pioneer daguerreotypist who introduced the daguerreotype process to Philadelphia in 1839. He served as a professor of physics and chemistry at the University of Pennsylvania between 1839 and 1843.

Johnston   Frances Benjamin Johnston (1864–1952), one of the first of America's documentary photographers, a pioneer woman photographer, and one of the first photographers to make a business of supplying pictures to magazines. Her major journalistic work was accomplished between 1889 and 1910, and thereafter she specialized in photographing places of architectural interest, as late as the 1930s doing a series on architecture in the state of Virginia. Her most notable work includes documentaries on iron ore mining operations, the women workers of Lynn, Massachusetts, and a series on the public schools of Washington, D.C. In 1899 she photographed Admiral George Dewey and his men on board the *Olympia* returning from their historic victory at Manila Bay. Her other photographs of notables included those of members of society in Washington, including the members of the President's own family. In 1901 hers was the last photograph made of President McKinley before his assassination. Miss Johnston also produced a sympathetic series of photographs of black institutions including most notably Tuskegee and Hampton Institutes. At a time, around the turn of the century, when Photo Secession secured the allegiance of many studio photographers, she apparently remained outside the movement, engaged in her daily round of varying assignments. "Her contribution to photography was not in technology or in artistic innovation but in excellence as a practitioner of her art," according to her biographers Daniel and Smock, in *A Talent for Detail*. Today a single one of her published photogravures may be worth over $100.

Joly   John Joly, in 1893 the inventor of the first successful method for making a photograph in realistic color, by a process of putting the negative through a screen microscopically checkered in red, green, and blue.

Kasebier   See page 83.

Keighley   Alexander Keighley (1861–1947), a Yorkshire photographer who from around 1880 for fifty years produced romantic and Impressionist pictures, many of them showing Mediterranean scenes. Keighley is particularly identified with the carbon print.

Keiley   Joseph T. Keiley (1869–1914), an American photographer (and Wall Street lawyer) identified largely with the platinotype process. He was active in organizing Photo Secession and a member of the Linked Ring. One dealer has asked $100 for a photogravure from a glycerine-developed platinotype titled "Shylock" made in 1900.

Keith   Dr. Thomas Keith (1827–1895), a highly skilled Scottish-born amateur calotypist and a leading exponent of the wax-paper process. Keith took up photography in 1854, late for the calotype, and probably gave up this hobby two years later. His pictures of architectural subjects were generally made by soft summer light in the early morning or late evening.

Kern   Edward Myer Kern (1823–1863), artist, explorer, and daguerreotypist who served in the 1853-54 China Seas exploration. Kern was the official artist for the 1856 Ringold expedition to the North Pacific, and the U.S. Navy's survey of a China route in 1858–60.

On April 19, 1903, Miss Frances Johnston, herself a member of the Daughters of the American Revolution, was present at the laying of the cornerstone of the Memorial Continental Hall in Washington, D.C. Born into a proper Victorian world but a Bohemian by choice, she was capable of conveying a tart social comment in her photographs. Frances Johnston was one of the first professional photographers regularly to undertake journalistic assignments. (Courtesy of the Library of Congress J698-1040E.)

Kilburn   The Kilburn brothers, B. W. and Edward, formed a partnership at Little-ton, New Hampshire, at the end of the Civil War to market B.W.'s photographs, including many he had made of views in the White Mountains. Eventually the Kil-burn Brothers' collection of negatives amounted to around 100,000, and after 1909 they became the possession of the Keystone View Company.

Krausz   Sigmund Krausz, a later-nineteenth century Chicago photographer known for his photographs of the types of people to be seen on city streets, such as the organ-grinder, iceman, matchboy, newsboy.

Kuhn   Heinrich Kuhn (1866–1944), member of the Linked Ring and founder of a German-Austrian school of photography and an important innovator working with the multiple gum technique of color printing. Some of his work was reproduced in *Camera Work*, to demonstrate the possibilities of the various photo-mechanical processes available at the time.

Langenheim   Among its other distinctions, the firm of Langenheim Brothers was the first American firm to market stereographs, beginning in 1854, the firm finding an especially receptive market for its views of American scenery. The Langenheims had started in business some time before, with the daguerreotype. In 1849 the firm purchased Talbot's U. S. patent for the calotype process and in 1850 secured an American patent for the albumen transparencies (lantern slides) marketed as the hyalotype. Later the firm marketed its stereographic views both on glass and on paper. Frederick Langenheim (1809–1879) initiated his career with two years of study of photography in Paris. William Langenheim (1807–1874) had a long-standing interest in scenic photography beginning with his own early photographs of Niagara Falls. The firm of Langenheim Brothers, according to contemporary Marcus A. Root, writing in 1864, was for several years "the leading photographer, not only in Philadelphia, but probably the world." Two portraits by the Langenheim brothers recently made auction-room history. The audience at Sotheby Parke Bernet sat in stunned silence one day recently as an item estimated at $200 generated a bidding duel which ended with a leading collector paying $1,900 for the two small portraits, rare prints from about 1849, providing a demonstration of the Langenheim interest in paper photography at that early time.

Lawrence and Houseworth   The successor to the firm of Thomas Houseworth & Co., a San Francisco firm selling photographs of western scenery, for which the earliest copyrighted was 1865. Although their photographers included such pioneers of western photography as Muybridge and Weed, the photographers were not generally credited, only the firm's logo "L&H" appearing, thereby setting a puzzle of identi-fication for collectors in the future.

Lea   M. Carey Lea of Philadelphia, who made a significant improvement in the collodion emulsion process by the addition of mineral acids. He was also the author of an important manual on photography, of which the second edition is known to have been published in 1871.

LeGray   Gustave LeGray (1820–1882), French inventor of the wax-paper process, announced at the end of 1851, a modification of the calotype, by which a waxed and sensitized paper for printing made it possible to store paper for up to two weeks rather than having to use it within 24 hours. His own photographs, after the manner of paintings, include large seascapes with clouds. He may have been the first to pho-tograph clouds effectively. "Brig Upon the Water," an albumen print made in 1856, was at the time widely shown and admired as a demonstration of his skill. Today, this same print, in the larger of the two known sizes, may be worth as much as $3,500.

Lerebours   N. P. Lerebours (1807–1873), possibly the first to open a daguerreotype studio in Paris. Lerebours was an early collector of daguerrean views of Europe and the Near East, and prints from his collection of copperplate engravings were made and published in *Excursions Daguerriennes* (1841–42). It is worth noting however, that sometimes the engraver gratuitously added a tiny figure—just to enliven the scene.

Le Secq   Henri Le Secq (1818–1882), both a painter and a photographer, especially known for the wax-paper negatives made in the late 1850s.

Leutgib   Karl Leutgib, a leading German professional photographer and an expert on retouching. Leutgib was brought over to the United States in 1868 by J. F. Ryder to work in his Cleveland studio and teach the art of retouching. Leutgib is thus supposed to have exerted considerable influence on portrait styles in American photography.

Levy   Albert Levy, possibly the first to manufacture and market a dry plate, in 1878.

Lichtwark   Alfred Lichtwark (1852–1914), a German leader in the movement to have photography recognized as an art in its own right. He was director of the Kunsthalle in Hamburg where, in 1893, he organized an international show for the display of over 7,000 photographs.

Lindt   J. W. Lindt, Melbourne photographer best known for his portraits of New South Wales aborigines and, later, the inhabitants of New Guinea.

Lippmann   Gabriel Lippmann (1845–1921), inventor in 1891 of a process which enabled him to reproduce colors from nature in a photograph. Lippmann, a professor of physics at the Sorbonne, did not, however, succeed in developing a technique which could make his discovery commercially viable.

Llewelyn   John Dillwyn Llewelyn, who married into Fox Talbot's family and, after experimenting with various photographic processes, in 1856 published an account of his oxymel process, by which collodion plates were treated with a syrup made of vinegar and honey to improve the keeping qualities of the plate.

Lowrie   J. F. Lowrie, an English portraitist during the last half of the nineteenth century. His work includes mounted ferrotypes.

Lumiere   Auguste (1862–1954) and Louis (1864–1948) Lumiere, the inventors, in 1895, of the cinematographe, which projected film for audience viewing—the first of a series of projectors they devised within the next few years.

Lummis   Charles F. Lummis (1859–1928), in 1888, gave up being a newspaper editor in Los Angeles to live among, and photograph, the Pueblo Indians of New Mexico for five years. He is listed in *Who Was Who* as an "Americanist, author, explorer."

Lytle   A. D. Lytle, a Confederate photographer during the Civil War, who specialized in photographing the Union troops and installations.

Maddox   Dr. Richard L. Maddox (1816–1902), the British inventor credited with having produced the first dry plate using gelatin to bind the light-sensitive silver salts to the glass. The announcement of his discovery appeared in the September 8, 1871, issue of the *British Journal of Photography*. By 1880 the gelatin dry plate had rendered the use of collodion obsolete.

Marey Etienne Jules Marey (1830–1904), a French physiologist who was inspired by Muybridge's work to invent a single camera which was capable of making a series of exposures on the single plate and, later, devised a camera which had a moving plate for photographing objects in motion. By clothing the subjects of his photographs in black and painting white lines down their arms and legs, he was able to make an effective demonstration with his camera of just how the body does move. In 1893 Marey published *La Photographie du Movement*.

Martin Adolphe Alexandre Martin (1824-1886), the French inventor of the ferrotype, in 1853, at just about the same time that the ferrotype (melainotype, tintype) was being independently developed in the United States.

Martin Paul Martin (1864–1942), a British photographer who, in the 1880s and 1890s became a pioneer photo-journalist, famous for his unposed photographs of city street scenes and particularly for a series titled "London by Night." Martin has been called the first "candid cameraman," but he operated nearly forty years before the phrase was coined.

Marville Charles Marville, a Parisian photographer especially known for his picture of the ruins of the Hotel de Ville following a fire there in 1871. An architectural photographer, his earlier series of photographs of Paris, made around 1865, earned him a reputation as a perceptive and especially sensitive photographer.

Mascher J. F. Mascher, of Philadelphia, an ingenious designer of daguerreotype miniature cases, who in 1853 patented a folding case to hold twin lenses for viewing a set of daguerreotypes stereoptically.

Mason William G. Mason, in 1839 one of the first Americans to try making a daguerreotype. Mason is credited by Rinhart as being the first to take a daguerreotype by artificial light rather than sunlight.

Maxwell Sir James Clerk Maxwell (1831–1879), an English inventor who in 1861 worked out the additive system for color photography, imposing three different lantern slides over one another to achieve a three-color image. A physicist, Sir James thought he had shown that by adding red, green, and blue light in various combinations new colors would result, but a century later it was discovered that some of Maxwell's success had depended upon the fluorescent nature of the red dye in the ribbon he had used for his demonstration. Sir James, the first professor of experimental physics at Cambridge, conducted extensive research into electricity and magnetism and was the author of many papers on the constitution of matter and theory of gases.

Mayall John Jabez Edwin Mayall (1810–1901), in 1843 one of the first to take "art"—allegorical—photographs. Mayall was first a daguerreotypist in Philadelphia and then later moved to London, where he affected the pseudonym of "Professor Highschool." He is especially known for his portraits, for the unusually large daguerreotypes which he exhibited in 1851 at the Great Exhibition at the Crystal Palace in Hyde Park, and for his earlier (1845) series of ten daguerreotypes illustrating the Lord's Prayer. Mayall also later made photographs on paper. Some years ago Mayall daguerreotypes were bringing $100 on the London market, but the much later Mayall cartes de visite made in the 1860s now also interest collectors. His work and especially his portraits of the British royal family helped start the craze for collecting cartes de visite.

Mayhew   W. C. Mayhew, who accompanied the expedition led by Lieutenant Lorenzo Sitgreaves in 1850 to survey the Creek and Cherokee Indian boundary west of Arkansas.

Mayberry   J. H. Mayberry, an American photographer active in Wyoming in the last part of the nineteenth century, known for his work depicting the life of the cowboy.

Meade   Charles R. Meade of New York, a prominent early American daguerreotypist.

Merlin   Henry Beaufoy Merlin (1830–1873), early photographer of the mines in New South Wales, mining towns and miners. With his patron B. O. Holtermann, Merlin produced a five-foot negative, one of the largest single wet-plate negatives ever to be made, and this was exhibited in 1876 at the Centennial Exhibition held in Philadelphia.

Moffat   J. Moffat, a Scottish photographer active after 1853 and best known for the portraits he made of Fox Talbot.

Mora   Jose Maria Mora, a Cuban-born photographer and entrepreneur who in 1870 established a popular photographic studio in New York where he specialized in the portraits of stage personalities. He became famous for the great number of painted backgrounds he made available, said to have numbered around 150. At one time the Mora gallery may have been doing more business in cabinet photography than any other studio in the country.

Moran   Thomas Moran (1837–1926), a painter who accompanied the U. S. Geological Expedition to the Yellowstone country in 1871 and a similar expedition in 1873, painting pictures which became an important influence upon the way photographers of the early West saw similar scenes. A brother, Edward, was also a famous painter, known both for his landscapes and marine paintings.

Morrow   Stanley J. Morrow, a Wisconsin veteran of the Civil War, a photographer who may possibly have been trained by Brady, who settled in Yankton in 1870 and is known for his photographs of pioneer life.

Morse   G. D. Morse, who established a photographic "Palace of Art" in San Francisco at the end of the nineteenth century.

Morse   Lemuel Morse of Lowell, Massachusetts to whom, with Benjamin R. Stevens, was issued the first American patent for coloring a daguerreotype.

Morse   Samuel F. B. Morse (1791–1872), generally accorded the title of "father of American photography" for his early interest, his enthusiastic advocacy, and his introductory instruction of some of the most eminent daguerreotypists, including Mathew B. Brady, Edward Anthony, and Albert S. Southworth. In 1805–10 as an undergraduate at Yale, Morse conducted some of the first photo-chemical experiments in the United States. In 1839, months before the formal announcement of the daguerreotype process, Morse met in Paris with Daguerre and wrote home enthusiastically about this encounter. A letter published in the *New York Observer* in April declared that the daguerreotype was "Rembrandt perfected." When, in September of that year, information reached America on how to make a daguerreotype, Morse became one

In the spring of 1839, Samuel F. B. Morse (1791-1872) visited Daguerre in Paris. The daguerreotype, he announced in letters back home to America, is "Rembrandt perfected." A few months later, in New York, Morse became one of the first Americans to experiment with producing his own daguerreotype, and he remained an influential enthusiast for many years. This portrait was taken at a Brady studio in 1866. Twenty-seven years have passed and the daguerreotype is already outmoded by the glass plate. The inventor of the telegraph, Morse was also well-known and highly respected as an artist. (Courtesy of the Library of Congress BH82 1963.)

of the first to experiment with this new medium, achieving his first daguerreotype
on September 28th. Morse, best remembered as the inventor of the telegraph, was,
however, an artist by profession. Because of the variety and extent of his many and
varied accomplishments he has been called "the American Leonardo" by his biographer Carleton Mabee. Claiming that he was not especially familiar with the "chemical or optical sciences," and adding that his interest in photography was centered
more on its artistic possibilities, Morse said, "The daguerreotype is undoubtedly destined to produce a revolution in art, and we, as artists, should be aware of it and
rightly understand its influence." Morse, incidentally, was the first to take a picture
of a college class: his group portrait made in 1840 shows the members of his own
Yale class of 1810.

Mudd   James Mudd, an Englishman who in 1854 turned from textile design to
photography and subsequently became well-known for his landscapes. His early
work, wax-paper negatives, had the sky blacked out with either ink or varnish—a
practice not uncommon in those days.

Muybridge   Eadweard Muybridge (pronounced "Moo-eye-bridge"), born Edward
Muggeridge (1830–1904), credited as the father of the motion picture by some, the
first important experimenter in the photography of motion, and an important photographer of various aspects of the American scene, including the West. Born in England,
his professional life was mostly conducted in the United States. Best known for his
pioneering work in photographing motion, he attracted international attention with a
series of pictures that proved there were times in a horse's gait when he lifted all four
feet off the ground at once, contrary to the way in which, for centuries, artists had
been depicting horses in action. Starting with one camera, Muybridge eventually
came to use a battery of 24 to take a series of pictures, developing a method for
triggering the shutter successively by means of electricity. After the initial experiments, sponsored by Leland Stanford, ex-governor of California, and conducted with
the wet-plate under the brilliant California sun, Muybridge moved East and between
1884 and 1887 was associated with the University of Pennsylvania, where he adopted
the use of the dry plate. In displaying his series of photographs on a moving apparatus, he anticipated the motion pictures. In 1887 he published *Animal Locomotion*,
and, in 1893, *Descriptive Zoopraxography*. These and his other works are important
not only to the history of photography but to science and art as well. Single collotypes
from *Animal Locomotion* have sold for $100. The original photographs would com-
mand a great deal more. One of Muybridge's albumen prints clearly identified on the
reverse as the product of the "Helios" studio would be worth $200. There are Muy-
bridge cabinet views, such as those of western mountain scenery, still to be found
and usually worth around $20.

Nadar   Gaspar Felix Tournachon (1820–1910), known professionally as Nadar.
An important person in the history of photography because of his various innovations,
Nadar is also admired for his numerous portraits of various celebrities, including
Gustave Dore, Honore Balzac, Eugene Delacroix, Charles Baudelaire, and George
Sand. Nadar took up photography in 1853 and thereafter maintained a studio in Paris
until he handed the business on to his son, who adopted the same name. Using plain
backgrounds and a minimum of props—unusual for his day—Nadar pere produced
portraits outstanding for their sense of liveliness and a feeling of intimacy: many of
his sitters were his good friends. Nadar was one of the first to employ artificial light
for making a photograph. In 1858 he began experimenting with the use of electric
light in the studio and in 1860 descended into the sewers and catacombs beneath

Paris to take photographs by electric light there. Nadar was also an enthusiastic balloonist and claimed that in 1856 he became the world's first airborne photographer. He took out a patent on the use of photography in map-making. He pioneered also in the use of microscopic photographs for airborne communication both by balloon and by carrier pigeon. In his later years, in collaboration with his son Paul, in 1886 he invented the technique of the photo-interview. As he conducted a lively interview with the one-hundred-year old scientist Michel-Eugene Chevreul, his son took a series of pictures which they later published with the appropriate captions. Active in the art world of Paris, Nadar pere, in 1874, personally sponsored the first exhibition ever held of the new Impressionist style of painting.

Neff Peter J. Neff, an assistant to Hamilton L. Smith in the development of the ferrotype (tintype) and in securing a patent in 1856. Neff appears to have originated the term "melainotype": a photographic portrait on metal. His exhibition of some of his melainotypes at the 1856 American Institute Fair earned him a medal and did a great deal to promote interest in this type of photography. Neff became the first manufacturer of metal plates for tintypes.

Negre Charles Negre (1820–1880), inventor of a process for photoengraving on steel, and a painter who took up photography in 1851. His prints, frequently signed in the plate, include both architectural subjects and pictures of street people.

Niepce Claude Niepce, the brother of Joseph Nicephore and also, like him, an inventor.

Niepce Isidore Niepce (1795– ?), not to be confused with his father, Joseph Nicephore. Following the death of his father, Isidore continued the association with Daguerre and in 1839 was awarded a pension by the French Government for his part in developing the daguerreotype.

Niepce Joseph Nicephore Niepce (pronounced "Nee'eps") (1795–1833), the world's first successful photographer, producing, in the 1820s, the first relatively stable images created by light. Working on a way to reproduce a design on the lithographic stone without the necessity of having to copy it by hand, Niepce had begun his photographic career in 1816, using both the silver salts—which later were routinely used in photography—and bitumen of Judea, a compound which hardens when exposed to light, and with which he, as it happens, achieved his best results. Various authorities assign various dates, but it appears to have been in the early 1820s that Niepce succeeded in producing his first negative, and in 1826 he became the first to devise a method for fixing the photographic image. Some examples of his earliest work remain: a faint image on a pewter plate made with an exposure of eight hours. Niepce tried in vain to interest the (English) Royal Society of his discovery, which he called the "heliograph." He then entered into a partnership in 1829 with L. J. M. Daguerre to develop the practical uses of his discovery of a method for making a permanent photograph. The partnership ended soon, however, with the death of Niepce.

Niepce de St. Victor See **St. Victor.**

Notman William Notman (1826–1891), born in Scotland, who came to Canada in 1856 to become that country's most famous nineteenth-century photographer and the first Canadian photographer to build an international reputation. Notman was also the first Canadian photographer to produce an extensive series for the stereoscope. By the late 1860s he had become the operator of a large chain of studios in Canada, extending also into a few cities in the United States. An important photographic publisher as well, Notman's own photographs appear, however, overladen with sentimentality. He is known for his three-volume *Portraits of British Canadians* (1865–68) with the accompanying text by John Fennings Taylor. Fine photographs from the studio of William Notman & Son have sold at auction for $100, although in 1977, $1,100 was paid at auction for a single composite print made in 1884, showing a group of eminent women.

O'Sullivan   Timothy H. O'Sullivan (c.1840–1882), a photographer principally of western scenery, particularly admired for his series of photographs made as a participant in Lieutenant George Wheeler's Geographical and Geological Explorations and Surveys West of the 100th Meridian, as well as his Civil War photographs. O'Sullivan was first employed at Brady's gallery in New York and then under Gardner at Brady's studio in Washington, D.C. After serving brilliantly as a photographer in the Civil War, where he was known for his daring, in 1867 he joined Clarence King's Geological Exploration of the 40th Parallel, photographing, among other subjects, the Great Comstock Lode mining operation. There he made the first American photographs underground, illuminated by magnesium powder which was ignited in an open tray. In 1869 King circulated a set of the "Exploration" photographs on uniform mounts with the government imprint. In 1870 O'Sullivan journeyed to what is now Panama to photograph the Darien Expedition which was assigned to study the feasibility of constructing a canal there. He then returned to the United States to join the Wheeler Survey in the Territories of Arizona and New Mexico. In 1875 the Wheeler Survey photographs appeared in a bound volume to accompany a limited-edition report consisting of just 50 sets of photographs each. Exploring and photographing regions of the West hitherto unknown to the white man, O'Sullivan was forced to make many of his pictures under extremely difficult conditions, as in the ascent of the turbulent Colorado River. With Wheeler he explored Arizona and New Mexico, making some of the earliest photographs of Indians in their cliff dwellings. In 1880 O'Sullivan served briefly as chief photographer for the U.S. Treasury Department. Single prints by O'Sullivan, mounted on board with the War Department emblem, have brought $250 at auction, and others have been valued at more than $500. A portfolio of 60 photographs by O'Sullivan and William Bell from the Wheeler Surveys has brought $6,000.

Palmer   Eli J. Palmer, an early Canadian photographer who established a daguerrean parlor in Toronto in 1849, where he remained in business for 30 years and after that continued as a supplier of photographic materials and equipment.

Pattinson   H. L. Pattinson, a daguerreotypist, possibly the first to photograph Niagara Falls. Arriving in the United States from Newcastle-on-Tyne, probably in the early 1840s, he remained in this country as a professional photographer.

Peck   Samuel Peck, the proprietor of a daguerrean parlor in New Haven who made history in 1854 by taking out a patent on his design for the American Union case for the daguerreotype. This case was the first product of plastic to be mass-produced in the United States.

Pennell   Joseph Pennell (not the artist of the same name who was born in 1860), proprietor of one of the first daguerrean parlors in New York City, who helped his friend A. S. Southworth advance his knowledge of photography and then, in 1840, with Southworth opened a studio in Chicopee, Massachusetts. From there Southworth went on to an association with Hawes in Boston, whereas Pennell later taught school and then was employed in the late 1840s at Waterbury, Connecticut, as a plate-maker.

Petzval   Joseph Max Petzval (1807–1891), Viennese inventor, in 1840, of a fast achromatic lens with a large aperture which appreciably shortened the time necessary for making a daguerrean portrait and thus gave the making of portraits great impetus. His lens, produced in quantity by Voightlander, also of Vienna, remained for decades the standard portrait lens.

Plumbe   John Plumbe, Jr. (1811?–1857), considered America's first native promoter of photography. In 1840 he was proprietor of a shop in Boston called the "Daguerreo-type Depot" which was possibly the first store for photographic supplies. He later expanded to operate a chain of daguerrean parlors in various cities, including Boston, Philadelphia, Cincinnati, Dubuque, and St. Louis. In 1843 he was advertising his "patent colored photographs," gilded by a method he had himself developed, a method which did not, however, ultimately prove practical. He originated the "Plum-beotype," by which a number of lithographic copies might be obtained from a single photographic portrait. Plumbe also manufactured a daguerreotype camera and minia-ture cases. In 1847 financial reverses caused him to sell out his interests.

Poitevin   Alphonse Poitevin (1819–1882), who in 1855 discovered the facts which made the process of photo-lithography possible, and also the inventor of the photo-mechanical printing process known as collotype.

Ponti   Carlo Ponti, a photographer of Italian ruins and, in 1860, the inventor of the megalethoscope, a panoramic viewer. Albumen prints attributed to Ponti have on occasion brought as much as $200.

Porta   Giovanni Battista della Porta (1538–1615), author of *Natural Magic* pub-lished in 1558, containing the first account of the use of a camera as an aid in drafting.

Porter   Edward L. Porter, an early experimenter in self-portraiture. In 1862 Porter devised a way for the photographer to take a picture of himself in the mirror.

Porter   William S. Porter, who in 1848 with Charles Fontayne produced a pano-ramic view of the Ohio River using eight large daguerreotype plates.

Prangey   Joseph Philibert Girault de Prangey, who between 1842 and 1844 made over 1,000 daguerreotypes of Arabic architecture in the Middle East.

Pretlove   David Pretlove, designer of miniature cases, known to have maintained an establishment in New York City for engraving, diesinking, etc., between 1844 and 1856.

Price   (William) Lake Price (1810–1896), an English painter also active in photog-raphy between 1854 and the early 1860s. Price introduced the idea that photography should imitate art and pioneered in the construction of combination photographs made from a number of negatives.

Quail   John Quail, in 1848 the inventor of a multiplying camera with a plate holder which might be moved both vertically and horizontally. Quail operated a daguerrean parlor in Philadelphia.

Reichenbach   Henry M. Reichenbach, a chemist employed by George Eastman, and inventor of the process which made possible the development of the Eastman trans-parent film, patented at the end of 1889.

Rehn   Isaac Rehn, the Boston daguerreotypist who introduced the ambrotype into the United States. Rehn, according to his contemporary Marcus A. Root in 1864, was a successful portraitist "from the small and exquisite stereoscopic picture, up to the life-size by the solar camera enlargement."

Rejlander   Oscar Gustave Rejlander (1813–1875) has been called the father of art photography. A Swedish photographer who took up practice in London in 1860, he became famous for his huge allegorical studies. He may be best known for his combination print—made from over 30 negatives—titled "Two Ways of Life," showing the rewards of industry as opposed to the evils of dissipation. Yet his more lasting legacy to photography may be his use of photography to explore the unconscious. Although some of his pictures combined as many as 30 negatives, his entire production was not large. Rejlander illustrated Darwin's *The Expression of the Emotions in Man and Animals.*

Rice   Sergeant George W. Rice, photographer with the Lady Franklin Bay Expedition in 1881 under the command of Greely and later with the rescue mission of 1884. In the course of his duties Rice succeeded in making some of the earliest photographs of Eskimo life.

Riis   Jacob A. Riis (1849–1914), journalist-photographer who made a documentary record of social distress in the tenements and sweatshops of New York City, primarily between 1887 and 1892. His photographs—shocking for their time—illustrate his books: *How the Other Half Lives*, published in 1890, and *Battle with the Slum*, 1902. The magnificence of his work was not, however, fully recognized until its publication, from the original glass negatives, in *U.S. Camera 1948*. Riis was one of the first to see the value of using a flash when it was introduced. Silver prints by A. Alland from the original glass negatives have sold at auction for $275.

Rinehart   Frank A. Rinehart, late nineteenth-century photographer of American Indians, one of whose platinum prints, signed in the plate, may be worth over $200.

Robertson   James Robertson, photographer of the Crimean War and, in 1857, official photographer for the British military expedition sent to India to put down the Bengal-Sepoy mutiny. In India, Robertson worked with Felice Beato, and their photographs, made in Lucknow in 1858, after the siege there effectively show the terrible ravages of war. At auction single salt prints by Robertson, signed in the negative, have brought between $150 and $500.

Robinson   Henry Peach Robinson (1830–1901), who has been called the uncrowned king of combination printing. Robinson became a professional photographer in 1857 and what is probably his most famous print, "Fading Away," was made the following year. The sense of realism imparted by this picture—actually posed and constructed from several negatives—showing a dying girl surrounded by sorrowing attendants, was found offensive by many at the time it was first shown. Yet Robinson's personal style started a fad for "art" photography. His own prints were often framed after the style of an oil painting, and he sometimes accompanied them with verse. His book *Pictorial Effect in Photography*, published in 1869, went into edition after edition; it is a manual for the production of photographs following the classic rules for composition in art. One of his familiar composite photographs might easily be worth $1,000 at auction. Other less important composites signed by Robinson on the reverse might be valued at around $500.

Roche   T. C. Roche, an American photographer active with Brady's staff during the

Civil War, present at many battles, and later a producer of stereographs showing the Union and Pacific Railroads and the Yosemite Valley, among other western subjects.

Root Marcus A. Root (1808–1888), a daguerreotypist who learned the art in 1843 and became successively active in Mobile, New Orleans, St. Louis, Philadelphia, and, finally, New York City in 1849. In 1864 he published *The Camera and the Pencil of the Heliographic Art*, a popular book which went into numerous editions. Root is said to have coined the word "ambrotype."

Rulofson William Herman Rulofson (1826–1878), a pioneer daguerreotypist of California during the Gold Rush days. He was born in St. John in the Canadian province of New Brunswick. After 1863 he was in partnership with Henry W. Bradley and in 1874 became president of the National Photographic Association.

Ruskin John Ruskin (1819–1900), noted English writer and critic who, learning of the daguerreotype process in 1840, used it to record the details of architecture in which he was interested, as a form of note-taking for drawings he wished to make later.

Russell Captain Andrew Joseph Russell (1831–1876), a photo-journalist who served in the Civil War and later became well-known also for his western scenes. An artist as well as photographer, Russell found the use of the camera aesthetically satisfying, sometimes adding human figures to a scene for the dramatic effect or adjusting his camera angle in order to be able to repeat visual themes. Along with Alexander Gardner, Russell became famous for his photographs of the building of the transcontinental railway. Employed by the Union Pacific Railroad between 1868 and 1869, he was present at the driving of the final spike to connect East and West. The best known photograph of this event was for a long time erroneously credited to Charles R. Savage rather than to Russell. Russell joined the King Survey in 1860. A number of his photographs were published in Ferdinand V. Hayden's *Sun Pictures of Rocky Mountain Scenery* in 1870. Subsequently Russell returned to the East, where he set up a photographic studio in New York.

Russell Charles Russell, inventor in 1861 of the tannin process, a modification of the wet-collodion method of photography.

Rutherford Lewis M. Rutherford, who, beginning in 1857 and for 20 years thereafter, took numerous photographs of celestial bodies including the moon. Rutherford has been called the father of celestial photography although not the first to photograph the sky.

Ryder James Ryder, a photographer who settled in Cleveland in 1850 and maintained a well-known gallery there. An influential advocate of negative retouching, he published his autobiography in 1902.

St. Victor Abel Niepce de St. Victor (1805–1870), a younger relative of J. N. Niepce who was also interested in photography. He developed an albumen process which proved to be the first practical method of photography on glass. Together with methods worked out by Fox Talbot, this process provided the basis for Frederick Langenheim's patent for the hyalotype in 1850.

Sarony The Canadian-born brothers Oliver F. X. (1820–1879) and Napoleon (1821–1896) Sarony, who together made the Sarony cabinet photograph famous throughout the world. The older brother, Oliver, in 1857 established a business in Scarborough, England, which developed into one of the most fashionable studios producing the carte de visite, expanding into a number of other cities. In the United States, Napoleon Sarony became a photographic entrepreneur at the age of 43, after a successful career in printing and after having retired for six years to study art. Establishing the first of his studios on Broadway in New York, he specialized in the portraits of popular stage personalities, selling his cabinet cards through a diversity of outlets, including mail order. Sarony's personal flair for photography encouraged his theater people to pose dramatically, frequently in costume for their roles, and Sarony's lively pictures helped to create a great fad for collecting cabinet cards. It has been estimated that Napoleon Sarony's studios produced about 40,000 portraits of theatrical personalities.

Savage   Charles R. Savage (1832–1909), an Englishman who emigrated to the United States, eventually settling in Salt Lake City to become one of the best known photographers of his day, especially admired for his stereoptic views of the Rocky Mountains. A famous photograph of the driving of the golden spike to complete the transcontinental railroad was for a long time erroneously attributed to Savage, who apparently at one time had worked for the railroad. Savage is best known today as a Mormon photographer, and $525 has been paid at auction for a single photograph made around 1872 showing Mormons quarrying rock for the building of the Salt Lake City Tabernacle.

Saxton   Joseph Saxton, probably the first to take a daguerrean view of Philadelphia, showing an old arsenal, exhibited in October, 1839. Saxton, later employed by the U.S. Mint, devised a method for transferring the daguerreotype image onto a metal plate for engraving.

Sayce   B. J. Sayce (1839–1895), inventor, along with W. B. Bolton in 1864, of a dry plate process of photography. In 1867 the firm of Sayce & Bolton became the producers of the first successful collodion emulsion plate.

Schultze   Johann Heinrich Schultze (1687–1744), who around 1725 experimented with light-sensitivity and discovered that light could darken a solution of silver nitrate, a principle which would later become the basis for modern photography.

Seager   C. W. Seager, who may have been the first person to make a successful daguerreotype in America, at the end of September, 1839. During the fall of that year he exhibited his work in New York City and lectured on the new art of making a daguerreotype. In March of the following year he became the first to publish a table of the time required for exposure under varying conditions: five minutes at noon on a bright and sunny day, one hour or even longer on a cloudy afternoon.

Sellers   Coleman Sellers (1827– ?), a Philadelphia amateur photographer and correspondent of Oliver Wendell Holmes, by profession a "dynamical engineer," the holder of many patents, professor of mechanics at Franklin Institute, and as well for a number of years, its president. In *Photography and the American Scene*, Taft has called Sellers "the most energetic amateur of his day." Sellers' many accomplishments included the invention of a crude form of cinema projector for the stereoscopic viewing of photographs of moving objects.

Shew   William Shew, in the 1840s a daguerreotypist and casemaker in Boston. In the early 1850s Shew moved his studio to San Francisco, where he took some of the earliest scenic views of that city.

Sigriste Guido Sigriste, a photographer, in the 1890s, of the action of racing horses and speeding automobiles.

Silvy Camille Silvy, a French photographer who in 1859 established a studio in London which became one of the most fashionable of its day. Silvy specialized in the carte de visite but also personally produced outstanding lovely landscapes. His portrait work included a famous series titled "The Beauties of England."

Simons M. P. Simons, a leading Philadelphia daguerreotypist in the 1840s and, in partnership with others, also a manufacturer of miniature cases.

Skaife Thomas Skaife, inventor in 1858 of a miniature camera so small that it used plates only one-inch square.

Smith Hannibal L. Smith, the inventor of the melainotype (tintype) in 1856. Originally a professor of chemistry at Kenyon College in Ohio, he later served as professor at Hobart College from 1867 to 1900.

Smith Samuel Smith (1802–1892), amateur photographer of Cambridgeshire, England, whose paper-negative process prints made before 1864 were shown initially at the 1872 exhibit held at the Albert and Victoria Museum in London.

Smyth Charles Piazzi Smyth (1819–1900) Scottish photographer of celestial bodies who, with publication of *Teneriffe . . .* in 1858 became the first to publish stereoscopic photographs as illustrations. In 1865 Smyth made history by photographing the interior of the Great Pyramid in Egypt, and in 1870 he published a pamphlet titled *A Poor Man's Photography of the Great Pyramid*. Smyth was also the inventor of a method for taking miniature photographs by sensitizing one square-inch of a microscope slide.

Snelling Henry Hunt Snelling (1817–1897), author of a popular manual of photography titled *The History and Practice of the Art of Photography* published in 1849 and thus thought to be the first all-round American manual on the subject. In 1843 Snelling had been employed as general sales manager by Edward Anthony. Among his numerous inventions were a blue glass filter, a camera, an enlarger, and a method for ventilating the operating room to rid it of noxious mercury fumes in developing daguerreotypes. Beginning in 1851 he was both editor and publisher of *The Photographic Art Journal*, and, from 1854 to 1859, the *Photographic and Fine Art Journal*. In 1854 he published an illustrated *Dictionary of the Photographic Art* and, in 1858, *A Guide to the Whole Art of Photography*.

Soulier Charles Soulier, a French photographer of the second half of the nineteenth century, especially known for his glass stereopticon slides of the Alps.

Southworth Albert Sands Southworth (1811–1894), with his partner J. J. Hawes one of the best known of the American daguerreotypists. Southworth began his career in photography in partnership with a Joseph Pennell, opening a daguerrean parlor in central Massachusetts but moving to Boston the following year. From 1845 through 1862 the firm of Southworth and Hawes conducted a highly successful business in Boston, dealing in photographic supplies and offering courses in daguerreotypy as well as producing its own daguerreotypes, mostly—though not exclusively—portraits, of exceptionally high merit. The partners personally posed the subjects who came to sit for their portraits, and their work, for which they were able to command the highest rates, is famous for its character delineation

The Boston firm of Southworth and Hawes not only was well-known and greatly admired for its daguerreotype portraits, but also ventured outside the studio with its cameras, producing this scene of a ship in drydock as well as many others notable for their depth and detail. Daguerreotypes, ambrotypes, and even tintypes made out of doors are fairly unusual, and they are particularly prized when they show the evidence of daily life as it was once lived. (Courtesy of the International Museum of Photography/George Eastman House.)

and the informal air achieved with some of the most prominent men of the day, such as Daniel Webster and Horace Mann. Southworth's firm is also, however, known for its portraits of children as well as its outdoor scenes, having frequently undertaken assignments thought almost impossible, such as photographing children in a classroom and ships idle at dock.

Stanford   Leland Stanford (1824–1893), American railroad builder and the governor of California from 1861 to 1863, who in 1872 sponsored the successful experiments of Eadweard Muybridge in photographing animals in motion; Stanford's own particular interest was in race horses.

Stanley   John Mix Stanley (1814–1872), a well-known painter of Indian subjects but also an earlier daguerreotypist. Stanley may have been the first cameraman to be employed on any U.S. Government expedition to the West. In 1853 he was engaged to make daguerreotypes of a survey for a northern railway route into Washington Territory, under the command of I. I. Stevens.

Steichen   See page 86.

Stelzner   Carl Ferdinand Stelzner, a German remembered along with Hermann Biow for their daguerreotypes showing the results of a fire which had devastated the city of Hamburg in 1842. Their pictures are thought to be the earliest surviving photographs of any taken showing a newsworthy event.

Stephens   John Lloyd Stephens, who in 1841 made daguerreotypes showing some of the architectural ruins of Central America.

Stevens   Benjamin R. Stevens, who with Lemuel Morse secured the first American patent for coloring the daguerreotype.

Stewart   John Stewart, a prolific English photographer who worked with the calotype and who apparently did most of his work in Europe.

Stieglitz   See page 87.

Stoddard   Seneca Roy Stoddard of Glen Falls, New York, who from the end of the nineteenth century until 1915 made a specialty of photographing mountain scenery and vacation life in the area. Scenes from Stoddard's Adirondacks studio made between 1875 and 1890 have brought about $20 at auction.

Stone   Sir Benjamin Stone (1838-1914), a prolific documentary photographer of British folkways and, in 1895, the founder of the National Photographic Record Association, for the preservation of a record of passing manners and old customs.

Sutcliffe   Frank Meadow Sutcliffe (1853–1941), English naturalistic photographer who specialized in scenes from Yorkshire life and whose work has been described as both unaffected and haunting. After 1875 Sutcliffe successfully operated a commercial portrait studio, producing cartes de visite and cabinet photographs. Original prints may be worth up to $250, and contemporary prints from the original negatives, around $75.

Sutton   Thomas Sutton (1819–1875), editor of *Photographic Notes*, who was granted a patent in 1861 for a single-lens reflex camera. With Sir James Clerk Maxwell, he also experimented with color photography.

Swan   Sir Joseph Wilson Swan (1828–1914), inventor of a perfected carbon print process based on the work of Alphonse Poitevin, patented in England in 1864 and introduced commercially two years later. His carbon process had the great advantage of producing prints in permanent pigments.

Szathmari   Carol Popp de Szathmari (1812–1887), both a painter and photographer of the Romanian nobility, who should also be credited with having been the first to photograph the Crimean War. Known to have compiled albums of his work, he remains relatively unknown today.

Talbot   William Henry Fox Talbot (1800–1877), inventor of the photograph as we know it today, a negative from which may be made many prints on paper. Experimenting with silver salts on paper, in August 1835 he succeeded in producing the first negative which has survived, a tiny picture of a latticed window, taken with an exposure of about half an hour. In 1839 Fox Talbot described his work at a meeting of the Royal Society of London. In his book *The Pencil of Nature*, published in 1844, he recalled: "This method was, to take a *camera obscura* and to throw the image of the objects on a piece of paper in its focus—fairy pictures, creations of a moment, and destined as rapidly to fade away. It was during these thoughts that the idea occurred to me—how charming it would be if it were possible to cause these natural images to imprint themselves durably, and remain fixed upon the paper." Talbot succeeded in making positive prints by his new method, called at first "photogenic drawing," but his earliest attempts were so highly fugitive that sometimes today little more remains than the photographer's signature. By 1841, however, he had devised improvements in his technique and that year patented his method as the "calotype" process, a process he later permitted to be known as the Talbotype. The Talbot method of photographing on paper was announced almost simultaneously with the daguerreotype, made on a copper plate and originating in France. Unlike the daguerreotype, the calotype had the advantage that it might be duplicated, but the use of the calotype was protected everywhere by patent restrictions and closely controlled by its inventor. In the next few years the most notable use of the calotype would be made by D. O. Hill and R. Adamson in their remarkable series of portraits and in other pictures. Talbot himself was a pioneer in making photo-micrographs of tiny subjects such as the wings of a butterfly and even of botanical sections, and he foresaw that the microscope would in the future also become a camera. Some of the most valuable of the calotypes made by Talbot are identified with a notation on the back, "L.A." standing for Lacock Abbey followed in some cases by the serialized number of the plate appearing in *The Pencil of Nature*. Usually somewhat faded and slightly foxed, Talbotypes by their originator have brought up to $1,000 at auction; one in fine condition would be worth twice that, although there is a record of others bringing only $300.

Taupenot   J. M. Taupenot, a French chemist who in 1855 invented a dry plate which could be stored successfully for several weeks before being used. However, his original plates required a long exposure time.

Thomson   John Thomson (1837–1921), with Adolphe Smith the author of *Street Life in London*, published in 1877, one of the earliest examples of the documentary use of photography to indicate a need for social reform. The joint project documented the life of the poor in London and contained 36 prints produced by the Woodburytype photomechanical process. Thomson later traveled extensively and took pictures in the Far East, spending five years in China and later publishing the four-volume *Illustrations of China and Its People* (1873–74), among other works. In 1880 he pioneered in producing his portraits of celebrities against the natural setting of their own homes. The Woodburytypes from *Street Life* have brought $200 to $375 at auction.

Tournachon   See Nadar.

Underwood   Two brothers, Elmer and Burt Underwood, who maintained the most popular American firm of photographic publishers at around the turn of the century, specializing in stereoscopic slides and equipment. The brothers started in business in 1880 selling their slides from door to door. In 1891 they moved the home office from Kansas to New York City, and in 1896 the firm added news photography to its other lines. Finally, with a declining market in 1921, the manufacture of both stereographs and lantern slides was discontinued.

Vacquerie   Auguste Vacquerie (1819–1895), who accompanied Victor Hugo and his wife to Jersey and, in collaboration with others, produced a photographic album on the author's life in exile; the photographs are particularly interesting for their symbolism.

Vance   Robert Vance, an early western daguerreotypist and one of the first to record the Gold Rush; Vance was the operator of the First Premium Gallery in San Francisco in the 1850s. Originally an Easterner, he returned to New York in 1851 to exhibit his photographs. When they did not sell, he returned to California leaving them behind. Today we have a catalogue of 131 fascinating items, but the whereabouts of the daguerreotypes themselves is unknown. The catalogue is reprinted in William Welling's *Collectors' Guide to Nineteenth Century Photographs*.

Villeneuve   Julien Vallou de Villeneuve, an early French photographer who around 1840 published a series of prints of nudes intended as guides for artists, from poses said to have been arranged by the artist Eugene Delacroix.

Vogel   Hermann W. Vogel (1834-1898), professor of chemistry at Berlin, a champion of pictorial photography, and especially important as an influence on Alfred Stieglitz.

Voightlander   Peter Friederich Voightlander (1812–1878), an early manufacturer of optical instruments and the first to produce an all-metal camera, in 1841. In the 1840s and 1850s the most popular cameras were those made by Voightlander incorporating a lens invented by Josef Max Petzval, "the German lens" considered by far the best for daguerreotype portraits.

Wakely   George D. Wakely, American photographer known especially for his photographs of a flood in Denver, Colorado Territory, in March, 1864.

Ward   Charles V. and Jacob C. Ward, brothers, were both painters and daguerreotypists and became itinerant photographers traveling through several South American countries at a very early period, between 1845 and 1848.

Warren   John C. Warren, author of what has been considered the first American book to be illustrated with photographs, *Remarks on Some Fossil Impressions in the Sandstone Rocks of the Connecticut River*, published in 1854, with a single folding salt print.

Warstat   Willi Warstat, author of *Allgemeine Asthetik der Photographie*, published in 1909, possibly the first systematic analysis of photographic aesthetics from a modern point of view.

Watkins   Carleton E. Watkins (1829–1916) a landscape photographer highly regarded especially for his pictures of the American West. In 1861 he established a high standard for such photographs, obviating any need for enlargement by printing directly from his mammoth plates. Watkins may have been the photographer responsible for some of the best work which was offered on the market by the firm of Thomas Houseworth and which won praise at the Paris International Exposition of 1867. Watkins' friend Thomas Keith designed a personal logo for him the next year. A rival of C. L. Weed, particularly in photographing the area known as "Yo-Semite," it seems quite possible that some of the work of each was attributed to the other. However, Watkins had begun publishing portfolios of his work as early as 1863. In 1868, 50 of his original photographs appeared in the report of the California State Geological Survey which had been lead by Josiah D. Whitney in the summer of 1866. Watkins' scenic pictures became some of the earliest to be considered grand enough for framing and hanging in the parlor. Among the very few portraits which were made by Watkins there is a handsome one of Louis Agassiz made in 1870. Watkins instructed E. Muybridge in photography and was his partner for a short while. An individual albumen print of the West by Watkins might be worth $150.

Wattles   James N. Wattles, who was reported by historian Snelling to have experimented with photography as early as 1828 and to have succeeded, at that very early date, in fixing the image.

Wedgwood   Thomas Wedgwood (1771–1805), one of the earliest experimenters with photography who published his results in 1802 in the *Journal of the Royal Institution.* In collaboration with his friend Sir Humphry Davy, he developed a method for copying a painting on glass by exposure to the rays of the sun. By throwing shadows onto the specially prepared surface, Wedgwood achieved an effect which anticipated contact printing. But the image was not permanent, and Wedgwood's prints were so highly fugitive that they had to be kept away from the light in a dark closet. It is reported that Wedgwood dared peep at them only once a week by the weak light of a single candle.

Weed   C. L. Weed, one of the first to photograph the Yosemite Valley. Many of his photographs, made by the wet-plate technique beginning around 1859, were printed and distributed by the San Francisco firm of Houseworth in the 1860s, although Weed was not generally credited as the photographer, as well as by Anthony's of New York. Weed's photographs were instrumental in helping to launch the fad for stereographic viewing.

Wheatstone   Sir Charles Wheatstone (1802–1875), discoverer of the principle of stereo or binocular vision before the invention of the photograph. In 1838 he devised a stereographic outfit for restoring binocular vision in looking at a picture —diagram or painting. During the following decade his invention found its most successful application in the calotype, but it was only after the invention of the wet-plate method of photography and the stereoscopic camera that the stereoscope would become a part of the standard furnishings of the Victorian parlor.

Whipple   John Adams Whipple (1823–1891) of Boston, eminent daguerreotypist and, in 1844, one of the first Americans to experiment with the glass negative. Whipple invented many photographic devices, including a buffing machine for the daguerreotype plate. He tried installing a steam engine in his Boston gallery to help run his plate-polishing devices. In 1849 he made daguerreotypes of a group of double stars and a few months later again used the Harvard observatory telescope to make a fine daguerreotype of the moon. Also in 1849 Whipple patented a screen which might be moved about to blur the edges of an image as the picture was being taken, to achieve a result he called "crayon portraiture." At his Boston gallery he was the first to enlarge daguerreotypes to life-size. In 1850 he was granted a patent for a process using the whites of eggs in the preparation of the glass plate and named his new process the crystallotype. Later becoming an instructor in the new paper photography, he personally influenced many other photographers to switch to the wet-plate method. Whipple gave up photography around 1874. A single photograph made in 1872 of the ruins which had resulted from the Great Fire in Boston—an unsigned print attributed to Whipple—has been offered by a dealer for $1,500.

Whitehurst Jesse H. Whitehurst, operator of a chain of daguerrean parlors in a number of American cities at the height of the popularity of the daguerreotype. According to Rinhart, Whitehurst sometimes employed a moving background for his daguerreotype portraits to approximate "the appearance of a beautifully clouded sky." Whitehurst's photographs of Niagara Falls were among those which helped create the popularity of the Falls as a subject for photography.

Willis William Willis (1841–1923), who in 1873 was granted a patent for the platinotype process and the founder, in 1878, of a company for the manufacture of platinum printing paper.

Wilson George Washington Wilson (1823–1893), Scottish photographer and entrepreneur, one of the first, in 1859, to take a successful photograph of persons walking about a street—"instantaneous" stereoscopic views. Later Wilson became the proprietor of what may have been one of the world's largest establishments for the production of stereo views and lantern slides.

Winter and Pond A photographic firm established in Juneau, Alaska, by Floyd V. Winter and Edwin Pond, at around the turn of the century, to produce views of the Klondike. This firm produced some of the first photographs of the Indians in Alaska.

Witteman The firm of Witteman Brothers, following the Civil War, conducted a flourishing business in postcards and souvenir photographs, over the years producing pictures of practically every aspect of American life. Later this firm became the Albertype Company of Brooklyn, New York. For many years the Witteman brothers themselves traveled throughout the United States, taking photographs, seeking local color; their pictures include some of the earliest to show airplanes.

Wolcott Alexander S. Wolcott (1804–1844), an American daguerreotypist and the inventor of numerous devices for improving the process of making a daguerreotype. Wolcott claimed to have been the first to make a daguerreotype portrait, in October of 1839. Wolcott and a partner, John Johnson in 1840 set up the first professional daguerreotype studio in the United States, in New York City. Using a camera which they had designed themselves, at first they produced portraits that were only tiny miniatures, later increasing the size of the image to 2 by 2½ inches. The partners also devised an ingenious system of mirrors to increase the light in the camera but reduce the glare in the sitter's face.

Woodbury Francis S. Woodbury of Woodbury & Page, active in photographing scenes in Java in the middle of the nineteenth century with headquarters at Djakarta.

Fifty Twentieth-Century Names in Photography

Many photographers have accomplished important work over a span of 50 or even 60 years. It is difficult to decide whether some of these long-lived photographers more properly belong with the list of "historic" photographers or with the twentieth century names which follow here. This is true, for example, of both Edward Steichen and Alfred Stieglitz, and for many of the others also associated with Photo Secession. It is certainly true of Frances Benjamin Johnston, who began as a pioneer photo-journalist at the end of the nineteenth century and continued working well into the twentieth century as a witness to architectural history. In making the division between earlier and later photographers it has, admittedly, been necessary to make arbitrary decisions. In general, however, those photographers who had already accomplished their most important work before the turn of the century have been placed with the earlier group, and those whose significant influence was perhaps most strongly felt in the present century have been placed in the later period.

It would be impossible to compile even a long list of the important names in the twentieth century which would be inclusive enough to satisfy everyone. In limiting our own list to a scant 50 names, we have endeavored to include only those photographers about whose work there appears to be a unanimity of praise. The inclusion of any name indicates that this particular photographer would be difficult to ignore. The absence of a name, on the other hand, does not indicate any lack of achievement or even of considerable critical acclaim.

More museums are, each year, arranging exhibits of photographs. More galleries are showing photographs along with the more conventionally accepted forms of art. New galleries are being established solely for the exhibition of photographs. And, as a result, new photographers are receiving the attention they deserve, to the extent that—happily—

any list one compiles today will no doubt tomorrow have to receive additions.

Abbott Berenice Abbott (1898–), portraitist and documentary historian, especially known for her photographs of street scenes in New York. In 1926 she had her own studio in Paris, where she took the portraits of some of the most fascinating artistic personalities of the day. The photographs of New York, made after her return to that city in 1929, revealed she thought, a "native fantasia"; despising pictorialism, she had found her perfect subject. A book titled *Changing New York*, with the text by Elizabeth McCausland, emerged from her work for the Federal Art Project in New York City between 1935 and 1939. An advocate of realistic photography, she also published several technical manuals including *A Guide to Better Photography* (1941). Prints from her Arts Project days may now be worth up to $300. Some of the portraits made earlier, such as that of James Joyce in 1928 or thereabouts, have sold consistently in the $200 to $400 range, as have various of the Manhattan scenes. However, a single vintage silver print made around 1936 and hand-colored by Marcel Duchamp has brought $4,000; the title: "The Bride Stripped Bare by her Bachelors, Even." The value of her work, like that of a good many other twentieth-century photographers, is rapidly rising. Berenice Abbott has also been extensively praised for rescuing the previously unknown work of the Paris photographer Atget. The quality of her own prints from the original Atget negatives has won critical acclaim.

Adams Ansel Adams (1902–), west coast nature photographer, lecturer, and the publisher of numerous books including manuals of instruction. Along with Willard Van Dyke and others, he was a founding member of Group *f* 64 in the early 1930s. In 1940 Adams helped Beaumont Newhall establish the photography department of the Museum of Modern Art in New York City. In 1948 he began publishing his Basic Photo Book series, which includes an exposition of his "zone system." Today any individual Adams print from one of his numbered portfolios is likely to be worth as much as $500 from a dealer. Matted and framed photographs have brought over $500 at auction. One of his most famous pictures such as "Moon and Clouds," brings more. Adams' *Portfolio VI*, with ten original photographs, published in 1974 and limited to 110 copies, has been worth $4,500 at auction. The retail price for a *new* signed photograph by the aging Adams rose to around $800 in 1975. A bona fide Adams print is signed by the master; one by a student from an Adams negative is initialled.

Allen, Sidney See **Hartmann.**

Arbus Diane Arbus (1923–1971), American photographer of the unusual and the strange, whose images included many made of eccentrics and of freaks. She has been called by critic Anne Tucker, "a huntress stalking photographs." Beginning her career in photography as a fashion photographer, her major work, however, was accomplished during her last ten years. The well-known print titled "Jewish Giant at Home with His Parents in the Bronx, N. Y."–titled and signed by Arbus–has brought $2,000. Some of her other prints may be worth about $1,000, and the Arbus prints made and signed by her daughter may be valued at $100 to $150.

Atget Eugene Atget (pronounced "Ah-jay") (1856–1927), a Frenchman who took up photography only in his middle years but who managed, working with an old view camera, to take a remarkable series of pictures of his native Paris. "In Paris, working in obscurity from 1898 to 1927 was Eugene Atget. His influence on his photographic contemporaries was nil, and not until his rescue from oblivion by Berenice Abbott in the early 30's was his power felt. Essentially a romantic, he photographed Paris with the single-mindedness of a man in love. Working with a large camera on a tripod, he examined its people, shops, buildings, interiors and exteriors, palace and pauper's place, street signs, vehicles, and vegetation. Here are lyrical images, peaceful pictures. A man's examining with tenderness and understanding the symbols of a fast-vanishing nineteenth century. In the 1930s the widespread publication of Atget's pictures affected many photographers. His directness of vision, his richly organized tones and textures were adopted by many photographers for their own purposes."—Arthur Siegel, in an article titled "Fifty Years of Documentary" (1951) reprinted in *Photographers on Photography* edited by Nathan Lyons. A print made by Berenice Abbott from an Atget plate (8 by 10 inches) may bring $200. The original Atget gold-toned prints have brought over $1000 at auction.

Avedon   Richard Avedon (1923–), a well-known fashion photographer also acclaimed for his highly original portrait work.

Beals   Jessie Tarbox Beals (? –1942), an early female press photographer active from 1900 to 1942, whose prints are now worth $200-$300.

Bellocq   E. J. Bellocq (1873–1949), a commercial photographer in New Orleans from 1895 to the 1940s, best known for his series of plates showing prostitutes in the red-light district there. The glass plates, later rediscovered and printed by Lee Friedlander, became known through the 1970 publication of *E. J. Bellocq: Storyville Portraits*. A "Storyville" print by Friedlander may be worth about $200.

Boughton   Alice Boughton (1865?–1943), a New York photographer for more than 40 years, chiefly a portraitist, early associated with Gertrude Kasebier and published in *Camera Work*. Possibly not as well known as some of the other women photographers of the early part of this century, she was, however, one of the most active. She opened her own studio in 1890. She is the author of a book, *Photographing the Famous*, published in 1928. One of her signed portraits of a famous person of her day, such as that of Henry James, may be worth $250 or more.

Bourke-White   Margaret Bourke-White (1904–1971), an intrepid and imaginative photo-journalist, one of the four original photographers for *Life* magazine, known both for the excellence of her work and the wide range of her subject matter, which included wartime scenes showing the battlefronts which she visited. She said that the experience of being assigned to photograph scenes of a drought in the Midwest in 1934 had forced her to realize that man was more than "a figure to put into the background of a photograph for scale." In 1937, with Erskine Caldwell, she published *You Have Seen Their Faces*, a report on poverty in the South. She was associated with *Life* in 1936, and her photograph of a dam in Montana appeared on the first issue cover. She is the author of six books describing her various assignments, as well as an autobiography, and four other works in collaboration with others. Prints with the Bourke-White red-ink stamp on the reverse have sold for $100 to $300.

Brandt   Bill Brandt (1905–), a pioneer of 35 mm. photography who has been called a "poet of London and industrial England" by critic Gene Thornton. Brandt has used his camera both to investigate the meaning of family life and class relationships and to photograph landscapes particularly notable for their surrealist quality. His point of view has sometimes been compared to that of Blake. Individual signed prints have sold for $200.

Brassai Gyula Halasz (1899–), a Frenchman known professionally as Brassai, who has specialized in reporting on the underworld and night-life personalities of Paris. Brassai is also known as an artist, sculptor, and producer of motion pictures. Identified with Brassai's stamp and with the title hand-written on the reverse, a single photograph may be worth $300 to $400.

Bullock Wynn Bullock (1902–), American photographer and teacher who took up photography in 1937 and held his first one-man show in 1941, in Los Angeles. Bullock has patented a number of photographic processes and published articles on photography in scientific journals. Prints have sold at over $350 at auction. (There is also a **John Bullock**, page 38.)

Callahan Harry Callahan (1912–), photographer of the obscure, who has often managed to fuse the documentary with the abstract for a stunningly sparse effect. Callahan has been a teacher of photography since 1946.

Capa Andre Friedman (1913–1954), known as Robert Capa, a modern documentary photographer killed on assignment in Indochina. A single Capa portrait has brought more than $200 at auction.

Cartier-Bresson Henri Cartier-Bresson (1908–), who began a serious career in photography in 1930, influenced initially by Man Ray and then by Atget. He became one of the best known of the modern photo-journalists. He is especially admired for his sympathetic insight into the nature of his subjects. Cartier-Bresson was early identified with the Leica, which he called "the extension of my eye." Cartier-Bresson has traveled throughout the world on a variety of photographic assignments and has published extensively.

Coburn Alvin Langdon Coburn (1882–1966), an American photographer who as a young man was a founding member of Photo Secession and active in the movement to have photography recognized as an independent art. Coburn is credited with having elevated the technique of photogravure to a fine art, personally supervising the production of the plates for *Camera Work* from his own gum-platinotype prints. Coburn also illustrated a number of books, including the 22-volume series of the novels and tales of Henry James and *The Door in the Wall* by H. G. Wells. One dealer has recently asked $900 for the Henry James series and $1,500 for the H. G. Wells book. Coburn held his first one-man show in 1903, in New York, and exhibited in London three years later. His "vortographs" produced in 1917 may be the first intentionally abstract photographs and are notable for revealing a Cubist influence. Hand-pulled gravure plates by Coburn sell for up to $400, many at around $250. Sources for these plates include not only *Camera Work* but also his *London*, published in 1909, and *New York*, in 1910.

Cunningham Imogen Cunningham (1883–1976), a strong aesthetic influence on other photographers, excelling at portraiture. Imogen Cunningham spent over fifty years in photography, moving from soft-focus images to her later characteristically spare and realistic style. In the early 1930s she was one of the founding members of Group *f* 64, along with Edward Weston, Ansel Adams, and others. On her ninetieth birthday in 1973 the Metropolitan Museum of Art exhibited 64 of her photographs. Images by Cunningham have sold for over $300.

Curtis Edward S. Curtis (1868–1952), a photographer active from 1890 to around 1930, especially known for his pictures of the Indians of western America and Alaska. His work was published between 1907 and 1930 in a 20-volume work titled *The North American Indian*, accompanied by 20 portfolios containing 722 of his photographs. It is believed that only about half, or possibly 300, of the projected limited edition were actually printed. On imported Holland paper, Japon vellum or on tissue and mounted, an individual plate from this series may be worth over $100, some bringing up to $900. The original photographs for this series have been lost. Curtis recorded Indian life only shortly after the Indians came into contact with the mainstream of American culture, and therefore his images, made with a reflex camera on heavy glass plates, are appreciated not only for their great photographic beauty but also for the ethnological information they present. A complete set of the photogravure plates from Curtis' *North American Indian* on the preferred Holland paper, along with the 20 volumes of text, has brought $60,000 at auction. A set in poor condition, dampstained, might be worth as much as $11,000.

Davison   George Davison (1856–1930), a founding member of the Linked Ring Brotherhood, in 1892, and credited with having initially encouraged the development of an Impressionist school of photography. From 1898 to 1912 he served as the managing director of Kodak, Ltd., but was asked to resign because of his anarchistic views.

Demachy   Robert Demachy (1859–1936), a French "art" photographer, many of whose prints were deliberately made to resemble drawings. Demachy has been called the father of gum printing, "that most elastic of photographic printing mediums" according to the notes for his first *Camera Work* portfolio. Demachy exerted an important influence on twentieth-century photography both through his images and his writings. Some of his earliest portraits and Impressionist landscapes appeared first in *Camera Notes* and then in *Camera Work*. Demachy photogravures bring up to $100.

De Meyer   Baron Adolph de Meyer (? –1946), a flamboyant photographer whose work published in popular fashion magazines between 1913 and 1920 set a new style in fashion photography. Earlier, however, his work had appeared in *Camera Work*, in 1908 and again in 1912. In 1976 a silver-print portrait of Chaplin, signed by both photographer and subject, brought $1,200 at auction.

Duncan   David Douglas Duncan (1916–), photographer of the Korean War who published *This Is War!* in 1951, a book of photographs left uncaptioned to speak for themselves. Later he joined the staff of *Life* magazine and, in 1958, published *The Private World of Pablo Picasso*.

Eisenstaedt   Alfred Eisenstaedt (1898–), a modern photographer, particularly noted for his use of natural light. A pioneer in press photography, he was one of the early *Life* magazine photographers. His work includes a documentary history of the rise of Hitler and of events leading to World War II, *Witness to Our Time*, published in 1966.

Evans   Walker Evans (1904–1975), who, beginning in the 1930s, set a new style for documentary photography, using "essential spareness and flat reportage" for a new effect, according to critic Jerry Tallmer. The poor of the eastern seaboard of the rural South were Evans' primary subjects. His best-known work was that which appeared in *Let Us Now Praise Famous Men*, a 1941 collaboration with writer James Agee which documented the lives of tenant families. Collectors will find useful a catalogue of prints available from the Library of Congress titled *Walker Evans: Photographs for the Farm Security Administration, 1935–1938* published by Da Capo Press in 1975. Signed prints from the Evans *Portfolio* published in 1971 in a limited edition of 100 copies are each worth more than $300. F.S.A. prints, signed, bring around $650.

Genthe See page 49.

Gilpin Laura Gilpin (1891–), who since 1902 has singlemindedly been concentrating on photographing American Indian life. Vintage platinum prints are worth around $500.

Hartmann Sadakichi Hartmann (1867?–1944), contributor to both *Camera Notes* and *Camera Work*, involved throughout his life with experimental art, known as the archetypal Bohemian.

Hine Lewis W. Hine (1874–1940), "free-lance conscience with a camera," who documented conditions in mills and mines and reported on child labor throughout the United States from around 1903 to 1917. In 1918 he photographed the American Red Cross Relief operation in middle Europe. In 1932 he published a notable collection of photographs titled *Men At Work*. The term "photo-story" was probably first applied to his work. A vintage print, with Hine's own identification on the back, might be worth $200 to $400.

Hinton A. Horsley Hinton (1863–1908), editor of *The Amateur Photographer*, a British publication, and a spokesman for the Linked Ring, known especially for his landscape photographs. Hinton is considered one of the great pictorialists.

Johnston See page 55.

Karsh Yousuf Karsh (1908–), Canadian portrait photographer especially noted for the fine composition in his work. Karsh has made a specialty of photographing celebrities, and his portrait of Winston Churchill is especially well-known. Single prints of his work are worth several hundred dollars.

Kasebier Gertrude Kasebier (1852–1934), one of America's most important photographers, who opened her own studio in New York in 1897. She was featured in *Camera Work*'s first issue and again in Issue No. 10. Kasebier was a founding member of Photo Secession and also of the Linked Ring. When she sold one of her early "art" photographs for $100, the sale was thought at the time to have set a new price record. Best known for her romantic scenes on the subject of motherhood, she liked to dwell on emotional content and employed dramatic swathes of light and shade to achieve the effects she wanted. Kasebier gave many of her images significant titles. There is now a new appreciation of her extensive commercial work which was published in magazines, including *The World's Work, Everybody's Magazine*, and *McClure's*. Kasebier photogravures from either *Camera Notes* or *Camera Work* have sold for over $100, to $250. The larger images, sepia, platinum or gum prints, many 8 by 6 inches, in the photographer's original folder and possibly signed, may be worth as much as $500.

Kertesz Andre Kertesz (1894–), a modern photographer who began taking pictures in Hungary in 1915, moved to Paris in 1926, and later resided in New York City, where he adopted Washington Square as a special subject. He has been called the father of candid photography. It has also been said of him that he is a photographer who can make even the great cities of Paris and New York seem as small and intimate as a village. A collection of his photographs covering the sixty years from 1912 to 1972 published recently included portraits of famous people, numerous of his outdoor scenes, and some of his "distortions." Single images have brought $400 at auction.

Kuhn Heinrich Kuhn (1866–1944), known for his gum prints, some of which have recently brought over $700 at auction.

Lange Dorothea Lange (1895–1965), identified with the photographic essay and influential in setting a style for photo-journalism reporting the bitterness of life. She opened her own studio in 1919, but it was not until the 1930s that, critics are agreed, her work gained strength. Along with Walker Evans and others she was employed in the photographic division of the Rural Resettlement Administration, later the Farm Security Administration. She is especially known for some of her earlier work of this period depicting the migrant poor of California, in which she sought to shock the conscience of the nation. She is also admired for a later, more thoughtful essay titled *The American Country Woman*. Individual portraits identified as among those published by the Farm Security Administration have sold at auction for between $100 and $200.

Lartigue Jacques Henri Lartigue (1896–), a French photographer acclaimed for his sympathetic pictures of ordinary people. In 1975, when he was in his eighties, he was hailed as a kind of "Maurice Chevalier of the lens" for his exuberant record of French life.

Man Ray Man Ray (1890–1976), an important influence on modern photography, a painter who switched over to photography in 1920. He produced his first experimental "Rayographs" in 1922. Associated with the Surrealist movement, in 1929 he began experimenting with solarization. As a professional photographer, he did both fashion illustration and portraits, and after 1940 he combined his interests in painting and photography. A self-portrait, one of only 150 printed from a broken glass negative, has brought $450 at auction. His portraits of well-known celebrities often bring $1,100 or more. *Electricté*, a portfolio of just 10 photogravures from rayograms (1931), has brought $3,600 at auction.

Moholy-Nagy Laszlo Moholy-Nagy (1895–1946), the Hungarian-born moving spirit in the Bauhaus movement in photography, noted both for his inventiveness and his daring techniques. During the 1920s Moholy-Nagy produced many abstract photographs, generating new interest in the aesthetics of photo-micrography, the use of multiple images, and in the deliberate distortion of an image. He also showed the way to a new application of the photographic image to advertising and display.

Morgan Barbara Morgan (1900–), known especially for her series of photographs of Martha Graham, the dancer, published to constitute her first book, and another series with a different subject published under the title of *Summer's Children*. Single images have sold for over $300.

Outerbridge Paul Outerbridge, Jr. (1896–1958), a successful commercial color photographer in the 1930s and 1940s, but also identified with black and white photography. A single platinum print by Outerbridge may be worth up to $500.

Salomon Erich Salomon (1886–c.1944), a German news photographer and an early exponent of the use of the miniature camera. During the late 1920s he dra-

Art. His exhibition titled "The Family of Man," combining the work of many photographers, had a world-wide impact. In spite of a lifetime in photography during which he produced many brilliant portraits of fashionable and powerful people, one of his most familiar portraits still remains that made of J. Pierpont Morgan in 1903. Steichen photogravures or halftones taken from *Camera Work* may be worth anywhere from $150 to $850. For example, one of the hand-toned photogravures, from *Camera Work* No. 19, has brought $600 at auction; Steichen personally treated such plates to achieve the effect of the original bromide print. The halftone titled "The Flatiron," made in 1906, also brought $600. A silver print with the Steichen stamp and his pencilled notes brought $1,900 at a 1976 auction, and the pigment print "Nocturne—Orangerie Staircase, Versailles" (c. 1910), $4,750.

Stieglitz Alfred Stieglitz (1864–1946), one of the most important influences on modern photography, founder of the Photo-Secessionist movement, editor and writer on photographic subjects, and the founder and editor of, first, *Camera Notes* and then *Camera Work*. Stieglitz also pioneered in combining the gallery showing of art and photography together. In 1893 he undertook the editorship of the *American Amateur Photographer*, the publication of the Society of Amateur Photographers. In 1897 this organization joined with the New York Camera Club, and Stieglitz became the editor of its *Camera Notes*. In 1902 he resigned his post to help in the founding of Photo Secession and the establishment of *Camera Work*. With Stieglitz as editor, this journal became an important showcase for photographic, literary and art work. It finally ceased publication after exactly fifty issues, in 1917. In 1905, with Edward Steichen, Stieglitz founded the New York gallery properly called the Little Galleries but more generally known as "291," its Fifth Avenue address. An exhibit of Stieglitz's own photographs shown in 1921 after an absence of several years won him a renewal of the praise which his work had begun to earn him twenty-five years earlier. In 1925 he opened the Intimate Gallery in New York and, in 1929, the American Place. He remained the center of a coterie of admiring younger photographers until his death in 1946. At the turn of the century he had been a leading exponent of "straight" photography, known especially for his views of New York, many deliberately made in the most adverse weather and in extremely poor light. After some critics ascribed the great effectiveness of his portrait work to his rapport with his subjects, he turned to what he called "equivalents," in which he was to demonstrate that the photographer, like the poet, deals in abstracts, the cameraman using light and time for his effects. By photographing clouds he felt that he had refuted the criticism that his own personal magnetism had vitally contributed to his previous success.

Original Stieglitz prints are now extremely rare. Stieglitz's own standards were so high that few of his efforts satisfied him. Out of repeated efforts he might wish to save only two or three prints, or possibly no more than one. After his death much of his work was divided among various museums. His published work, most notably that which appeared in *Camera Work*, commands some of the highest prices in today's market. "The Steerage," a photogravure on Japanese tissue from the "291" deluxe issue of *Camera Work* Nos. 7–8, 1915 has sold several times at over $3,000. The sum of $2,300 was paid at auction for a single "equivalent," a chloride print, double-mounted and signed. Prints from his late "Lake George" series have brought $3,000-$4,100.

Strand Paul Strand (1890–1976), photographer and film-maker, a major influence in twentieth-century photography. Strand's first one-man show was held in 1916 at the "291" galleries. The following year, the last two issues of *Camera Work*, edited by Alfred Stieglitz, devoted to Strand's work, demonstrated his interest in abstract

One of the best-known of Alfred Stieglitz' photographs is this one, titled "The Terminal," showing a horsedrawn streetcar waiting at the turnaround, steam rising from the backs of the horses. This picture was made in 1893, when Stieglitz spent several days experimenting with a borrowed four-by-five inch hand-held camera. The so-called "detective" camera was not at the time generally considered an adequate instrument for the serious photographer. (Courtesy of the International Museum of Photography/George Eastman House.)

design as related to photography. Traveling widely on a variety of types of assignments, Strand produced a body of work which included documentaries on towns and people and portraits which were of an experimental nature. His books include *Time in New England*, with Nancy Newhall, published in 1950. With Charles Sheeler in 1921 he produced the first American avant garde film, "Manahatta." Individual photogravures by Strand have been offered by dealers for around $200, his *Mexico Portfolio* at $500.

Ulmann Doris Ulmann (1882–1934), a photographer especially known for her images of backwoods and other poor people. A collection of some of her work made in the 1930s titled *The Darkness and the Light* is especially interesting for its picture of plantation life for blacks. A platinum print by Ulmann may be worth $350, a photogravure, $100.

Uelsmann Jerry N. Uelsmann (1934–   ), contemporary photographer known for the mystical and haunting character of his experimental work, often attained with multiple images.

Vroman Adam Clark Vroman (1856–1916), best known for his photographs of Indian life in the American Southwest. A beautifully bound album of just over 50 platinotypes from photographs taken in New Mexico and Arizona in 1902 sold at auction in 1976 for $7,000; another for $9,800, and a third for $12,500.

Weegee Photographer Arthur Fellig (? –1968), New York City news photographer famous for his candid pictures of the seamy side of city night life. Weegee, who made a business of answering police calls, said of his work in the 1930s and 1940s that it was the essence of "straight" photography . . . "I didn't know any tricks." Sometimes outrageous, often poignant, and frequently funny, his work now hangs in museums. Weegee once likened himself to Atget in his devotion in recording the life of a city. Weege was also a portraitist and a photographer, on occasion, for fashion magazines, as well as a specialist photographer for movie companies. A Weegee print, stamped "Weegee the Famous" (he had the stamp made up long before he became well-known) may be worth $150 or more, depending both on its subject and the rarity of the print.

Weston Edward Weston (1886–1958), a much-admired twentieth-century photographer who, in 1911 at a studio located in what is now Glendale, California, made something of a false start with what have been termed "exalted" portraits. Although the photographs he made then won prizes, he ceased to exhibit and only renewed his work in photography in 1922 after three years of study in Mexico. Returning to California in 1927, Weston then made a series of photographs of natural forms in the landscape. Advocate by then of the "straight" approach to photography, he traveled, exhibited, and generally won acclaim for his work until illness, in 1948, forced him to discontinue his activities. Weston found some of his most exquisite subjects in the female nude and the sculpture-like forms of vegetables: the artichoke, a pepper, a cabbage. A signed vintage print made by Edward Weston in the 1940s may be worth $1,000 today. A series of eight working prints along with the final portrait, the set considered both "important and unusual," has sold at auction for $3,400. Just one of Weston's working prints would be considered a great find. Many of his vintage prints, signed, dated, and titled, bring between $500 and $1,000, though at auction in 1976 a portrait of Tina Modotti commanded $5,100 and another a nude brought $2,700. A Weston image printed by his son is also valuable, worth maybe $250 to $400.

White   Clarence Hudson White (1871–1925), American "art" photographer from around 1890, and a founding member of the Photo-Secessionist movement. His own career in photography was fairly short, terminating around 1907, but he continued as a teacher, at Columbia University, from 1906 until his death. He also founded his own school of photography, in 1914. His work is amply represented in photogravures made directly from original negatives, such as those published in *Camera Work*. A single one of these photogravures may be worth more than $100, possibly to $400. A dealer was recently asking $1,000 for an inscribed vintage platinum print, in the original paper folder bearing White's monogram.

White   Minor White (1908–1976), photographer and a major twentieth-century influence on other photographers, one of the founders, in 1952, of *Aperture* magazine and then its editor. White helped Ansel Adams establish the photography program at the San Francisco Art Institute in the late 1940s, and he was instrumental in establishing the department of photography at the Massachusetts Institute of Technology.

Talking About Old Photographs:
A Glossary

Abat-jour An aperture, window, or kind of skylight for admitting light into the photographic studio, sometimes an opening added to a top-story room not originally intended for photography. Designed to admit an indirect and softened light, this opening might be equipped with a mirror or its surrounding area painted white to deflect the rays of the sun. The proper construction of the abat-jour was a matter of great debate in the 1850s, and photographic manuals might devote a whole chapter to this subject.

Aberration A blurring or other type of distortion caused by some optical defect in a camera's lens.

Abstract photography A modern concept, unknown to nineteenth-century photography; in abstract photography the photographer may ignore literal reality to concern himself primarily with the composition of his picture and its technical production. Perhaps the leading characteristic of nineteenth-century photography was its attempt to capture on the photographic plate the simple reality of what could be seen.

Accelerating buff A device developed in the United States as a means for polishing the daguerreotype plate. The American photographers' use of such gadgets of their own invention helped them produce the prize-winning daguerreotypes at the International Crystal Palace Exhibition held in London in 1851. The buffs, of leather saturated with organic materials, produced a brighter picture.

Accelerator A substance which was added to the developing solution to shorten the development time and bring out the image more quickly. Dubbed "quickstuff" or "quick," accelerators were already popular with daguerreotypists by 1841. Wolcott's American Mixture was one of the most popular of these quicks, but there were also various others in use, some of which had the reputation of acting particularly fast, and others, although slower, had the virtue of producing a finer tone in the picture.

Actinic impression Actinism is the property of light that causes chemicals to combine and change, and therefore, in photography, the actinic impression is the chemical reaction which is caused by light rays. In the early days of photography it was thought that the only actinic rays (those chemically active) were the ultra-violet, violet, and blue.

Additive process A natural-color process in photography discovered in 1861 by Sir James Clerk Maxwell, utilizing the primary colors of red, green, and blue to form a colored positive picture.

Aerial photography   The art/science of taking photographs from the vantage point of a vehicle in flight. The first airborne vehicle was a kite or balloon. The first man to take a photograph as he was aloft in a balloon was the professional photographer known as Nadar, in 1856. Nadar patented his idea of making use of photography from a balloon for the purposes of map-making. Although some of his aerial views have survived, the only photographs of the jaunty aerialist himself were patently taken on the ground. In October 1860, a daring photographer from Providence, Rhode Island, J. W. Black, sailed over Boston in a balloon which was owned by Professor Samuel Archer King and not only got pictures of Boston "as the Eagle and Wild Goose see it," but, since he was using the wet-plate method, also made history by developing his plates while in flight. This exploit was widely reported in contemporary journals.

By the time of World War I aerial photography was widely accepted for use in enemy surveillance. It has been reported that in a single month the British army took almost 16,000 aerial photographs. Today aerial photography may be used for mapping and surveying, for geological research, archeological work, and biological surveys as well as military reconnaissance. Pictures of the clouds taken from satellites help predict the weather. Today, as in the nineteenth century, not only are aerial photographs utilitarian and informative, they also often produce feelings of wonder and awe.

Agfacolor   Along with Kodachrome, one of the first commercially successful methods for color processing, introduced in the 1930s.

Airbrush   Used for finishing both negatives and prints, a mechanical sprayer using liquid color, invented in 1892 by Charles L. Burdick of Chicago.

Airgraph service   An airborne system of communication. The original service was operated in 1870–71 by the exiled French Delegate Government, to keep open communications with the beleaguered capital city of Paris. Pigeons carried messages which had been photographed and reduced to less than three inches in size, printed on very thin paper. Later messages were printed on collodion pellicles. Too few pigeons, however, survived to deliver their messages to make this system practical. By the time of World War II messages on microfilm were being routinely delivered by airplane.

Alabaster process   Also called alabastrine, a method of improving the quality of positives made on glass by the wet-collodion method, and later, occasionally, used on a thin gelatin negative. The negative is bleached in a solution of mercuric chloride, washed, dried, backed with a dark material, and then copied.

Alabastrine   A type of photograph popular around 1860 for a brief period: a positive on a surface of polished glass with the underside colored; the shadows appear velvety, purple or red, and the highlights of the picture are dramatized by the use of calomel. The successful alabastrine is somewhat underexposed. According to Marcus A. Root, in 1864, "there is nothing to compare with a well-colored alabastrine portrait" for delicacy and detail.

Albertype   The reproduction of a photograph by one of the first in the series of processes later to be known collectively as collotype. The process was invented by J. Albert of Munich in 1868, and an American patent was granted in 1869 and soon acquired by Edward Bierstadt. Like the Woodburytype, which the Albertype resembles in appearance, is is notable for the fine quality of its continuous intermediate tones. On plain salted paper, an Albertype might even be mistaken for an albumen print, and it was sometimes glazed to heighten the similarity. One of the great advantages of the Albertype was that it was not subject to fading, in this respect again also similar to the Woodburytype. Both were popular for book illustration, though it is possible that more use was made of the Albertype. Two thousand copies might be printed from a single plate.

Album A blank-leaved book designed for the storage and display of a collection of photographs. These photographs might be inserted into the album pages or pasted down. The popularity of photography on paper gave rise to the accumulation of collections of photographs which required some means of display. The first albums were made for the cartes de visite in the 1850s, although it does not seem that a patent was issued for a specific type of album until 1861. The passepartout method of enclosing a photograph within a frame, sometimes six or even more on a single page in the case of tintypes, became standard for the Victorian family album, which usually included both pictures of members of the family and card photographs of public figures such as the members of European royalty and the statesmen whom one most admired. As Helmut Gernsheim has pointed out, the album might both serve as an illustrated genealogy and express a form of hero-worship. Often the family album was very large, and the shape might be oblong. It was frequently bound elaborately in red velvet, with brass clasps, or perhaps bound in full morocco. It might be decorated with mother-of-pearl. Some were even made to resemble prayer books, and others contained music boxes which would begin to play when the front cover was lifted.

Eventually the term album also came to include the travel album as, in the late nineteenth century, more Americans traveled abroad and brought back photographs as souvenirs, or returned with picture books extolling the wonders of a foreign place, which also were called albums.

Albumen A complex organic compound, important to the history of photography in several ways. (See also the next several entries.) The albumen used in photography is the animal albumen to be found in the white of the egg. An albumen process capable of producing either a negative or positive on glass was the invention, in 1848, of Niepce de St. Victor. At first his invention was not enthusiastically received since at least initially it required a long exposure time, from six to eighteen minutes, making it too slow to be used for making portraits, thus severely limiting its use. In the United States, in 1850, John A. Whipple was granted a patent for making glass negatives with albumen. In addition to being used along with light-sensitive agents as a means of preparing the photographic plate, albumen is used in print paper and for preparing the zinc plate for photo-etching.

Albumen paper A kind of photographic printing paper prepared with the whites of eggs, the invention, in 1850, of Louis D. Blanquart-Evrard, a French photographer and publisher. This paper was popular for printing collodion negatives from the 1850s to around 1895. It had the advantage of being resistant to fading as well as having a gloss and thus was found highly superior to the salted paper previously used. Even after the introduction of gelatin-bromide paper, albumen continued to have its devotees.

According to the popular manual on photography published by N. G. Burgess in the 1860s, the photographer who wished to prepare his own albumen paper should proceed as follows: "Take the whites of three or four fresh eggs, and beat them with a glass rod or flat piece of glass until the article becomes of a frothy consistency. Remove the froth, and place it in a cool place, and allow it to return to its liquid state again, in a long bottle. (Then combine with water and hydrochlorate of ammonia, and filter this.) For salting paper with albumen, it should be floated three or four minutes."

Albumen plate   A photographic plate which has been coated with a thin layer of albumen (egg white) before the collodion is flowed on, to prevent the curling or slipping of the collodion film around the edges.

Albumen print   A photographic print made on a thin coated paper which has been especially prepared with egg white to receive the image. The albumen process was most commonly used for obtaining prints from wet-collodion glass negatives. The process for making a print on albumen paper was announced in 1850 by L. D. Blanquart-Evrard. Albumen paper, unlike the plain salted paper previously used, has a smooth surface and a slight sheen, permitting greater detail. The earliest albumen prints were fairly dark, but it soon became standard practice to wash them with a chloride of gold solution. Later prints may have a grayish rather than brown cast. The carte de visite and the cabinet card are two good examples of the albumen print. Albumen prints are usually found mounted.

Aluminum flash   The so-called "silver-bronze," an aluminum bronze powder used for flashlight camera work, sometimes in conjunction with magnesium. Burned in a bottle, it would provide a very bright light where natural light was not sufficient to permit picture-taking.

Amateur Photographic Association   An organization established in London in 1861 under the patronage of the Prince of Wales. The Association remained active and influential until 1905.

Amateur Photographic Exchange   An American club established in 1861 to encourage nationwide amateur participation in photography. One of its rules required the regular exchange of mounted stereoscopic prints. However, the initial interest generated in the first two years of the Club's existence was soon drained off by the events of the Civil War.

Ambrograph   A photographic image produced by the collodion process on japanned bristol board. Although reported to have produced a highly effective picture, it was extremely difficult to make.

Ambrotype   Produced by an early wet-plate process; a faint negative image on glass which was viewed as a positive when placed against a dark background. This image has been described as a creamy gray with the black areas forming a rich contrast. The dark background is customarily provided by a separate piece of black cloth such as velvet, paper, or japanned metal, though black color may be painted on the reverse. A poor appearance may be caused by a shabby background or a flaking back, and the replacement or repair of the backing may produce a great improvement in the picture. Ambrotypes are usually, although not always, portraits, and were customarily made in the same sizes as the daguerreotype, to fit into the same kind of miniature case. Like the daguerreotype, the ambrotype is reversed from right to left, but an ambrotype may, however, be flipped over to correct this. Patented by James A. Cutting of Boston in 1854, the ambrotype was popular for a brief period of about six years. At first it was hailed by many as an advance over the daguerreotype since it could be viewed at any angle. Another advantage was that it required a relatively short exposure time, of no more than 20 seconds at the most. The ambrotype, however, lacks the crispness of detail characteristic of the daguerreotype and many connoisseurs consider it relatively flat. According to M. Carey Lea: "A really fine ambrotype is a very beautiful thing, but for the most part, they want contrast and breadth of effect." Ambrotypes, at first made on plain glass, were later made on tinted glass as well. It was also a common practice to tint the cheeks in a portrait a delicate pink for lifelike effect. Marcus A. Root claimed to have thought of the name "ambrotype," meaning an imperishable picture. The ambrotype may, however, easily be destroyed by attempts to clean its surface.

American film The invention of George Eastman: paper coated with a gelatino-bromide emulsion over plain gelatin. This is the type of film first marketed along with the original Kodak camera, in 1888. The film was loaded into the camera at the factory and, after exposure in the camera, was returned, still in the camera, to the factory where it could be developed.

American Institute Sponsor of an annual fair held in New York City which, in the middle of the nineteenth century, did much to encourage excellence in photography by awarding prizes to fine examples such as, in 1844, the daguerreotypes entered by Mathew B. Brady. A Photographic Section was organized in 1859 with Henry J. Newton, president.

American Photographic Society An organization established in 1858 with J. W. Draper as first president, but lasting, apparently, only briefly. Its membership consisted mostly of amateurs.

American Place The American Place was the name of a gallery opened by Alfred Steiglitz in 1930 in a New York City office building, after he himself had, for the most part, ceased activities as a photographer. The American Place served both as a showroom and a gathering place for younger photographers. Stieglitz is reported to have once informed a potential customer that he was "not a salesman, nor are the pictures here for sale, although under certain circumstances certain pictures may be acquired." The American Place continued to show photographs and play an important role in encouraging new talent until 1946, the year of Stieglitz's death.

American Stereoscopic Company A major producer of sterescopic views, a firm which succeeded that managed by the Langenheims (q.v.) and in which they had at first a substantial interest.

American Union The American Union miniature case, one made especially to enclose a daguerreotype and, later, any other form of photograph of the same size. This case was made of a thermoplastic material consisting mostly of a mixture of sawdust and shellac which could be molded into elaborate and often fanciful shapes and designs. The American Union case was patented in 1854 by Samuel Peck. These cases are collected independently of any photographs they may now or have once contained.

Ammonia fuming A method for increasing the speed of the very slow paper in use in the middle of the nineteenth century. Particularly after 1863 when enlargements became popular, ammonia fuming was used to add brilliance to a print.

Amphitype A print produced by a process discovered by Sir John Herschel and announced in 1844, but which proved to be of little practical value. The process produced a vigorous print which could be viewed as a negative or positive from one side or the other, and the positive aspect frequently resembled a fine engraving. However, it required an exposure time of up to six hours. Amphitypes were rarely produced in the United States. Amphitype is also the name of a photolithographic process.

Anaglyph   By a stereopticon process patented by the Frenchman Louis Ducos du Hauron in 1891, two pictures, one red and one blue, are combined in the viewer to be seen through special lenses for a single three-dimensional effect.

Analytical portrait   Also known as a composite or average portrait, a style of photograph achieved by printing several portraits of the same size on a single sheet of paper, to produce one fused—and entirely typical—picture. This style had a vogue in the United States in the late 1880s. A composite print of the heads of 51 different bank managers, made by Oliver Lipincott of New York and completed in July, 1909, was hailed as a true rendering of the characteristics of "the King of Finance."

Anastigmat   A type of lens introduced by Zeiss in 1889, free of the defect known as astigmatism.

Anecdotal photography   Story-telling by means of a series of still photographs which have been arranged in a series. Popular in Great Britain beginning in the early 1860s and a predecessor of the lantern slide presentation, the sequence of photographs frequently employed trick photography to make the story more thrilling.

Aniline process   A process patented in 1864 by W. Willis of Birmingham, England, for the photographic reproduction, without a negative, of a drawing made on transparent paper. The print is of a blue-black color, primarily suitable for copying plans or other simple line drawings.

Anthony process   A method for processing the daguerreotype patented by Charles Anthony in 1851.

Anthony's   The American firm of E. and H.T. Anthony Company, established in 1852 by the two brothers. By 1870 it had become the country's largest dealer in photographic materials and supplies, a major publisher of photographs, and a leading purveyor of stereoscopic views and equipment, to the extent that it was a major factor in creating the popularity of the stereoscope. Anthony's was also a major vendor of the photographic album from its earliest introduction. Of particular interest to collectors of the work of Mathew B. Brady is the fact that Brady presented Anthony's with a set of his wartime negatives to help meet an outstanding bill for photographic supplies, with the result that Brady stereographs often bear the Anthony imprint.

Anthotype   Surely one of the slowest means ever devised for taking a photograph: the juices of various flowers or other vegetable substances, possibly alcoholic, are used in various approaches to the chemistry of making a photograph. One of the leading experimenters in this medium was Sir John Herschel, who found that it might take him one full month to achieve a single positive. Furthermore, he discovered that almost all the pictures he obtained, no matter which kind of plant he tried, proved to be highly fugitive—little reward for the amount of patience required.

Anthrophotoscope   Invented by two San Franciscans, Rowell and Mills, in 1867, a device for viewing portrait photographs to enhance the illusion of perspective.

Anthropomorphic photograph   Any photograph made showing the parts of the body for the purpose of identifying them. This kind of photography might be employed, for example, by a police department for the purpose of identifying criminals, through a comparison of noses, ears, etc. The use of photography for such a purpose dates from the middle of the 1880s, when it had quite a vogue.

Anti-graphic photography A term which has been specifically applied to the work of Henri Cartier-Bresson, especially his work shown in New York City in 1933 when it was charged that luck, rather than planning, had had a major part in producing some of his dramatic images.

Antihalation backing A coating of dye or pigment applied to the back of a film support to prevent extraneous reflection which might affect the light-sensitive material.

Aperture The lens opening: the area of adjustable opening in the lens of a camera which determines how much light will reach the sensitive photographic materials. The size of the lens opening is regulated by the diaphragm and is expressed as an $f/$stop.

Aplanatic lens A type of lens which is capable of defining well at a large aperture, first designed and introduced by Thomas Grubb of Dublin in 1841. A series of improved versions was designed in the late nineteenth century by A. Steinheil of Munich.

Arched print A photograph which has been trimmed on the top so as to represent the curve of a Gothic window, as was frequently done with the cabinet card and stereograph.

Archival processing A method of processing for the purpose of preserving a photograph, similar to the customary methods of developing, fixing, and washing but involving extra steps introduced for the purpose of totally removing any chemicals which might eventually harm the image of a negative print. The chemicals that must be entirely removed include those which were essential to making the photograph. The purpose of archival processing is to render a photograph as durable and thus permanent as possible.

Argentotype An early name for a print on bromide paper.

Aristotype A print produced on a gelatino-chloride printing paper, a type of photograph, apparently introduced in 1888, which achieved some popularity at the end of the nineteenth century.

Arrowroot paper A type of photographic printing paper prepared from arrowroot and sometimes preferred for large portraits or for landscapes in which fineness of grain and sharpness of detail are major considerations.

Artificial negative A factitious negative, one achieved by a hand process rather than by photography. Such a process might be used, for example, to produce the lettering to title a series of lantern slides.

Artist's Camera The trade name of a twin-reflex camera first marketed in 1891 by the London Stereoscopic Company.

Artotype A development from the Albertype (q.v.), the Artotype was even more popular than its predecessor for use in book illustration. The Artotype was particularly liked for the reproduction of portraits.

Art photography In the simplest sense, photography divorced from consideration as a science or as the entirely literal translation from the visual. "Art" photography, for most people, however, means the type of photography associated with the Linked Ring Brotherhood in England and, in America, Photo Secession. Art photography has at various times been associated with the combination print, allegorical poses, the soft focus, and the altered print, as well as with efforts to force photography to comply with the conventional rules of classical painting. The art photographer, whatever may be his techniques, is one concerned with aesthetic theory.

Art Union   An association for the distribution of art, popular in the 1840s in the United States, when there was at least one such association for the distribution of daguerreotypes, the Daguerreotype Art Union and Photographic Association of Chicago, founded in 1845.

Astigmatism   An aberration of the lens which prevents equal focus for lines at right angles to each other in the same plane.

Astronomical photography   See **Celestial photography.**

Astraphograph   Meaning "not reversed," a collodion positive on glass treated so that, while still tacky, it might be rolled off onto black paper, thin card, or even highly polished japanned leather. The process was invented by James M. Letts of Dundee, New York.

Autochrome   The first generally popular color process in photography, invented by the brothers Auguste and Louis Lumiere, patented by them in France in 1904 and introduced commercially in 1907 when a good color emulsion became available. By coating a photographic plate with tiny grains of starch in equal parts dyed red, green, and blue, with further treatment a color transparency might be obtained. The first American showing of the results of this process was at the Little Galleries of the Photo Secession in 1907. The examples exhibited had been produced by Steichen, Stieglitz, and Frank Eugene. However, this was an additive process, and truly successful color photography was not developed until the 1930s when the alternative subtractive system began to be marketed.

Autographic   Capable of being written upon, but, specifically, the trade name Kodak gave to the feature which permitted the introduction of a stylus into the back of a camera so that, directly after exposure, the picture might be identified or dated. Such an autographic camera was produced between 1914 and 1934.

Automatic photography   Picture-taking without the intervention of a photographer. According to the 1911 *Encyclopedia of Photography* edited by Bernard E. Jones, the first machine to take pictures automatically was that invented by M. Enjalbert and demonstrated at the Paris Exhibition of 1889. The sitter dropped a coin into a box, the end of the exposure time was indicated by the ringing of a bell, and "a finished ferrotype picture was delivered in about five minutes." Semiautomatic cameras had previously been used with some success by itinerant photographers in the United States with the aim of turning out portraits quickly.

Autotype   An image which has undergone, in the carbon print process, a double transfer to correct the original reversal of the image.

Barrel distortion   The magnification of an image at its center.

Bas relief   A print made from a positive and a negative transparency of the same subject, the two bound together slightly out of register for a third-dimensional effect.

Bates   A photographic company in Boston which in the nineteenth century specialized in purchasing negatives from photographers to make stereoscopic views, which it marketed.

Beauties of England   The title of a series of cartes de visite issued by the London photographic firm of Camille Silvy, in the 1880s.

Belinograph   A photograph transmitted by telephone.

Bellows   In a camera, a collapsible unit which is light-tight and accordian-pleated, connecting the lens to the back of the camera and permitting the focusing of the lens.

Berlin portrait   A photograph made on a piece of glass which has been coarsely ground on the underside, to give the image a soft and fuzzy look, considered flattering in a portrait.

Bezel   A favorite kind of mid-nineteenth century style for the trimming of a finished photograph by lopping off the corners.

Bi-Gum   A nickname for the gum-bichromate process (q.v).

Black vignette   A style of portrait invented by the Russian photographer Bergamaso and thus also known as a Russian vignette. On a glass negative, the sitter's head appeared as well-lighted against a perfectly dark background. This effect was achieved by placing a card to cut off some of the light either outside or inside the camera.

Blue bosom boy   A daguerreotypist not sufficiently skilled in his craft to be capable of making a portrait that records a white shirt or other white area as a true, clear, and sparkling white.

Blueprint   A white image on a clear blue background produced by a process utilizing the reduction of potassium ferricyanide, by light, to its ferrous compound, Prussian blue. The blueprint or "blue" is used commercially to produce maps, drawings, and other line-work. (See also **Cyanotype.**)

Border printing   "This is an alternative to mounting a print," according to the Encyclopedia of Photography (1911). "A sheet of paper and a printing frame, both larger than the actual picture are used, and by masking the negative the print appears in its first stage with a plain margin. Masks are next used to cover the picture itself, and also the plain margin with the exception of an edge all round the print. The second exposure then gives a narrow border to the picture . . . Used with discretion and taste, good effects may be secured by surrounding borders of varying width and tint, the great advantage being that the tone and quality of the tints are the same as in the picture itself. The great pitfall is over-elaboration, resulting in distracting attention from the picture itself." We have all seen examples of such over-elaboration, and to us today border printing seems one of the hallmarks of the early twentieth-century studio photograph.

Boston School   A school of landscape photography that emerged in Boston in the early 1860s with Barnum and Soule its leading exponents, and with counterparts in both New York and Philadelphia.

Boudoir   The boudoir size in the cabinet card became popular around 1890. Larger than the usual cabinet card, the card itself may be around 5 by 8 inches and up to 7 by 10 inches, with the mounted print also larger than that for the standard cabinet card. The origin of the term seems to be unknown.

Box camera   A camera of the type introduced by George Eastman in 1888 (the Kodak), consisting of a light-tight box, with lens, shutter, and view-finder, and employing film rather than a plate.

Brewster   A type of stereoscopic viewer popular in the early 1850s, manufactured for Frederick and William Langenheim by the American Stereoscopic Company, and consisting of a tapered box with lens at the back and a slot at the top for the insertion of the stereo slide.

Brightness   A personal and subjective interpretation of the degree of brilliance of a photographic print.

Brilliancy   A quality present in a print which is bright and very clear, generally having a long range of tones from very dark shadows to white highlights.

Bromide paper   A type of ready-to-use photographic printing paper available in several grades of sensitivity which supplanted albumen paper and came into general use in the 1880s. Its advantages included greater versatility and certainty. The Eastman Company was the first to market it. The term "bromide" comes from the use of silver bromide in the manufacture of the emulsion with which this paper is coated. Modern "bromide" papers may be chlorobromide, with varying amounts of both silver chloride and silver bromide.

Bromide print   Historically, a print made on paper coated with an emulsion of silver bromide in gelatin, used for either contact printing or enlarging, in either artificial or natural light.

Bromoil Process   An elaborately controlled process for producing a positive print, based on the principal that oil and water do not mix, the invention of E. J. Wall in 1907. Basically it is a bromide print which has been extensively treated by bleaching and pigmenting to achieve a special artistic effect. This process remained in popular use with "art" photographers until around 1930.

Bronzed print   Any print made on a paper which, in certain lights, has a rather metallic appearance.

Brownie   First marketed in 1900 by the Eastman Company, the Brownie No. 1 was a six-exposure camera which sold for one dollar, the first of the modern simple rollfilm box cameras made available at such a low price that a camera might be within the reach of almost everyone. As a matter of fact, its advertising was primarily directed toward children. So reliable and so simple to use, the Brownie helped launch the modern era of popular photography.

Buffalo   The impressive Buffalo Exhibition which was held in the Albright Art Gallery in 1910. The exhibits were chiefly arranged by Stieglitz, and the exhibit was reviewed in *Camera Work*, No. 33. Beaumont Newhall has stated that the year of the Buffalo Exhibition definitely marked a turning point in the history of photography. It became apparent that from then on photography would have to be judged on its own terms rather than as the little sister of more conventional art, and of painting in particular. As Stieglitz was to point out a bit later, "Photographers must learn not to be ashamed to have their photographs look like photographs."

Buff stick   In the shape of a paddle, usually about three feet long and only some three inches wide, with a convex underside well-padded and covered with buckskin or velvet, this was the photographer's tool for polishing the daguerreotype. The buff stick might be used with jeweler's rouge to impart an especially high polish. Essential to the photographer's trade in the 1840s, the buff stick became an emblem of his studio.

Burning in   A mechanical process employed in the darkroom to darken a portion of a print, by means of additional exposure.

Burnishing   Treating a finished collodion print with a patent glaze and then running it through a device which pressed it between rollers, a process introduced in the late 1870s.

Button-pressing   A derisive term employed by some professional photographers with regard to the use of the early "detective" (hand-held) cameras by relatively unskilled amateurs.

Cabinet card   A card of the type which became popular in the mid-1860s, the card itself measuring 4½ by 6½ inches with a mounted photograph only slightly smaller. As the fad for the just slightly smaller carte de visite began to wane, the photographic studios launched a vigorous and successful campaign for the new hobby of collecting the larger card. It was possible to have one's own portrait taken and mounted on the card, but the big trade was in the sale of portraits of the admired public personalities of the day. Thousands of these cabinet cards poured out from the studios, and the public began eagerly to collect them, exchanging choice ones by the tens and even hundreds with friends, and proudly making up albums for their display. The fad for cabinet cards swept not only the United States but England and the European continent as well. Photographs of actors and actresses, midgets and kings, statesmen, and of pretty girls in native costume were among the so-called "sure cards" which sold well. The albums were designed to hold more than a hundred of these cards. Individuals patronized the photographic studios to have themselves photographed after the popular style of the day, which favored elaborate dress, romantic backdrops, and a stylized pose. To pull in the most clients, the studios competed to devise the most attractive settings. Waterfalls, castles in the distance, and jungle foliage were all considered suitable backgrounds for a full-length portrait: a lady in formal evening attire might thus be portrayed standing with her toes perilously close to an improbably cascading waterfall as she gazes off dreamily at distant battlements. Today the poses seem trite, the scenery vastly overworked, and most of the photography routine. Even so, the diligent collector may still turn up the unusual pose, the interesting personality, the unusually well-composed photograph, or the picture which contains some especially interesting detail.

Cabinet size   The reference is to the size of the cabinet card's mounted photograph, approximately 4 by 6 inches. The cabinet card, larger than the carte de visite, was more convenient for displaying a full-length portrait, and one story is that the cabinet card attained its popularity because it was so much more effective for displaying a lady's full skirt.

Calotype   A silver chloride print on paper, invented by the Englishman William Henry Fox Talbot. Fox Talbot began experimenting with "photogenic drawing" around 1833 and by 1840 had improved his original process to produce a latent image on prepared writing paper, an image which could be revealed by a process of development, and thus the first negative-positive process. Calotype prints are characteristically of a soft reddish-brown tone and have, to our eyes today, a delightfully gentle quality, the result of a combination of the technique with the quaint old-fashioned dress of the subject or the English rural background. Most of the calotypes produced were made in the British Isles during the 1840s. Because the process was slow, many photographers preferred to take pictures of buildings, ruins, and still-lifes rather than portraits, yet the portraits made by Robert Adamson together with David O. Hill, including their studies for Hill's "Disruption" painting, are generally considered among the most outstanding portraits ever made in any medium. Fox Talbot made his prints on the only paper available to him, writing paper, which he sensitized by brushing on a solution of crystallized nitrate of silver dissolved in distilled water, dried, and sometimes treated further. This basic process would remain the only negative-positive process available until the invention of the wet-collodion process in 1851. Talbot, however, kept a tight rein on the use of his English patent, and the calotype—later called the Talbotype—was not accessible in the United States until it was imported under patent by the Langenheim Brothers of Philadelphia in the late 1840s. By the time that Fox Talbot relaxed his patent restrictions in 1852, the wet-collodion method had already been invented, and the calotype never did become popular in the United States. (See also **Collotype.**)

Cameo print   A carte de visite photograph which has been raised, like a medallion, by pressure applied to its backing.

Cameotype   A vignette daguerreotype of the kind which was introduced by New York photographer Charles Williamson, known to have a studio in Brooklyn after 1851.

Camera   A device for revealing "a particular cone of space during a specific parcel of time," a darkened chamber or box into which light is admitted to form an image of external objects on a surface placed at the focus of the lens. The term camera comes from the Latin word for "room." The camera itself is an optical device known long before a way was finally found to fix the image which it trapped. The modern camera is a light-tight container designed to hold film and to provide a system of viewing and focusing. The basic nineteenth-century camera differed by having a plate of glass or metal upon which the image was registered, rather than using film, and lacked a shutter, employing only a lens cap which the photographer snatched off for what he hoped might be the appropriate length of time.

Camera Club   "The" Camera Club was a New York association formed by the amalgamation, in 1897, of the New York Camera Club and the Society of Amateur Photographers. Alfred Stieglitz was its vice president and the editor of the Club's journal, *Camera Notes,* an important publication in the history of photography, containing not only photographs but the reviews of current exhibitions. Stieglitz withdrew in 1902 to found a movement known as Photo Secession and to establish his own quarterly journal, *Camera Work.*

Camera lucida   An aid to sketching and not, properly, a camera in the modern sense. The camera lucida, invented in 1807 by William Wollaston, enabled an artist to simultaneously see both his subject and the paper on which he was drawing by peering through a peephole at the edge of a prism.

Camera obscura   An early optical instrument: a room—or box—with a single small opening through which an inverted image is projected from objects outside the box onto the opposite interior wall, thus reducing three-dimensional objects to a two-dimensional plane. Described in 1553 by Giovanni Battista della Porta in his book *Natural Magic*, the principle on which the camera obscura operates had, however, been known even as early as 300 B.C. The camera obscura is considered a true camera (light box) except that no light-sensitive material is employed to retain the image. Thomas Wedgwood was one of the first, in 1802, to apply this camera to photographic use but did not, however, succeed in producing an image that was not highly fugitive. The term camera obscura means, in Latin, a dark room.

Canvas effect The canvas effect may be achieved by first printing from a negative made of a piece of canvas which has been photographed with a strong side light.

Canvas photograph A photograph made directly on canvas or other heavy cloth. In the mid-1850s when paper photographs eclipsed the daguerreotype, various experiments were made with making photographs on different substances including not only cloth but also leather.

Caption The words which accompany a photograph, provide information, and usually include the name of the photographer and the date of the photograph, possibly also a title. Such information may appear on the mount or on the back, and occasionally it has been written in below the photograph in the margin or even on the negative itself. Story-telling captions for photographs did not become popular until well into the twentieth century.

Carbon print A highly durable photographic print produced by a process which was invented in 1855 by Alphonse Louis Poitevin and subsequently improved upon by Sir Joseph Wilson Swan in 1864, as well as by others. A positive carbon image on a fine film of insoluble gelatin is transferred to another sheet of paper and rinsed in an alum solution to harden. The carbon process is different from all other photographic processes in that the final image is composed of a gelatinous pigment, which may contain carbon, rather than metallic silver. The technique, although known in the United States shortly after its discovery, was, however, seldom used here. The print which results is more distinctly black and white than of a brownish cast and the image is often rich in tones. Various colors of prints are also possible, since a finely ground color may be added to the gelatin used to coat the paper. The heavy paper needed for carbon printing was available until around 1930. Although an early successful use was for copying old masters, the carbon print is more closely associated with "art" photography of the turn of the century.

Card picture See **Carte de visite.**

Card stereograph A stereograph (paired photograph) on paper or cardboard. At first, in 1850-51, the calotype was used, but within a year or so, the collodion process was universally adopted. The first card series to be produced in the United States was issued by the Langenheim Brothers in 1854. By the 1860s card stereos were published in great quantities, literally covering just about every subject under the sun.

Caricature A card photograph which has the subject's head inserted into a prepared picture, usually for comical effect, as, for example, an outsized head upon a small drawing of a torso.

Carte de visite A relatively small photograph about 2½ by 3½ inches, usually a portrait, which is mounted on a slightly larger board, 2½ by 4¼ inches. Cards of this type, first introduced in Europe, reached the United States around 1859 and met with an immediate enthusiastic response. The carte de visite, or visiting card, was apparently never actually used as a visiting card anywhere, but was so named because of its small size. The French photographer Andre A. E. Disderi secured the French patent and was a major force in making this form of photography popular throughout Europe. In 1859, on one highly publicized occasion, he took the portrait of the Emperor Napoleon III who had interrupted a parade just passing by the Disderi studio to pop in for his picture. During the following year, the Mayall portraits made of the English royal family also helped to spur the fad for collecting card photographs. In the United States, the infatuation with these cards grew to such proportions that the word "cartomania" was coined. The carte de visite was the first form of photography, along with the stereograph, to take advantage of the fact that many copies could be produced from a single collodion negative on glass. In addition, special cameras were developed to make it possible to record a number of images simultaneously at one sitting. The several pictures were then simply snipped apart. Actors and actresses and other prominent persons who might benefit from the distribution of their pictures posed for the "publics," cards made specifically for wide distribution, sometimes paying for their own copies by authorizing this distributon.

Carte de visite camera   The special camera equipped with from two to four lenses to take as many photographs simultaneously. By means of the introduction of a special holder, the plate might be moved within the camera either vertically or horizontally to permit as many as eight, sometimes even sixteen, photographs to be made at one time from a single pose. The resulting images, clipped apart, were then mounted separately.

Carte de visite viewer   A device for looking at card photographs, consisting of a wooden box with a hinged lid into which a lens was set. Since looking over one's collection of cartes de visite and showing them off to guests was a popular Victorian pastime, many of these viewers were elaborately decorated.

Cartomania   A word coined around 1860 to describe the craze for collecting and exchanging cartes de visite.

Catch light   Those tiny reflections from a light source often to be found in the eyes of a portrait subject.

Case   A decorative container, usually hinged, specifically designed to house and preserve one, possibly two, or sometimes more, daguerreotypes or ambrotypes. The earliest cases were made of leather, but soon cheaper materials were used for their manufacture. Imitation leather cases were produced as well as plastic cases. The thermoplastic Union Case was patented in 1854 by Samuel Peck. Thereafter this type of case dominated the market. Thermoplastic, composed mostly of sawdust and shellac, could be stamped into attractive patterns and provided a strong and durable case as well. The elaborate designs for these cases included floral and geometric motifs, wreaths, cupids, medallions, allegorical and even realistic scenes. The standard work on the subject of these designs is *American Miniature Case Art* by Floyd and Marion Rinhart.

Cased   Enclosed in a miniature case. Daguerreotype and ambrotype portraits are generally found cased.

Casket photograph   A single image viewed by means of a special device invented by Sir Joseph Wilson Swan in 1862, by means of which two mounted collodion positives are, through the agency of prisms, seen as one. Sir Joseph called his invention the Crystal Cube.

C.D.V.   See **Carte de visite.**

Celestial photography   Obtaining photographs of the moon, sun, planets, and other subjects of astronomical investigation, as well as photographs of subjects of related and specifically meteorological interest, including clouds, water-spouts, etc. Celestial photography encounters special problems of illumination, magnification, and exposure time, among others. The first successful celestial photograph may have been that taken of the moon by an American, Professor John W. Draper, in 1840. Today's telescope is at the same time often a camera, and because long exposures can produce pictures of light too weak to be seen by human eyes, astronomers may learn more from the photograph than by studying the skies directly.

Celluloid   Celluloid film. Celluloid, invented in 1861, was first used successfully for the production of flexible film by John Carbutt of Philadelphia in 1888.

Centennial Photographic Company   The official body of photographers for the Centennial Exhibition held at Philadelphia in 1876. Three men, even though using the laborious wet-plate process, are said to have produced almost 900 portraits in a single day.

Ceramic   The photographic image transferred onto a substance such as china, porcelain, or enamel, such as was sometimes done for use in jewelry. The impression was burnt in and then protected with a glaze. In the latter half of the nineteenth century there was a fad for ceramic jewelry of this type. The earliest patent may have been that taken out in England in 1854.

Change-box camera   A type of camera with a device attached to the back to permit the shifting of the plate or film into the proper position for exposure—by daylight. One of the first of the change-box cameras was that invented by H. Cook in 1867, his so-called "opera-glass camera." Later cameras of this type have a counting device to tally the number of exposures made.

Chemical toning   The use of gold—or the compounds of other chemical elements—for the purpose of preserving a photograph and also to impart a rich red-brown or other warm-colored hue.

Chiaroscuro   Any monochromatic style of pictorial art, usually black and white, which gains its effect from the contrast of light and dark.

Chloride paper   A photographic printing paper that may require a relatively long exposure. The emulsion is rendered sensitive with silver chloride.

Chloro-bromide paper   A printing paper containing a balance of silver chloride and silver bromide and generally used only for enlarging. Announced by Eder in 1883, this paper has been in use ever since.

Chocolate plate   A brown-tinted ferrotype, the plate for which was patented by the Phoenix Plate Company in 1870. This plate had an instant success. The chocolate-tinted surface was made available in three shades: a light chocolate, yellowish with red overtones recommended for light-colored clothing and drapery; a medium brown imparting a warm overall hue; and the dark chocolate scarcely different from the black plate hitherto in use.

Chromatic background A special effect achieved in daguerreotype portraiture by means of a background of black or brown lace draped over a tall frame behind the subject.

Chromatint A colored photograph achieved by tracing a photographic image on paper, applying color, and then adhering it to the back of the original so that color shines through.

Chromatype A process invented by the Frenchman M. Ponton, and further developed by Robert Hunt in 1843, which produced a negative on paper chemically changed to a positive deep orange in color.

Chromo-ferrotype Another name for the chocolate plate (q.v.).

Chrono-photography The art/science of making a photographic record of the motion of an object or animal in proper chronological sequence. E. J. Marey and E. Muybridge were among its pioneers.

Chrysotype A modification of the calotype process, devised by Sir John Herschel and announced to the Royal Society in 1843 but even then admittedly inferior to Talbot's calotype.

Cinema film Following upon the experiments on animal locomotion made by E. Muybridge, cinema film for producing sequential photographs was offered commercially, after 1896.

Circle of confusion An optical term designating the permissible size of an image point formed by a lens: .01 inch in diameter. Less technically, a cluster of light rays projected on a focal plane by a point of light outside the camera. The tighter this cluster, the sharper the image.

Clay's Farewell "Clay's Farewell to the Senate," in 1845 the first notable engraving from daguerreotypes, based on the portraits made of various members of Congress by the firm of Anthony, Edwards & Clarke in 1843–44.

Cliche-verre According to Helmut Gernsheim, although painting and photography must be considered totally different media, there is a legitimate combination of the two in cliche-verre, in which pictures drawn or painted on glass are copied onto photographic paper. This process was the subject of numerous experiments conducted in England from around 1839 and the invention of the calotype. However, as far as is known, none of the early attempts at photography through glass has survived. A caricature by George Cruikshank made in 1851 is thought to be one of the few early examples remaining.

Closeup A photograph of a subject placed at no more than four feet from the camera.

Cloud effect The inclusion of clouds in an outdoor scene by means of combining two different negatives of the same view. In wet-plate photography, cloud effects were particularly difficult to achieve on a single negative. Some of E. Muybridge's early photographs of the Yellowstone area, for example, employed this technique. (See also **Equivalent.**)

Coating box A tightly fitted wooden box into which the daguerreotype, already cleaned and polished, was rendered sensitive by chemical means. The box was equipped with heavy glass jars and a sliding cover usually of thick glass and was airtight to prevent the escape of vapors. From the coating box, the plate was directly transferred to the camera.

Cockling The curling of a paper photograph.

College album An album containing photographs of interest to the members of a college class, the faculty, and alumni, among others. Such albums began to be popularly produced in the late 1860s.

Collodio-bromide print A print made on collodio-bromide paper which, between 1890 and 1920, was a standard type of printing paper.

Collodio-chloride paper A photographic printing paper invented by Simpson in 1864 and in use until around 1895.

Collodion Guncotton dissolved in ether and alcohol: a transparent glutinous solution of pyroxyl, alcohol, and ether used as a vehicle for light-sensitive particles and coated onto an emulsion support to produce the "wet-plate" photograph and later used in the preparation of a "dry plate" as well. Collodion has the advantage of being strongly adhesive. Its introduction by F. Scott Archer in 1851 revolutionized photography. For about thirty years, from the mid-1850s to the mid-1880s, the collodion wet-plate method dominated photography. Although as early as 1862 the dry collodion plate was being recommended—for "views" for example, which required travel to the location—its general use was deferred until the way was found to manufacture a plate which could be stored for some time. In 1864 B. J. Sayce invented the first truly successful dry collodion emulsion.

Collodion print Any print made by the use of the collodion process which was introduced in 1851. This process, producing a negative on glass, made possible —for the first time—the production of satisfactory paper prints in quantity. Most photographs made between 1854 and 1885, when a successful dry plate was introduced, are made by the wet-collodion method. They include the ambrotype and the tintype (ferrotype). The wet-collodion process requires that a glass plate be exposed and developed in one continuous action while the plate is still wet. The advantages of the collodion print over the calotype included its being more reliable and providing greater detail and more subtle intermediate tones. A major advantage over the daguerreotype, which was a unique image, was that more than one print could be made from the negative. The collodion print on a transparent surface, such as glass (the ambrotype) or mica, presents aspects of both the negative and positive. Those made on japanned iron plates (tintypes) or other substance such as leather or cloth can only be viewed as positives.

Collodion transfer A collodion positive transferred from its original glass plate to another support, usually paper.

Collodion wet plate The type of photographic plate in general use from 1854 to around 1885. The process of preparing the wet plate involved the photographer's cleaning a glass plate thoroughly and then coating it with iodized collodion. While the plate was still damp and tacky, it was sensitized by being dipped into a bath containing silver nitrate. It was then necessary to expose the plate in the camera before it had a chance to dry out. Furthermore, this plate had to be developed immediately, within half an hour at most, necessitating the outdoor photographer's carrying a portable darkroom into the field. (See also **Collodion.**)

Collotype A process invented by Alphonse Poitevin and patented in England in 1855. The inventor called his process photo-lithography since his own experiments were limited to the use of the lithographic stone. Collotype may mean, however, any of the photo-gelatin methods for reproducing a photograph, including the Artotype, heliotype, Albertype. The "phototype" or collotype process is based on the principle that if a film of bichromated gelatin is exposed to light under a negative and then the unaltered portion washed out, the film will then have that property of attracting ink in some parts and absorbing water elsewhere to repel the ink, as does lithographic work, with the difference that the effect of the ink and the water depends upon the result of the action of the light. The first practical use of the collotype was made in 1865, and the collotype was used extensively for book illustration until outmoded by the halftone and photogravure.

Color print   A photograph taken in the colors of nature. It was not until the 1890s that the production of photographs directly from the colors of nature became a practical possibility. The color prints made before that time were largely of an experimental nature. Interest in color printing had been evidenced earlier, but early efforts were limited to varying the chemicals used in printing to obtain various monochromatic effects. Salts of uranium, for example, might be combined with different chemicals to produce a picture which was an overall shade of red, green, violet, or blue. It was also found that a picture in color could be produced through the use of salts of iron; in this case the picture is of a purplish color. It is thought that the first truly successful attempt at directly producing the colors of nature was made by Sir James Clerk Maxwell, employing the additive system, in 1861. In 1869 Louis Ducos du Hauron announced his discovery of the subtractive system of producing color. This was not to be greatly improved upon until 1904, when the Lumieres developed their color-screen process. (See also **Additive process, Subtractive process,** and **Hand-coloring.**)

Combination print   The print resulting from the use of two or more negatives to create a single positive print, as in a print showing a landscape made up from separate negatives of the sky and of the other parts of the scenery. An advantage of such combination printing is that different exposures might be used for different parts of the picture. It would also be possible to produce a more complicated picture than would be possible with a single exposure, even one not possible at all. The technique was first employed by Oscar G. Rejlander of Sweden, then working in England, for making up elaborately designed allegorical scenes. His great triumph was the combination print titled "Two Ways of Life" in which he employed no fewer than 25 models appropriately posed to demonstrate the ways of virtue as opposed to those of evil. The cumulative print, 31 by 16 inches, was entered in the Manchester Art Treasures Exhibition in 1857, where, even though the "evil" part was draped for modesty's sake, it was purchased by Queen Victoria. Another famous example of combination printing is "Fading Away," by Henry Peach Robinson, made up from five different negatives and showing a dying girl surrounded by her grieving attendants. The fact that this was a photograph rather than a painting lent it a painful reality in the eyes of many viewers, to the extent that some felt it was in bad taste. Robinson has been called the "uncrowned king" of combination printing. There appears to have been a lag of about ten years before many Americans began to experiment with the technique. The first to do so may have been John L. Gihon, in the late 1860s. The ultimate commercialization of the technique was the sale of negatives in which the center had been left blank, to be filled with a portrait.

Compensating positive   A thin, translucent positive bound in contact with a contrasty negative, in register to reduce gradation of tone.

The Haunted Lane is an example of the type of trick photography which delighted the Victorians. Between 1875 and 1890 large numbers of "sentimental," or story-telling stereographs were published to satisfy an eager public. (Courtesy of the Library of Congress USZ62-11053.)

Composite photograph   See **Combination print.**

Compositional case   A case designed to hold one or possibly more daguerreo-types or ambrotypes, composed of a mixture of glue and sawdust fused under high heat in a mold. Such cases are sometimes mistaken for gutta percha.

Contact   A print made by exposing a sensitive photographic surface to light beamed directly through a negative; thus, a contact is the same size as the original negative.

Contrast   In a print, the difference between the minimum and maximum densi-ties. It is, fundamentally, contrast which makes the image visible. A "contrasty" print is one with sharp differences in brilliance and density—between the white and black areas.

Controlled-process photography   So-called "art" photography, in which the pho-tographer deliberately seeks an effect and manipulates the printing process to that end. The turn-of-the-century pictorialist photographers, for example, used such processes as gum-printing and bromoil to alter print density values, often to make the photograph more closely resemble a painting.

Copper daguerreotype   A photograph achieved by the daguerreotype process directly on polished copper which has been especially treated so as to produce a picture which is a shimmer of colors.

Copper toning   A process for toning bromide prints first introduced in the 1870s.

Copy print   A photographic copy made from a work of art, usually a painting, sometimes a print; or, any print produced by re-photographing an original print to produce a negative from which new positives can be made.

Copyright photograph   As early as 1846, photographs—in those days the da-guerreotype—were used as an aid to describing an invention for which a U.S. patent was sought. Thus, among old patent records there are photographs of con-siderable interest to the photographic historian. In addition, of course, photographs themselves may be registered for copyright, as may other types of visual and printed material.

Costume card   A cabinet card depicting the local costume of an area, such as Switzerland, Germany, or Italy, and often realistically colored by hand. Such cards were among those popularly collected in the 1880s and later.

Crayon daguerreotype   A daguerreotype portrait in which the edges are delib-erately blurred so that the effect may resemble that of a simplified drawing. This might be achieved by the use of a special screen, the invention of J. A. Whipple. During the relatively long exposure time, the screen might be jiggled or otherwise moved about. Whipple patented his screen in 1849.

Crayon enlargement   A type of portrait popular in the years before World War I and for some time thereafter, sentimental and "arty" in effect. Its characteristic shape is oval, and it may be stretched on a frame or pressed into a convex mount. It is almost invariably "finished" with a liberal use of the airbrush and colored in pastels. Sometimes we find that the artwork has survived whereas the photograph has faded.

Crayon portrait   A thin positive printed on glass and then shaded by an artist to imitate crayon work. A crayon portrait often consists of an enlargement from a card negative.

Crayon sauce A black powdery substance used in retouching paper negatives.

Crop To trim or cut away portions of a print to improve the overall effect.

Crystallotype The English term for the American hyalotype; or, an American adaptation of the calotype process, resulting in a photograph which was characteristically brown in color, the result of gold toning. The process was so slow, however, that for the most part it was considered appropriate only for copy work.

Crystal Palace The landmark Crystal Palace Exhibition held in Hyde Park, London in 1851, attracting world-wide attention. Designed as a showcase for the latest inventions and technologies, the daguerreotypes entered by Americans attracted admiration and medals were awarded to Mathew B. Brady, M. M. Lawrence, both of New York City, and to J. A. Whipple of Boston. This exhibit spurred interest in photography as a technology and secured wide recognition of its artistry.

Crystoleum A photograph which has been specially colored to produce the effect of a painting on glass: a chromo-photograph. The crystoleum may be backed with white cardboard and framed.

Culinary period A term used to characterize the period of experimentation in photography which took place between 1850 and 1865, when a wide variety of efforts were being made to discover a really satisfactory dry plate. Among the common substances used in these experiments were such kitchen items as honey, beer, vinegar, tea, sherry, caramel, and skimmed milk.

Cyanotype Popularly known as a blueprint, this is the familiar white-on-blue photograph of the type often used for charts, drawings and the plans of architects and engineers. It was one of the many inventions of Sir John Herschel, who announced its discovery in 1842. It took more than 30 years, however, for the practical possibilities of the cyanotype to be realized. Although, in general, too slow for anything but copying by superimposition, the blueprint does, however, have the advantages of being relatively cheap to produce, simple to accomplish, and permanent. A prepared blueprint paper is placed in contact with a negative or drawing on tracing paper and exposed to light. The resulting print is washed in water, which serves both as its developer and fixer. The image is a bright white against a violet-blue background. The cyanotype was the subject of some amateur experiments from around 1885 to about 1910, and there remain some family pictures in this manner in the nineteenth century is *Billy Blew Away's Alphabetical Orthological and Philological Picture Book*, published in Boston in 1882. Anonymous, the author was probably Edward Winbridge, whose nickname was "grasshopper" (this emblem appears along with the silhouette drawings). The earliest book ever to be produced by this method may have been Anna Atkin's *Photographs of British Algae*. Undated, this book may have appeared as early as 1843 and, if so, would be the first book ever in the world to be illustrated with photographs.

Cyclograph A panoramic camera by means of which the outer circumference of a cylindrical object may be registered on a single flat surface.

Daguerrean artist The name by which the professional photographer, in the 1840s, preferred to be known. The daguerrean artists of America, according to Floyd and Marion Rinhart, should receive credit for having established a truly new native school of art.

Daguerrean Association The Daguerrean Association of New York, a group formed in 1851 but apparently lasting only a few years.

Daguerreotype A positive image produced directly on a silvered copper plate which has been sensitized with iodine or bromine vapor, or both, exposed to the light to secure an image on the plate and then developed through the use of mercury vapor. Invented by the Frenchman Louis J. M. Daguerre and announced by the French government in August, 1839, the daguerreotype was introduced into the United States the following month and became, for more than a decade, the most popular type of photography in America. Indeed, in this country it was close to the only known type of photographic process.

A positive on a mirrored surface, the daguerreotype reflects light and thus may be viewed only at certain angles. In direct sunlight the daguerreotype appears to be no more than a shiny piece of metal. Because of this and because the image is so fragile, the daguerreotype is commonly protected under glass and encased in its own miniature case (q.v.).

The designations for daguerreotype size are derived from the size of plate originally used by Daguerre. The plate he used was 6½ by 8½ inches, and this size became known as the whole plate. The quarter-plate and sixth-plate size, 3¼ by 4¼ inches and 2⅔ by 3¼ inches, became the most popular for portraits in this country. Plates which were larger than "whole" size could, however, be made by a skilled operator, and some as large as 15 by 17 inches were offered by a few daguerrean parlors (photographic studios).

In the United States, the inventor and artist Samuel F. G. Morse to some extent earned his title of the father of American photography through his early enthusiasm for the daguerreotype. He was among the first to attempt to make his own pictures in this country, and he subsequently instructed others. The first daguerreotype portrait, however, was probably one made by Professor John W. Draper of New York, who was a friend of Morse. The first daguerreotype studio was one opened in New York City in March, 1840, by Alexander S. Wolcott and John Johnson. By 1845–46 the professional daguerreotype portrait had become popular, and Mathew B. Brady undertook to make portraits of all the most prominent men in American life, including all the past presidents still living. Although most daguerreotypes were portraits made indoors in the studio, some outdoor photography was attempted, even though the camera was slow and the preparation of the plates away from the studio difficult.

Daguerreotypy in America, where it reached its pinnacle of achievement, achieved the height of its popularity in the early 1850s. By the middle of the decade the ambrotype and the ferrotype on glass and metal, respectively, had been developed and were already popular. The use of the collodion method of wet-plate photography to produce a negative on glass from which a paper negative or negatives might be made spelled the end of the daguerreotype. One of the greatest drawbacks had been that a single image was produced, an image which could not be duplicated by the same process. Yet the "mirror with a memory" had possessed not only an exemplary brilliance but such a sharpness of detail that it invited examination through a magnifying glass. So devoted were some of its adherents that when the daguerreotype was no longer fashionable many adopted the wearing of black armbands to signify their sorrow. Although in greatly diminished numbers, some daguerreotypes were still being produced during the Civil War years.

Dallastype An early kind of photoengraving developed by C. D. Dallas and introduced, in England, in 1863.

D & P Developing and printing: a form of business enterprise for the finishing of photographs. It was created in the 1890s with the marketing of cameras designed for film and the resulting enthusiasm of amateurs eager to snap pictures but impatient with the details of processing. It was only in 1891 that Eastman began to market the "Daylight Kodak" with an arrangement which made it possible to change the film without sending the whole camera back to the factory.

Darkroom A room, closet, or other enclosed area devoted to the development and processing of photographs, from which all white, or actinic, light is excluded. The darkroom is not, in fact, completely dark, but the color of the light is carefully chosen (red or orange) to match that part of the spectrum to which the particular sensitive photographic materials used is least responsive.

Dark slide A protective device to shelter a plate from light until it is ready to be exposed to light within the camera. In preparing to take a daguerreotype, for example, the photographer places a coated plate in a special holder which is then covered with the dark slide. Once the plate has been inserted in the camera and the camera closed, the dark slide may be slipped out.

Death portrait A photograph taken of a deceased person. Among daguerreotypes and tintypes there are many showing dead persons, most frequently children. The child may be propped in his cradle or bed and the impression often intended to be conveyed is that he is only sleeping. Sometimes a mourning parent also appears in the picture. Another death portrait might be of a young woman reposing in her coffin or lying on a sofa with flowers in her hand. The deceased may even be pictured propped up in a favorite chair. Such final photographic records were sometimes permanently displayed in tombstones, and several patents were issued for recesses or frames to make this possible.

Defiance A kind of gelatin dry plate used in the 1880s.

Definition The degree of sharpness in a negative or print, its fineness and clarity of detail.

Demon A type of English detective camera, for which wildly extravagant advertising claims were made.

Density A term signifying the opacity of a negative: the logarithm of the opacity. (The two terms density and opacity represent different mathematical concepts.) In a negative, density is the light-stopping power of the blackened silver deposit.

Depth of field That area from the point closest to the camera's lens to the point furthest from the camera within which everything is acceptably in focus.

Detective camera A type of light and portable camera using the dry plate and designed to be relatively easy to use. This type of camera may have taken its name from the hand camera devised by the Englishman Thomas Bolas in 1881 for the use of a police department in photographing criminal suspects, apparently without their knowledge. A prism before the lens meant that the camera need not be pointed directly at the person whose picture was being taken. Eventually a "detective" camera came to mean any which was disguised as to function. Such a camera might look like a book, a handbag, a parcel, or it might be concealed in the hat which the photographer wore on his head. It might be a doctor's satchel or a pair of opera glasses. The use of such a hidden camera during the nineteenth century helped solve the tricky social problem of taking the picture of a lady to whom one has not been properly introduced. In the United States, the leading manufacturers of this light portable camera were the Scovill Manufacturing Company and the firm of E. & H.T. Anthony. These cameras remained popular from the mid-1880s to around 1896. Possibly the oddest shape of all assumed by any of these cameras was that of a pistol, certainly, at least, the most difficult to ignore.

Detroit   The Detroit Publishing Company, owner of about 2,500 photographs many of which it published around 1900 in a series constituting a splendid record of American life.

Developer   The chemical that turns exposed silver halide crystals into black metallic silver, thus allowing a latent photographic image to become visible; or, any other substance that performs the same function in photography.

Development   The process of rendering visible a latent photographic image.

Diaphanotype   According to M. A. Root in 1864, the diaphanotype, similar to hallotype, is a paper photograph cemented to glass and painted on the back to produce an enamelled effect, after a process originated by E. C. Hawkins of Cincinnati. Extremely difficult to manage, the process was rarely used.

Diaphragm   That part of a camera which controls the amount of light allowed to pass through the lens. This variable opening is calibrated in f/stops, each numbered f/stop admitting half as much light as the preceding numbered stop.

Diazotype   Any one of several photographic processes developed in the 1890s based on the light-sensitiveness of diazo compounds. A special use for these processes was in printing on silk.

Diorama   A device to enable an audience to view a series of pictures, often photographs, and sometimes pictures prepared by artists in reliance on information furnished by photographs. Daguerre was one of the first to experiment extensively with the diorama, not surprisingly since Daguerre was interested in stage scenery and was himself an artist. The audience may be invited to move past a series of still pictures arranged in some appropriate sequence, or a series of such pictures may be unrolled in front of the audience. During the 1850s, in the United States, the diorama became popular as a means of viewing the magnificent scenery of the West which few easterners had as yet been privileged to see.

Direct positive   A positive obtained without the use of an intervening negative.

Distorted   A distorted negative or print is produced by the deliberate alteration of the photographic image. This may be accomplished either by mechanical or chemical means. Methods of distortion include increasing the size of the silver grains, changing the texture of a gelatin emulsion, possibly by melting it, and printing a negative and positive so that they overlap.

Documentary   A photograph which has a story to tell, often one with a message which the photographer wishes to convey in order to persuade the viewer of some truth about society. To paraphrase Dorothea Lange, one of the great practitioners of this form of photography, a documentary photograph is a mirror for the present and a document for the future. In "Fifty Years of Documentary," an article written in 1951 and reprinted in *Photographers on Photography*, Arthur Siegel states that "in photography, documentary is the term used to describe a specific attitude which sees, in the creative production and use of photographs, a language for giving a fuller understanding of man as a social animal. By examining closely, by isolating and relating his subjects, the documentary photographer penetrates the surface appearances and reveals the world about us. The documentary editor, either by working directly with the photographer or by assembling previously unrelated pictures, combines the photographic image with text to create meaning in some area of the social scene. In either case, the endeavor to influence human behavior by giving a deeper understanding of the social process is the same."

Dodging   A mechanical process used in the darkroom to make a portion of a print appear lighter by subtracting exposure and, thus, the opposite of burning in.

Double   A popular form of trick photography early in the twentieth century, printing two images of the same person in a single photograph, as of a person who appears to be playing cards with himself.

Double exposure   The intentional—or unintentional—recording of two images in a single picture.

Double whole plate   A daguerreotype plate size, 8½ by 13 inches, or double the size of the plate originally used by Daguerre, and abbreviated ¾ p. A daguerreotype of such size was very difficult to prepare and therefore only a few highly skilled photographers were able to produce it successfully.

Dry collodion   Collodion in the dry, or preserved form experimentally used in the preparation of a dry plate for photography beginning in the middle of the 1850s. One of the first of the really effective dry collodion processes was that developed by Dr. J. M. Taupenot, a French chemist, in 1855. His collodio-albumen plate was more convenient to use than the wet plate but because of its long exposure time, from two to ten minutes, it proved impractical for portraits and was therefore used only for views. The great advantage of the collodio-albumen plate was that it could be kept for several weeks before being used, but unfortunately the required length of the exposure time increased with the length of time the plate was kept. A more practical type of dry plate was invented by Dr. Richard Norris Hill and patented by him in 1856, in England. This plate was made commercially available the following year by the Birmingham Dry Collodion Plate Company which had been founded by Dr. Hill. It had the advantage that it might be stored for up to six months. In 1860 the company offered what it called its "extra quick dry plate" with the promise that it might be kept satisfactorily for a full year before use, and that it would even then still be as fast as the wet plate.

Dry mount   A method of affixing a print to a cardboard for display, using a tissue paper which is sandwiched between the print and board and then subjected to heat.

Dry plate   The successor to the wet plate, a glass plate delivered from the factory ready to use, already coated with a durable sensitized emulsion. At first collodion was used, later gelatin. Whereas it had been necessary to prepare each wet-collodion plate immediately before exposing it in the camera, now plates might be conveniently stored until ready to be used, and the photographer was relieved of some of the burdensome procedures in getting ready to take a picture. Although the earliest dry plates were slower than the wet plates, they were from the first somewhat less expensive. George Eastman, in 1881, entered the photographic business with his dry plate. By around 1885 the wet plate method of photography had definitely been outmoded. Improvements in the dry plate by then meant that, at last, a camera might be held in the hand rather than having to be mounted on a tripod, cameras were designed with shutters, and the term "detective camera" (q.v.) entered the popular vocabulary.

Dubroni   The Dubroni outfit, invented in England in 1864, was an attempt to get around the necessity of setting up a darkroom for wet-plate photography: the preparation and the development of the plate were both performed within the body of the camera itself. However, the success of the Dubroni outfit appears dubious, since there are few photographs remaining identified as having resulted from its successful use.

Eastman   The Eastman Kodak Company of Rochester, New York, since its foundation in 1880 by George Eastman, both an extensive innovator and supplier in the field of photographic supplies. Eastman Kodak was probably the single most important factor in the development of popular photography in the early twentieth century and has continued to play an important role in the development of both amateur and professional photography since then. "Electricity existed prior to Bell and Edison, as photography antedated Eastman, but each created a new science—telephony, electrical illumination, and film photography. They also originated new industries. These in turn brought new occupations, new policies, new professions, new publications, a wider distribution of knowledge, new channels of communications and understanding—perhaps, also, a new cycle of civilization," to quote Eastman's enthusiastic biographer, Carl W. Ackerman.

Eburneum   A photographic image which has the appearance of having been made on ivory, by a process invented in 1865 by J. M. Burgess. To achieve this effect, a carbon or collodion transparency is backed with a special mixture.

Ectograph   A photograph which has been elaborately finished by a process invented by William Campbell of Jersey City, requiring not only that the photograph be fine, but the finest glass plate, and utilizing a sun-bleached wax and non-fading colors.

Edge fog   The darkening at the edges of a photographic film or paper, either through the action of the chemicals themselves or of light, and frequently the result of improper storing.

Edge reversal   The result of using a special technique for distorting the camera image: a sensitive emulsion which has been developed but not fixed is exposed to naked light and then redeveloped so that the image will show a reversal of tone wherever there is a sharp edge. The print made from such a negative shows contours rimmed with black lines. The technique of edge reversal has been used for special effects by a number of twentieth-century photographers, including Man Ray.

Edging   Putting a narrow border of gelatin or gutta percha around a dry plate prepared by the tannin process, to help make the collodion adhere more satisfactorily to the glass of the plate.

Edinburgh   Either the Edinburgh Photographic Society, an institution established in 1861 with J. D. Marwick as president and continuing to modern date; *or* the Edinburgh Stereographic Company, a publisher of views including numerous ones of American scenes, many of which have now become rare.

Edition print   One of a collection, usually presented in a portfolio or album. "Edition" include collections of vintage prints, series prints, photogravures and reprints of historical photographs.

Electric flash   A burst of light produced electrically for the purpose of illuminating a scene for photography. From the earliest days of photography the possibilities in the use of such a flash of light seem to have fascinated photographers. In 1851 Fox Talbot conducted successful experiments to photograph a wheel while it was in motion, using the flash of light produced by a battery of Leyden jars. Many years later, Mach and Salcher, in 1885–86, succeeded in photographing bullets moving at a speed of about 765 miles-per-hour by shooting their projectile at a glass tube which was wired to set off a strong electric spark.

Electric light Artificial—electric—light as a source of illumination for photography rather than relying upon the sun seems to have come into general use only in the 1880s. During the 1860s the French photographer Nadar had experimented extensively in his Paris studio with the use of electric lights, even also moving outside the studio and underground to take successful pictures by electric light in the intense dark of the Paris sewers and catacombs. There appears to be some evidence that it was, however, a Russian by the name of Levitsky who, during a lecture he was giving in 1857, became the first to take a portrait by electric light, to the amazement and great excitement of his audience.

Electronic flash A system for storing electrical energy for a controlled flash of light, usually by means of xenon gas in a sealed glass tube.

Electrotachyscope A machine invented in 1890 by a German, Ottomar Anschutz. By means of this device, a series of photographs, as of a bird or some other animal, might be rotated to produce the effect of its moving.

Electrotype A reproduction of a photograph by a specific method which was developed early. According to Levi L. Hill, writing in 1850, the electrotype reproductions of daguerreotypes, first produced by M. F. Fizeau, had never been surpassed.

Emulsion A mixture of light-sensitive salts in suspension used for coating plates or film for photographic purposes. An important turning point in the history of photography came when, in 1864, Bolton and Sayce succeeded in producing the first emulsion which could be pre-mixed and stored satisfactorily until its use should be required. Until that time the photographer had to mix his own chemicals on the spot for the preparation of the plate.

Enamel A photographic image, usually of miniature size, which has been transferred to enamel, usually to be employed in jewelry or for some other decorative effect. A leading practitioner of the art of enamel photography was Lafon de Camarsac, who, in 1867, was honored for his work in this medium at the International Exhibition held in Paris.

Enamelled print One given a very high gloss with a collodion marketed for this purpose and best used on a collodion print.

Energiatype A negative on paper, for which ferrous sulphate has been used as the active developer. It was the invention, in 1844, of Robert Hunt but was a kind of photograph that never achieved popularity.

Engraved Daguerreotype The result of transferring the daguerreotype image to a metal plate for printing (counter-drawing) without injury to the original, a process which Marcus A. Root, in 1864, declared presented "no difficulty" but which apparently itself required as much care and time as any other kind of photographic process.

Enlargement A larger photograph produced from a smaller one: in 1840 John W. Draper of New York may have been the first to make an enlargement. Working with a daguerreotype, his purpose was to demonstrate that a small original photograph might be enlarged with more success than using a large camera to make a large picture in the first place. The first enlarger which was patented was the invention of Alexander Wolcott. In the 1850s, with the introduction of wet-collodion photography, paper enlargements began to be popular. With the enthusiasm for photographs of Imperial size, enlargements became larger and larger until they attained life size. For a while it seemed that the public might be convinced that bigger was better. With the introduction of dry-plate photography, the selective enlarging of just one portion of a photograph became fairly routine.

Enlarger   According to Feininger, "an enlarger is a camera in reverse." Like the camera, the enlarger has a lens which is focused to produce a sharp print as well as a diaphragm which permits the regulation of the brightness of the projected image. One of the most popular of the enlargers in use after 1857 was D. A. Woodward's "solar camera."

Ephemera   Material of lesser importance, or chiefly of a passing interest, and thus, for the photography collector, material of interest primarily because of its association. Ephemera may include items such as the old sheet music decorated with a photograph on the cover or the music for a song about some aspect of photography. It includes novels dealing in some way with the practice of photography, and children's books illustrated from photographs. Many types of ephemera are to be found in antique shops and shops where "collectibles" are sold. An example might be a lamp with a shade made up from several old photographs. Or, a lamp shaped to represent a camera on a tripod—or even one made from an antique camera. Prices for such ephemera have been steadily escalating in recent years.

Ephemeral   A kind of phosphorescent photograph made by a process introduced by W. B. Woodbury.

Equivalent   A photograph intended to stand as a symbol or metaphor. The term "equivalent" is applied to the symbol or to the photograph itself. The concept of equivalent photography was developed by Alfred Stieglitz. When critics complained that a great deal of the compelling power of Stieglitz's portraits might spring from his special empathy with his subjects, to prove them wrong he turned to what he called equivalents. He first photographed clouds and sun effects which conveyed emotional meaning and then turned to the photography of other expressive, though non-human, objects in nature. Stieglitz' equivalents have sold at auction for as much as $3,500.

Etched Daguerreotype   A daguerreotype prepared by a variation of the etching process so as to have a surface capable of holding ink. The print made from such a prepared plate is said to resemble an aquatint. One of the problems of printing from the daguerreotype was that its silver surface quickly wore off. One of the solutions proposed to meet this problem was to protect the surface with a thin shield of copper deposited by the electrotype process. Although several persons worked to develop an entirely satisfactory process for reproducing the daguerreotype, none, it is believed, really succeeded.

Excel Detective   The name of a twin-reflex camera first marketed by a Brussels firm in 1890.

Exposure   The effect that light has on photosensitive material. Also,the product of the time and the intensity of illumination acting on photographic material and thus the result of the combination of a camera's f/stop and its shutter speed.

Exposure by cap Rather than employing a shutter, as does the modern camera, early cameras registered a scene as the photographer whipped off the lens cap and then replaced it, in what he hoped would prove to be the appropriate number of seconds—or, earlier, possibly even minutes.

Exposure meter A device for gauging light intensities. Measuring the sensitivity of the photographic plate became important when the gelatin dry plate came into general use in the mid-1880s. The forerunner of the modern measuring devices was the Sensitometer developed by Leon Warnecke in 1878. It consisted of a transparent scale of 25 squares of different intensities for determining the rapidity of the action of the plate. In 1890 F. Hurter and V. C. Driffield introduced their new and different method for determining a plate's sensitivity, enabling the manufacturer to indicate this on an established scale of values.

f/ F-number, the numerical expression of the relative size of the lens opening: a lens's focal length divided by the effective diameter of the lens. Thus, "*f*" followed by a number expresses a ratio. If the diameter of a lens is one-half its focal length, for example, this ratio is expressed as *f*/2. The larger the *f*/stop number, the smaller the aperture opening. The aperture opening controls the depth of field, i.e., the area within which there is a sharpness of focus.

f/64 See *Group f/64* under *Names in Photography.*

Fading A gradual elimination of the photographic image, generally due to the effect of light. The impermanence of the photographic image was a major subject of concern especially in the 1850s and 1860s when, along with the introduction of the wet-collodion method of photography, there was interest in all types of paper photographs, including the calotype. An excessive tendency to fade, it was discovered, might be caused by any number of factors including the imperfect washing of the print, an insufficiency of hypo, the acidity of materials used for mounting a print, or even an excessive amount of sulphur present in the air. In the 1850s and later the almost routine measure taken to protect against fading was to tone the print with chloride of gold.

Fading Committee A committee of seven members which was established in 1855 by the Photographic Society of London to investigate why so many paper prints were disastrously subject to fading.

False image A "ghost": the appearance of a light spot in a photograph because of an error in focusing or a lens defect.

Family album A book specifically made to hold a collection of photographs showing members of the family. Such an album is often hard to date since the collection of photographs may range over many years. The first albums probably date from around 1860. The earliest albums commercially produced were generally set up to contain the carte de visite or cabinet card. The universal popularity of the album is explained by its being the most convenient system for examining one's collection as well as displaying it. In 1861, a Swiss, F. R. Grumel, patented the type of album which has slotted pockets for the insertion of two photographs back to back.

Farm Security Administration The reference is to the body of photographs produced by the F.S.A. under the Roosevelt administration during the depression years of the 1930s. Among the crew of photographers hired by Roy E. Stryker to document social conditions, particularly in the South, were Walker Evans and Dorothea Lange.

Here General U. S. Grant, in 1886, is surrounded by ten members of his immediate family. The General has been stricken with cancer of the throat and is, at the time, struggling to complete his memoirs from his sickroom. A recognition of the solemnity of the occasion seems to reside in each face. The photographer is unknown; the picture is credited to the U.S. Instantaneous Photo Company. (Courtesy of the Library of Congress USZ62-10909.)

Fast film   Film which is highly sensitive to light.

Fast lens   A lens with a small f/number and thus one capable of admitting a great deal of light into the camera.

Father of American Photography   A title bestowed by common assent upon Samuel F. B. Morse (1791–1872). Morse interviewed Daguerre in Paris in the spring of 1839 and wrote home enthusiastically of his technique in photography before the specifics of this technique had been made known. In the fall of the same year Morse became one of the first Americans to try his own hand at daguerreotypy. In the years that followed he instructed a number of others in photography, including some who were later acclaimed as among the greatest of all the nineteenth-century photographers, for example, Mathew B. Brady, Edward Anthony, and Albert S. Southworth. There is another candidate for this title, Professor John W. Draper of New York University, who was also one of the first to experiment with the daguerreotype in this country and who is believed to have been the first to make a portrait by this method.

Ferro-prussiate process   One of the oldest of the various printing processes, having been invented in 1840 by Sir John Herschel. Paper is coated with a mixture of ammonio-citrate of iron and potassium ferricyanide dissolved in water. After being dried in the dark, this paper is printed by daylight in contact with a negative or drawing on tracing paper, to produce an image in a bright blue. The print is then simply washed, leaving a finished print which is blue on a white ground. There is another blueprint process, called Pellet's process, however, in which blue is formed where the light does *not* strike, and this negative cyanotype process is considered more suitable for use with negatives generally. (See **Cyanotype.**)

Ferrotype   A direct positive made by the collodion process on tinned iron. The ferrotype was apparently independently introduced by several inventors in the mid-1850s, including the Frenchman Adolphe Alexandre Martin in 1853. It was patented separately both in England and in America in 1856. The American patent was granted to Hamilton Smith of Ohio, and the patent rights were bought out by Peter Neff the following year. Highly popular in the United States as a means of making relatively inexpensive portraits, the ferrotype became known as the "tintype," a misleading name since it is not on tin. Hamilton Smith had used the term "melainotype," the prefix meaning black. "Ferrotype" was, however, the term used by Victor M. Griswold, an early manufacturer of the plates. The word "ferrotype" had, incidentally, been applied somewhat earlier in England to an entirely different process. The ferrotype proper did not catch on in England until some time in the 1870s when it was introduced as a kind of cheap novelty from the United States.
During the American Civil War the tintype became the popular form of portrait. It was both cheap and quickly made, it might be sent through the mails or carried about on one's person, and it was highly durable. The tintypists followed the military and set up tents so that soldiers might have their pictures taken to send home. Furthermore, tintypes might be made in exceedingly small sizes and therefore were suitable for being incorporated into jewelry. They were sometimes mounted into rings, brooches, or pins. The first political button carrying the photograph of a political candidate was a tintype. Tintypes were even incorporated into tombstones after a patent was granted making it feasible.
As a photograph the tintype is less esteemed than either the daguerreotype or the ambrotype. It is characteristically of a grayish tinge and its surface may be faintly gritty in appearance. Because the gray color may produce an unpleasant effect in a

portrait, it was generally customary to tint the cheeks a pale pink. After 1870 the tintype might be made on a metal japanned dark brown rather than on the more customary black. Although each image, in a tintype, is unique, it was usual to employ a multiple-lens camera to achieve the economy of making a number of portraits at a single sitting. Quick service was offered by the tintypist, and a sitter frequently could leave the studio within minutes of having his portrait taken, the tintype in his hand still not quite dry.

Ferrotyping   A modern method of processing a paper print to impart a high gloss, by drying the emulsion surface flat against a polished metal surface such as stainless steel.

Film   A light-sensitive emulsion on a flexible base. The advantages of photography on film rather than on glass include the film's ease of use because of its light weight. In addition to being as smooth as the glass plate, film has the potential for being quite free from impurities. The introduction of film in photography outmoded the use of both glass and metal plates and ended, as well, the further development of the dry plate. The world's first commercially produced film was manufactured at the Eastman plant in Rochester, New York, and was placed on the market in March, 1885. In December, 1889, a patent was granted to Henry M. Reichenbach, and in 1892, two additional patents, to Reichenbach and George Eastman, for the production of the first transparent nitrocellulose photographic rollable film, thus ushering in the modern age of photography. (See also **Flexible film** and **Stripping film.**)

Film format   The size of photographic film. The modern camera film may vary from subminiature through 35 mm. to the larger roll film marketed in a cassette to sheet film and the single sheets which are sold in a wide variety of sizes.

Film speed   An indication of the sensitivity of a film to light. The faster film is the more sensitive, having a larger size of silver crystals existing in piles on the negative and visible in the positive as grain. The faster the film speed, the larger the crystals, and the greater the grain.

Film *und* Foto   The title of an international exhibit held in Stuttgart in 1929 under the auspices of an arts-and-crafts group largely influenced by the Bauhaus.

Filter   A round piece of colored glass, or sometimes gelatin, placed in front of a camera lens to achieve a desired special effect. Colored filters may be used at times to darken or lighten certain colors in a scene which is to be photographed. A sky filter, for example, holds back blue light, thus making the sky appear darker than it would otherwise in a finished print, with the result of dramatizing cloud effects.

First Premium Gallery   A daguerrean parlor operated in San Francisco in the 1850s by Robert H. Vance. The name of the studio was derived from the State Fair awards won by its proprietor.

Fisheye   An extremely wide-angled lens which produces a circular image with barrel distortion.

Fixer   The chemical agency, in developing, which removes the silver halide crystals not exposed to light from the surface of the image. What remains is a developed negative. Fixing is the process of stabilizing a positive print so that it will not fade or disappear.

Flare   A hole appearing in the photographic image caused by reflections of light inside the lens or along the edge of the lens mount.

Flash A burst of light induced to provide more light than is furnished by the existing available light. The first flashlight powder used magnesium and was made commercially available after 1887. A few photographers, seeking to make the flash yet more dramatic, added gunpowder—sometimes with dangerous results. Photographer Jacob Riis was one of the first to make effective use of the flash in modern documentary photography. The modern type of flashbulb came onto the market in the 1930s.

Flexible film A gelatin film having a sufficiently supple base so that the film may be wound upon a spool for the purpose of moving it along within the camera. Beginning around 1880 many efforts were made to produce a film of this type, and some flexible film was placed on the market although it was as yet both delicate and fairly unreliable. In 1892 the Eastman plant in Rochester, New York, became the first large manufacturer of a reliable flexible film.

Florence compound A plastic composition used for the manufacture of miniature cases, invented by Alfred P. Critchlow and after 1853 produced by him in his manufacturing establishment at Florence, Massachusetts. This compound was a hard and durable plastic believed to have been composed of a mixture of shellac, wood resin, and lamp black. It could be molded into a variety of designs, and many of the designs produced were both fanciful and extremely elaborate.

Flouisme A French school of photography favoring soft-focus effects and indistinct outlines, popular around 1900. Since it favored the photograph altered for artistic effect, its advocates were disparaged as "daubers and gum splodgers" by naturalistic photographer Peter Henry Emerson.

F/number See *f/*.

Focal plane The surface in a camera where the light rays come together to form the image.

Focal plane shutter A (light-controlling) shutter which operates immediately in front of a camera's focal plane to permit exposure of the sensitized photographic material.

Focus The point at which the rays of light from a photographic subject converge after passing through the camera's lens to form an image.

Focusing cloth Any black cloth which was used to drape both the camera and the head of the photographer to exclude extraneous light while focusing. Such a cloth was frequently made of black velvet or twill and lined with red or yellow cloth.

Fog A fault, in either a negative or print, evidenced by a deposit of silver other than that composing the actual image. Fog may be produced chemically or by the action of light, often simply by leaks in the darkroom.

Folio An out-sized photographic album, one more than 12 inches.

Formalistic photography The exploitation of some of the unique aspects of photography in an attempt to achieve artistic form. Among the first to grasp the possibilities inherent in this form of photography were Man Ray and Moholy-Nagy in the twentieth century. The characteristic result achieved has been at times compared to abstract painting.

Fotoform The general name given to the body of photographic work produced by photographers working in Germany following World War II, primarily under the leadership of Otto Steinart. The photographs produced by this school included many abstracts and graphic patterns.

Fotogram   A modern non-objective style of photography, or the product of this style, characterized by some as typically "destructive" of its subject.

Frame   An enclosure for a photograph. The custom of protecting photographs by framing them antedates that of placing them in an album. Ambrotypes and daguerreotypes were almost invariably framed in a miniature case, in which they were protected from both light and dust as well as from the possibility of surface damage such as scratches. Some collectors of nineteenth-century photographs are wary of the photographic image lacking a contemporary case or frame since there is always the possibility that the photograph remained unframed because it was rejected by the photographer.

Frena   A type of magazine camera exceedingly popular in England from 1892 to around 1910. In its advertising it was claimed that "anyone who can ring an electric bell and turn a key can take pictures with this apparatus."

Frontier photography   Although early photographers such as J. H. Fitzgibbon of St. Louis joined the American western migration and set up studios on the frontier, it was not until the "Era of Exploration" in the 1860s and 1870s that frontier photography could be considered to have unique characteristics. Frontier photography, with its use of the wet plate, and the venturesomeness of its photographers determined to secure pictures of hitherto unexplored wilderness, was created by the employment of photographers in government surveys.

F/stop   See *f/*.

F.T.   Family tradition: a term employed sometimes to signify that the identification of a particular photograph rests only with family legend.

Full plate   A daguerreotype size, about 8 by 10 inches, and, thus, larger than the so-called "whole" plate. It is abbreviated to "F." Occasionally one may find "full" and "whole" plate used interchangeably.

Fumination   The process of subjecting sheets of photographic paper to the fumes of ammonia as the last step in the preparation of the paper by hand for printing. Fumination had the purpose of making the paper a bit more sensitive and thus shortening the printing time at the same time as rendering tones more brilliant. This process was first suggested in the early 1860s by H. T. Anthony and it was thereafter the subject of a great deal of argument. However, fumination had been tried somewhat earlier by some working with the daguerreotype.

Fuming   The exposure of albumen paper, sometimes other paper or even plates, to the fumes of ammonia in order to achieve a brighter print.

Galerie Contemporaine   Produced between 1878 and 1884, a series of Woodburytype portraits of notables, the photographers including Carjat and Nadar. A single portrait from the series is probably worth more than $100-900.

Gallery   An early term for the photographic studio, as in daguerrean gallery.

Galvanism   A method of taking "instantaneous pictures" by attaching a galvanic battery to the back of a daguerreotype plate and allowing electric current to flow through at the moment that the plate was exposed. The purpose of this was to speed the action. In Henry Snelling's *History and Practice of the Art of Photography*, he informs us that a skilled operator, by this means, succeeded in taking a view of the steeple of the St. Louis courthouse *after sundown* and in photographing a man at the very instant that his foot was raised preparatory to taking a step.

Galvanized plate   A daguerreotype plate covered with a thin fresh coating of pure silver, by means of galvanism.

Galvanography   According to the *Encyclopedia of Photography* (1911), "Under this name there have been put forward several processes based on the idea of painting on a silvered copper plate with oil colour in thick masses so as to give relief," resulting in an intaglio printing plate, by a method discovered in 1842.

Gaslight paper   A kind of printing paper introduced around 1893 and a great improvement at the time since it could be used by artificial light. The gaslight paper was either chloride or chloride-bromide paper and was initially used with the dry plate. An old gaslight print may characteristically have a bronzed appearance or a metallic or silvery cast. Eventually "gaslight" came to mean a relatively slow paper.

Gelatin   A glutinous substance obtained by boiling animal substances, predominant in the twentieth century in the preparation of photographic emulsion, providing the vehicle for the light-sensitive silver salts.

Gelatin film   A type of film initially manufactured by Eastman and used in the Kodak No. 1 which was introduced in 1888. The early gelatin film is entirely gelatin, with uneven edges, and, unlike later film, brittle.

Gelatin paper   A coated paper about the thickness of writing paper, yielding a brownish-to-purple image. Two examples of photographs on gelatin paper are the Aristotype, which was introduced in 1888, and the familiar proof paper. Two enduringly popular types of modifications of gelatin papers are the gelatin bromide paper introduced by Mawdsley in 1873 and improved upon by Swan in 1879, and gelatin chloride paper invented by Eden and Pizzighelli in 1881.

Gelatin plate   A glass plate which has been prepared to receive the photographic image by flowing gelatin onto it. Chemicals have been added to the gelatin which is allowed to dry before use. The gelatin dry plate is thin, whereas a collodion negative is on a thick glass plate, and the coating, unlike that of the collodion plate, is black and smooth and of an even appearance. The gelatin plate was the first entirely successful dry plate. The initial work on a gelatino-bromide emulsion is generally credited to Dr. Richard Leach Maddox, who announced early results of his experimentation in 1871. In 1873 John Burgess became the first to market a gelatin emulsion and the first ready-made plate. However, its reception among professional photographers remained fairly tentative until the plate was substantially improved by Sir J. W. Swan of the firm of Mawson & Swan who tried ripening the emulsion with heat and thus succeeded in increasing its sensitivity. This new dry plate remained a valuable English export item for a number of years, its use finally being replaced by film.

Gem   A small—sometimes even tiny—tintype (ferrotype). The gem may be found mounted in a paper folder, in an album, or incorporated into a piece of jewelry such as a ring, pin, or brooch. Such jewelry was especially popular in the mid-1860s. These "gems" were usually produced in the studio with the use of a multiplying camera of four lenses and two or more successive exposures with four moves of the camera. The popularity of the gem continued until around 1880.

George Eastman House   At the time of its foundation in 1949, the only major museum in the United States exclusively devoted to photography, the George Eastman House of the International Museum of Photography is located at Rochester, New York, in the former home of George Eastman. Its collection includes over 50,000 photographs from all periods, antique cameras, and other materials illustrating the history of the motion picture. Exhibits are held regularly featuring the work of contemporary as well as earlier photographers, and a participating membership is open to the public. This institution also publishes material in its field and serves as a clearing house for the publications of other houses.

Gernsheim   The Helmut Gernsheim Collection of photographs acquired in 1964 by the University of Texas and housed in its Humanities Research Center in Austin, Texas. Helmut and Alison Gernsheim, who amassed this great collection, are the co-authors of an important history of photography covering the years to 1914, first published in 1955, and of a number of other similarly authoritative works on special subjects within the field of photography. The Gernsheim Collection includes nineteenth- and twentieth-century images by the masters of photography and an extensive collection of books and journals ranging from sixteenth century pre-history of photography to the present. The Collection is particularly interesting for its examples of early experiments in photography and the work of various Victorian photographers. The entire augmented collection of the University of Texas now contains over 150,000 photographs, 6,000 books and journals, and 1,600 pieces of antique equipment.

Ghost   A blurred effect left on the photographic plate, often purposely by an object moving too fast for its image to be registered properly in the camera. The production of such ghosts sometimes resulted accidentally from the long exposures required by the early cameras. Such a ghost might appear in a daguerreotype, for example, if the photographer had, in arranging his picture, stepped momentarily within camera range during the period the lens cap was off. The production of trick ghost photographs particularly delighted the public after paper photography became popular, during the fad for viewing stereographs.

Gigantography   The process of making an enlarged half-tone negative for a poster-sized print.

Gilding   Initially, the process of bathing the daguerreotype silver plate with a warm solution of gold chloride after development and fixing, by a process invented by the Frenchman M. Fizeau around 1840. Later, gilding meant generally the process of coloring, tinting, or stabilizing a photograph with a gold wash, after any number of different processes. The effect of gilding is usually to soften the overall effect of the photograph, as well as to stabilize the image, although gilding was at first devised for the daguerreotype in order to help make the plate more durable. The first American patent for thus treating a daguerreotype was issued in 1842 to Benjamin R. Stevens and Lemuel Morse, of Lowell, Massachusetts.

Glass House   The glass house or room was the photographic studio, usually possessing a skylight and generally arranged to utilize the sun to the full as a source of light for photography. A glass room, according to M. Carey Lea, in 1871, was needed to provide the portraitist with "the pure, soft, diffusive light that comes from a northern exposure. An abundant supply of this light is of the highest value." In his manual on photography, Lea devoted pages to discussing such details of the glass house as the proper pitch of its roof, adding that "few photographers succeed in their first attempts at building a glass house." In the photographer's studio, underneath the required expanse of glass, would be not only the posing chair itself, but various props and screens, the headrest on its stand, sometimes more than one camera, and often, as well, some of the paraphernalia for finishing the pictures and framing or mounting them.

Glass negative   A negative which has been produced on a piece of glass by the collodion process. In 1848 M. Niepce de St. Victor, a younger relative of Niepce, became the first to announce the details of the production of a negative on glass, achieved by using the white of eggs as a coating for the glass. Although he was not the first to try making a negative on glass, he had succeeded in producing the first relatively practical results, and his experiments were quickly followed by the work of others. In 1850 Frederick Scott Archer published the results of his work using wet-collodion to coat the plate, and within the next four years the glass negative sup-planted both the daguerreotype on copper and the calotype on paper as the popular means of photography.

Glass plate   The term glass plate almost always refers to the wet-collodion plate, which had to be flowed with chemicals, sensitized, exposed and developed all while still wet, within a short time, preferably no more than 15 minutes. It was not until the mid-1870s that plates were made available which could be stored for a later use, and although these were also made of glass, they are usually specifically referred to as dry plates. The introduction of the glass plate and its popular use from 1854 on meant a revolution in photography. It was now possible for a number of copies of a photograph to be produced from a single negative. For the professional photographer it opened up opportunities to sell numbers of each picture rather than having to sell each one separately. The earlier glass plate is considerably heavier and thicker than the later dry plate.

Globe lens   An early type of wide-angle lens covering about 90° and in use from around 1862.

Glycerine process   A process which was invented by Stieglitz and Keiley around 1900, to permit the local development of a platinotype, thus making possible the alteration of the photograph without its having been, literally at least, retouched by hand. Some of the most notable glycerine prints were produced by Gertrude Kasebier, whose prints frequently resemble etchings or drawings.

Gold toning   A method for treating prints with a solution containing gold chloride, used for albumen prints to keep them from fading and to impart an attractive soft tone to the print, possibly a wash of brown, purple, or a blue-black. A modern use of gold toning is made to protect the print but without necessarily altering its color. (See also **Gilding.**)

Goodwin Patent   A patent granted to the Rev. Hannibal Goodwin in 1898 follow-ing years of dispute, for his invention of the transparent flexible photographic film. This invention would eventually provide the basis for the entire film industry. Similar patent claims had been filed by George Eastman and Henry M. Reichenbach, and the Reichenbach formula was accorded its own patent at an earlier date, in 1889.

Gradation   The rate of increase in density when a sensitive material is exposed to produce a series of different tones. A negative of full tonal range, for example, from bright to dark, may be printed with a soft gradation on a soft grade of paper.

Grain   Small clumps of the black metallic silver which forms the developed photographic image. Grain may actually be seen under the microscope and some-times, in an enlargement, will even be apparent to the unassisted eye.

Graphoscope   A type of viewer for use either with cabinet cards or stereographs, popular around 1870, providing a magnified image of a transparent photograph.

Gravure   Photogravure: an engraving produced by means of a photograph, and thus the printed copy of an original photograph. Following earlier experiments with various methods of photo-engraving, Karl Klic of Vienna, in 1879, developed a process using a polished copper plate to etch in the tones of the picture at different depths, with the darker parts of the picture deepest and therefore holding the most ink. There are some cases in which an original photograph has disappeared and all the evidence that remains is the gravure. For example, the original photographs made by Edward S. Curtis for his monumental *The North American Indian* have been lost, giving added importance to the published plates. Gravures gain in stature if they have been produced under the direct supervision of the photographer himself, or even by him personally, as were many of those published in *Camera Work* (1903–1917) by members of the Photo-Secessionist group.

Great Exhibition   The first general international exhibition ever held, the Great Exhibition of the Works of All Nations opened in 1851 in London's Hyde Park, where it was housed in the Crystal Palace. After a formal closing, the building was re-established at Sydenham, South London, and the exhibition reopened in June, 1854. It was itself the first public event of which a substantial photographic record was ever made. In addition, through its exhibit of many photographs, it provided a stimulus to the further development of both amateur and professional photography and also set an international standard for accomplishment.

Group *f*/64   A loosely organized group of photographers who joined together in 1931. They were mostly professionals whose avowed purpose was to "act together towards strengthening of clean photographic thought," according to Ansel Adams, one of its founders and leaders. The name of the group, derived from the small aperture of lens in their large cameras, signified an attitude in favor of the sharp and clear image, not any specific technique. The group held an important inaugural show in 1932 at the M. H. de Young Museum in San Francisco.

Gum bichromate process   Dubbed "bi-gum," a complicated process for print control first popularly used around 1895. By contact printing, a solution of potassium bichromate mixed with gum arabic and a colored pigment is coated onto the paper and exposed under the negative. The paper is washed in water to bring out the image rather than developed in the more usual sense. Gum printing is used to condense light and dark areas, with resulting blacks and shafts of light which convey a special emotional intensity. The photographer may alter the image by applying sensitized pigment as he wishes, build up areas he considers too weak or wipe out detail he does not want. The principle of this process was first discovered by Alphonse Poitevin, but its chief advocate was Robert Demachy of Paris at the turn of the century. Demachy held that gum printing added the "vital spark" to any photograph, which otherwise might be too literal.

Gum print   A "photo-aquatint" or type of highly controlled print, either gum-bichromate or gum-platinotype, made in accordance with principles first explained by A. Poitevin in 1855. Since the gum print permits extensive alteration by the photographer during the process of printing, gum printing is chiefly associated with efforts to render a photograph more "artistic" along the lines of conventional art, particularly painting. Two of its leading exponents were Robert Demachy and Alvin L. Coburn. A definitive work on this type of print is *Photo-aquatint . . .* (1898) by Robert Demachy and Albert Maskell, a book now valued at around $50.

Gutta percha   A substance derived from the tree of that name and through the years employed for a variety of purposes in photography. F. Scott Archer, for example, used gutta percha in some of his earliest experiments with collodion, to help strip the sensitive photographic layer from its glass support. Since gutta percha may be softened in hot water and then hardened into the desired shape in a mold, some miniature cases were apparently made of it; however, almost all of those produced after 1854 were thermoplastic rather than made of gutta percha, or "hardened rubber."

Halation   A reflection of light producing a negative image which is not sharp and particularly lacking in the highlight areas. This reflection may take the form of a halo-like effect or a general blurring.

Half plate   Abbreviated ½ p, a daguerreotype size which is larger than the quarter plate but not larger than 4¼ by 5½ inches.

Half-tone   A term sometimes used to indicate the middle (intermediate) grey tones of the photographic image.

Halftone   A reproduction of a photograph by a photomechanical process which simulates the continuous tone gradation characteristic of the photograph by utilizing a finely patterned screen of dots of a size proportional to the densities of the various parts of the original image, and thus breaks down the image into a pattern of lines and dots. A method for accomplishing this was patented as early as 1852 by Fox Talbot. In the United States, in 1865, F. W. von Egloffstein took out a patent for a method which employed a screen ruled on glass with 300 lines to the inch. Until the technique was perfected, photographic book illustration had required mounting the original photograph or a copy of the photograph, such as a Woodburytype. The first halftone to appear in a daily newspaper was published in the *New York Daily Graphic* on March 4, 1880, showing, along with other possible methods of reproduction, a view of the city's shantytown by H. J. Newton. It would be many years, however, before the halftone would come into common use. In 1897 the *New York Tribune* began printing halftones regularly on its high-speed presses, and in 1904 London's *Daily Mirror* became the world's first daily newspaper to be illustrated exclusively with halftones.

Halftone negative   One exposed through a line screen so that the image is composed of vary-sized dots or tiny squares of silver, small in the highlight areas and large for the shadows.

Hallotype   The combination of two images to constitute one picture, by a process patented by J. Bishop Hall of New York in 1857. In its simplest form, two glass plates were sealed together at a slight distance apart. According to Marcus A. Root, sometimes a part of the image in back might be removed to let through more light, or the images might be colored.

Hand camera   A type of camera capable of sufficiently fast exposure times so that it might safely be used in the hand rather than on a tripod. One of the first of the hand cameras was the Kodak No. 1 which Eastman marketed in 1888. This type of camera was plugged as "no work and lots of fun"—a concept which purists such as Alfred Stieglitz found absurd. Stieglitz declared that he found the hand camera and bad results practically synonymous. Yet the hand camera helped create the hobby of photography as it is today, with all its equipment and its numerous publications, and engendered the huge photographic commercial enterprise. The advent of the hand camera, which used film rather than a plate and had a shutter rather than a lens cap, marks a watershed date in the history of photography: the modern era of photography was initiated around 1888, even though some of the major pictorialist work was yet to come.

Hand coloring   Beginning with the daguerreotype and continuing through the ambrotype and tintype, it was a fairly routine procedure to color photographs by hand. The coloring in a portrait might be no more than a faint tinting of the cheeks or a timid dab of color at a bow or ruffle. Although some studios might employ trained artists for this work, most engaged untrained women and girls for the finishing work, with the result that the color was often added with a relatively clumsy hand. Perhaps for this reason, many admirers of the daguerreotype felt strongly that coloring was unsuitable to the daguerreotype and marred its bright beauty. According to Henry H. Snelling in his 1849 *History and Practice of the Art of Photography*, "The method now pursued [of coloring] is on the whole ruinous to any daguerreotype, and to a perfect one absolutely disgusting." However, a bit of color was generally felt to improve the tintype because of its otherwise somewhat dead appearance.

Hard   An adjective which, when applied to print, indicates a very high contrast between the blacks and the whites.

Hayden   A United States Government survey ("the Hayden survey") made in 1871 under the leadership of Dr. F. V. Hayden which reported the natural wonders of the western region later to be designated Yellowstone National Park. The official photographer for this first expedition, as well as for the several later successive ones, was William H. Jackson.

Headrest   A structure of wood and/or cast iron designed to rest on the floor or be attached to the back of a chair, used for the purpose of holding steady the head of a person sitting for his or her portrait. The relatively long exposure time made this assistance necessary, since few could remain as perfectly still as the camera required. Alexander S. Wolcott, who together with a partner opened the first portrait studio, patented a headrest as early as 1840. Much later the headrest was still being employed for taking cartes de visite. It is sometimes visible in the finished picture, particularly in the portraits of children, even though the pose was intended to hide it. Photographers attempted to convince their patrons that the headrest was simply a gentle support against which one might lean the head, but clients complained vigorously that they did not like having their head "placed in a vise" or "screwed up" and claimed that they were capable of holding perfectly still for minutes without it.

Heliochrome   A single-color photograph produced by the subtractive color process developed by Louis Ducos du Haron of France in 1869.

Heliochromy   The art of taking a photograph in natural colors, the name applied by Niepce de Saint-Victor to the method of color photography he discovered in 1853. As early as 1840 Sir John Herschel had observed that paper exposed under red or blue glass would assume the color of the glass. In 1848 Edmond Becquerel reported that he had produced all the colors of the spectrum on a specially prepared silver plate. However, he had to admit that his colors proved "permanent" only so long as the exposed plate was kept in the dark. In 1850 Levi L. Hill, an American, announced that he had discovered a process for producing the daguerreotype in the colors of nature, claiming also to have found a method for making the colors permanent. His method for achieving this, however, remained secret, and the fixation of color in a photograph remained an unsolved problem for many more years. (See **Color print**.)

The photographer in the picture is W. H. Jackson, and the scene Observation Point in Yosemite Valley in 1876. Unfortunately, it is not known who took this stunning photograph. (Courtesy of the Denver Public Library, Western History Department.)

Heliograph   The name bestowed upon the earliest known permanent photographic image, produced by the Frenchman J. N. Niepce around 1825. The image was recorded on a pewter plate coated with bitumen of Judea dissolved in oil of lavender and even after an eight-hour exposure was still fairly faint.

Heliography   The original photographic process, discovered by J. N. Niepce around 1825, modified by Daguerre, but in use to a later date for the specialized printing of bank notes.

Helios   "Helios: the Flying Studio" was the trademark assumed by E. Muybridge beginning in 1867 when he first entered his photographs for copyright.

Heliotype   A photo-lithographic process developed by Ernest Edwards, a London portrait photographer, in 1869 and thereafter widely used for book illustration. As many as 1,500 heliotypes could, eventually, be obtained from a single plate; initially the rate was much less. The first book illustrated with heliotypes was Charles Darwin's *The Expression of Emotions in Man and Animals*, published in 1872 from the photographs of Oscar Rejlander.

Hellenotype   An American method for coloring photographs, employing two differently finished prints, one tinted and the second one superimposed on the other.

High Contrast Print   A print which has deep black shadows and bright high-lighted areas, with few shades of gray between. The ultimate high contrast print is simply black and white.

High key   Referring to a photograph in which most of the tones are lighter than a medium gray. Such a "white" photograph is sometimes sought to emphasize a portrait subject's innocence or youth.

Hillotype   In 1850 Levi L. Hill of Westkill, New York, announced that he had devised a process for reproducing the colors of nature directly in the daguerreotype. He called this the Hillotype. His initial announcement proved premature, however, and finally in 1856 Hill published a *Treatise on Heliochromy*, which proved to be more of a record of failure than success. It seems as though Hill was not the only photographer to find that although he might capture color, it would remain in the photograph only briefly.

Holmes-Bates   A hand-held viewer for looking at stereoscopic photographs, the invention of Oliver Wendell Holmes in 1861.

Holmes   A stereoscopic camera for taking daguerreotypes, invented by S. A. Holmes and patented in 1854.

Hologram   A modern invention: the hologram is a two-dimensional photographic plate or piece of film in which, through the agency of laser light, an image is made to appear in three dimensions, for either a monochromatic or rainbow effect. Holography was invented in 1947 by Dr. Dennis Gabor.

Holograph   A holograph list is one handwritten such as might accompany the contents of an album or collection of pictures; the term is not unique to photography nor does it refer to a photographic process.

Homes, Booth & Hayden   Along with the better-known Scovill Manufacturing Company, a firm manufacturing leather wood-frame miniature cases in Waterbury, Connecticut.

Honey process The subject of experimentation in the 1850s, a method for preparing the collodion plate which has the advantage of keeping it relatively moist and therefore not requiring almost immediate use; however, it attracted dust.

Horn silver The combination of chloride and silver which blackens under the rays of the sun or other strong light. The discovery of this phenomenon formed one of the bases for the development of photography. Horn silver derives its name from its appearance.

Hyalography Photographic etching on glass.

Hyalotype The name under which Frederick Langenheim secured the U.S. patent for the lantern slide, in 1850. He had journeyed to Europe to learn the secrets of the process developed by Fox Talbot and by Niepce de St. Victor, returning to patent the "hyalotype" which used the whites of eggs to bind light-sensitive materials to a glass plate, thus producing an albumen transparency.

Hypo The popular name for sodium thiosulfate, used for fixing a photographic image. Sir John F. W. Herschel discovered the chemical compound he called "hyposulphite" in 1819.

I The abbreviation for the Imperial daguerreotype plate size, 9 by 12 inches or larger, to about 14 by 16 inches; sometimes, however, defined simply as any daguerreotype plate larger than whole-plate size (6½ by 8½ inches). Few daguerreotypists cared to attempt the larger plate because of the difficulty in preparing it properly.

Identity card According to the historian M. F. Braive, the first time a photograph was used on a card for the purpose of identifying the card-holder was in Paris in 1867. Helmut Gernsheim tells us that the first pass issued to contain an identifying photograph was that issued in 1861 by the Chicago and Milwaukee Railway Company. Certainly any cards or passes issued before 1870 would be of special interest to collectors.

Image The two-dimensional picture as it appears in a photograph, as distinguished from the plate or film on which it is recorded.

Image A publication issued by the International Museum of Photography at the George Eastman House in Rochester, New York, made available to associate members of the Museum on a quarterly basis.

Image of America The title of a catalogue for an exhibit held at the Library of Congress in 1957, covering the years 1839–1900.

Image point The point at which the image of distant objects comes into critical focus.

Imperial An "Imperial" card is a photograph mounted on a card which is 6⅞ by 9⅞ inches in size, thus larger than the more conventional cabinet card. The date of its introduction is not known. The term "Imperial" originated with the daguerreotype, to indicate a plate larger than whole size. After the introduction of the wet-collodion method of photography in the mid-1850s, enlargements became popular, until the concept of Imperial had expanded to mean a photograph so big that it might be life-size, even sometimes full-length. Such grandiose portraits might be embellished and then colored by an artist, possibly highlighted with crayon or India ink.

IMP/GEH   The initials for International Museum of Photography/George Eastman House (Rochester, New York), often employed thus to indicate the source of a photograph.

Impressionist photography   A style of photography which followed that of the Impressionist painters and was based, at least, on a movement back to naturalism initiated by Emerson around 1889. One of the leading characteristics of the Impressionist style is the use of soft focus.

Incident light   Any light that may fall upon a subject to be photographed, whatever its source. Reflected light, on the other hand, is the amount of light reflected off a subject.

India tint mount   A type of mount in which the photographic print has a border of thin tinted paper.

Infinity   In photography, that area furthest from the camera in which objects still remain in focus for the lens.

Instantaneous exposure   In general, a camera exposure of very short duration, one so brief that the camera may be held in the hand (rather than mounted). Today this may mean an exposure time of 1/25th of a second or less, although in the 1850s "instantaneous" could mean a full second.

Instantaneous photograph   An "action" photograph, taken of subjects in motion without their being posed. In the 1850s there was considerable discussion of the techniques which might be used for stop-action photographs and a number of successful photographs were actually taken by the most skilled photographers using the wet-collodion method. The first real success, however, came around 1860 with stereographic views taken of city streets in which pedestrians were strolling about and traffic moving at the slow pace of the day. During the 1860s and 1870s manufacturers of stereographs frequently made a point of a series' including "instantaneous" (candid) shots. According to Towler in 1864, a sharp and clear instantaneous photograph can be made if the light is "very bright," the atmosphere "very clear," the glass plate also clear and free of impurities, the collodion "very ripe," the developer "very sensitive," and the lens properly corrected and capable of producing a sharp picture with a large diaphragm, "the shorter the focus the better within proper bounds." He makes the difficulties sufficiently obvious. Instantanteous photography is often equated with outdoor photography, likely, of course, to include moving objects. Just as the Impressionist style in painting had its influence on photography, so, it is thought by some critics, instantaneous photography in turn influenced the Impressionist painters, possibly to the same extent that Japanese art was an influence.

Instant dip method   A daguerreotype will be destroyed if you attempt to clean it with a cloth or directly with silver polish. Do not attempt it! However, a modern way of cleaning the daguerreotype plate has been devised using a cleaning agent which is readily available: the instant silver dip which does not require touching the plate. The image should be separated from its case, if there is one, and from any wrappings. Holding the edge carefully, rinse both sides of the plate in cool running water, then place it in a dish containing an "instant dip" solution of the kind which is sold in hardware stores for cleaning household silver. Agitate for about half a minute, or until the discoloration has disappeared. Then rinse both sides under running water again, for maybe half a minute, shake the water off and dry, using the mild heat of a candle or a domestic hair dryer, but not held too close. (See also **Missouri method**.)

Intensification The process of increasing the overall density—contrast—in a developed silver image by chemical means.

International Center of Photography A center exclusively devoted to photography, established in New York City in 1974, dedicated to "the appreciation of photography as the most important art-communication form of the twentieth century with the capacity to provide images of man and his world that are both works of art and moments in history." Regular exhibits are held, and the public is invited to membership.

International Museum of Photography. See **George Eastman House.**

International Society of Pictorial Photographers An English association formed in 1904 for the purpose of unifying work in photography in all nations.

Iron horse The mutoscope, a machine patented in 1895 by Herman Casler of Oneonta, New York, for viewing a quick succession of cards for an impression of motion. This is the familiar penny-arcade peep show.

Iron instrument of torture A name popularly applied to the headrest, made of wood or wood and iron, used to help a person sitting for his photographic portrait hold still long enough for the exposure. This headrest remained an essential part of studio equipment until well into the 1870s.

Iron photograph A print made by a process which was especially speedy for the nineteenth century, utilizing a preparation of iron; however, the process created special problems in achieving the desired tone.

Iron process Printing accomplished with the use of salts of iron.

Isochromatic photography Photography in which colors are rendered in a monochromatic picture according to their true brightness. An isochromatic plate is one sensitized for color.

Ivory photograph Unlike the Ivorytype, a photographic image actually made on real ivory, generally by a carbon transfer process for subsequent painting as a colored miniature.

Ivorytype Either a picture printed through a negative onto artificial ivory by a process introduced in London by J. E. Mayall and then colored in imitation of a miniature painting on ivory; *or* the "American ivorytype," a colored print mounted on a sheet of plate glass with the use of hot wax, then backed with white paper or cardboard. In the American method, introduced in 1855, a tiny distance is maintained between the glass and the paper backing, and sometimes a duplicate tinted print placed behind, to give the picture—usually a portrait—more color or vigor. Ivorytype portraits of contemporary heroes were once popular.

Kallitype A printing process invented in 1899 by W. J. Nichol, a development from the Chrysotype, producing a reddish-brown print capable of being bleached, redeveloped, and intensified.

Keystone The Keystone View Company, producer of stereographs including a "Stereographic Library" featuring a "tour of the world." This company remained active from the nineteenth century into the 1930s.

Kinematography An early term for the art of photographing objects in motion for the successive projection of images on a screen.

Kinematoscope   A relatively crude device for viewing photographs made of moving objects, and thus anticipating cinema projection. It was the invention of Coleman Sellers, who used his invention to produce a sometimes astonishing effect of reality.

Kinetoscope   The first practical form of the motion picture, invented by Thomas Edison in 1889. The kinetoscope uses flexible transparent roll film and shows a succession of positives, so rapidly that they appear to blend and thus produce the effect of motion. The kinetoscope, which must be hand-cranked is, however, for individual viewing and for this reason has been dubbed the "one-man peep show." Its successor in popularity was the Mutoscope, patented in 1895, which provided a picture seven times larger and which was equipped with a reel holding cards which proved more durable than the kinetoscope's film.

King survey   The first of an important series of geological surveys conducted by the American government in the West. The exploration of the Fortieth Parallel was made under the direction of Clarence King beginning in July, 1868, and continuing for several years. T. H. O'Sullivan served as the photographer with the expedition for the years 1867–69. The reports emanating from the expedition contained lithographic copies of O'Sullivan's photographs. Photographs later published on mounts with the King survey imprint were not, however, captioned in a consistent fashion. A limited number of stereograph cards was issued from his photographs in 1872.

Kodachrome   A color film first marketed commercially in 1935 which, along with Agfacolor, within a few years made color generally available to photographers. Kodachrome could be used in any camera and required only a single exposure. It was the invention of Leopold Mannes and Leopold Godowsky, who based their work on that done in 1912 by Rudolph Fischer. In 1941 Kodacolor came on the market, providing a negative with reversal not only of light and shade but also color. From this film any number of prints could be made rather than just one as previously.

Kodak   A revolutionary new type of camera invented by George Eastman, patented by him in 1886 and first marketed in 1888. The first Kodak on the market, Kodak No. 1, was a simple box camera 3¼ by 3¾ by 6½ inches, with a fixed-focus lens and an ingenious barrel shutter arrangement. It came from the factory already loaded with gelatin film for 100 negatives, and when the film had been exposed, the entire camera had to be returned to the factory to have the film processed and the camera re-loaded. Each of the first Kodak's circular negatives was 2½ inches in diameter, and the pictures were returned separately mounted, each within a gilt-edged chocolate-colored frame. For Kodak No. 2 (1889), a larger camera but with only 60 exposures, the image was enlarged to a circle 3½ inches in diameter. The photographs produced by the subsequent Kodaks would be rectangular or square. In 1891, Eastman devised a way for the film to be loaded in daylight, and cameras no longer had to be returned to the factory of origin for the film to be processed.

Kodak No. 1 was the first of a long series of cameras that made the snapshot an integral part of American life. Carl W. Ackerman, author of a definitive biography of George Eastman, has summed up the significance of the Kodak by quoting from the original Kodak ad, which said it all: "Ten years ago every photographer had to sensitise his own plates and develop and finish his negatives on the spot where the picture was taken. . . . Four years ago the amateur photographer was confined to heavy glass plates for making his negatives, and the number of pictures he could make on a journey was limited by his capacity as a pack horse. . . . Yesterday the photographer, whether he used glass plates or films, must have a dark room and know all about focusing, relation of lens apertures to light and spend days and weeks learning developing, fixing, intensifying, printing, toning, and mounting before he could show good results from his labors. Today photography has been reduced to a cycle of three operations: (1) Pull the string, (2) Turn the key, (3) Press the button." Of course, whether the result could be called art was highly debatable among those photographers who had labored long to raise photography to the level of salon showings. Yet the advance in technology was beyond the area of debate.

Said Eastman, "There is no jugglery about it; photography has simply been brought down to a point where the mechanical work can be entirely separated from the chemical work. Besides this, the part of the work left for the novice to do has been greatly simplified. Heretofore the so-called 'detective' camera has been the only instrument suitable for wayside photography, and even with this form of camera it has been necessary to perform upwards of ten operations in order to simply make one exposure, as the mere act of 'taking' the picture is called. . . . The Kodak reduces the ten or more operations heretofore necessary to make an exposure with detective cameras to three operations, reduces the weight and bulk in the same proportion, and increases the number of pictures that can conveniently be made on one trip from *six* to *one hundred.* . . ."

Kromskop The invention of Frederic E. Ives of Philadelphia in 1892, a device optically reuniting three stereoscopic transparencies for viewing as one. When each transparency was of a different and appropriate primary color, a naturalistic color photograph resulted.

Lafayette The name of a firm operated by a Frenchman in the middle of the nineteenth century, with studios in Paris, Dublin, and various cities in England, known for the high quality of its portraits and its cartes de visite and cabinet photographs.

Landscape, pure A photograph—or perhaps a painting—which appears to show an outdoor scene in nature presented without alteration simply for its own sake, and often a scene apparently untouched by the hand of man.

Lantern slide A positive transparency intended for projection, first developed by the Langenheim Brothers of Philadelphia around 1850. Lantern slides would remain popular for parlor entertainment throughout the nineteenth century and up to World War I. The Langenheims dominated the market until 1874, when their business was sold to Casper W. Briggs. Briggs' slides anticipated the movies in many ways, with a variety of slide sets of the story-telling variety on religious, literary, historical, and humorous themes. Most slides, including the American, are close to square, 3½ by 4 inches, and the English slides are 3½ inches square. However, slides were also made in novelty shapes and sizes. They might also be painted in either oils or watercolors, and sometimes were designed to be jiggled or otherwise moved about for an effect of motion. Occasionally the work of one of the great photographers—Frederick Evans, for example—may be found on the humble lantern slide.

Latent image The potential photographic image, which is made to appear when a photograph is processed, or developed. Or, more technically, that portion of the silver halide crystals in an emulsion which is developable by exposure to light. As Alvin Langdon Coburn said, "Pause for a moment and consider the mysterious quality of light registering itself in sensitized gelatine—all the scientific poetry in the words 'latent image'."

Laterally corrected   Rearranged so that right and left appear as normally viewed in life. The daguerreotype, for example, is a mirror image providing a picture in which everything is laterally reversed, so that the writing which appears on a sign in a daguerreotype will read backwards. The tintype, also, is naturally reversed. The necessary lateral correction may be achieved by shooting the picture through a mirror arrangement or through a prism, or by rephotographing. With a portrait, the reversal may be of little importance: the subject sees himself as he invariably does in the mirror. With landscapes, however, a lateral correction may be essential to achieve verisimilitude.

Leaf shutter   A concentric arrangement of overlapping metal plates which, when activated, moves to admit light into the camera; also called a diaphragm shutter.

Leather photograph   The problem of achieving a photographic image on leather has been of interest to experimenters since the very earliest days of photography. The initial experiments made by Wedgwood and others were on white leather. Much later, collodion positives were made on black patent leather, among other types of leather. Few examples of photography on leather have survived, however, because of the tendency of the leather to dry out and crack and the incompatibility of leather with the delicate photographic image.

Leica   A 35 mm. camera invented by Oskar Barnack and first marketed by the Leitz Company in 1924, one of the earliest of the "candid" cameras, followed by many imitators and numerous successors. The light, hand-held Leica freed the enterprising photographer to seek new images; among its most successful early users were Dr. Erich Salomon and Paul Wolff.

Lens   A solid piece of transparent material, that part of the camera which is capable of gathering and selecting light rays reflected by a subject to travel to the focal plane and there form an image. Lenses are customarily made of glass. They may be characterized as slow or fast. Accessory lenses such as wide-angle, telefoto, and zoom lenses, for example, have relatively small aperture openings and are therefore slower; a fast lens is one having a large aperture opening of $f/2$ or wider.

Lenticular process   A method for making stereo photographs by using a screen of interlaced strips; *or*, a color process introduced by Eastman Kodak in 1928.

Lettertype   The term lettertype—or lettergraph—was used to indicate the tintype, which was convenient for sending through the mails because of its light weight and virtual indestructibility. The tintype is resistant to damage from light, damp, and, to some extent, friction, although it may be dented or scratched.

Lightening process   A special collodion formula introduced into the United States by T. S. Lambert and licensed by the firm of Anthony. It was supposed to reduce exposure time by as much as one-fourth and made possible E. Muybridge's successful experiments with the wet plate in photographing motion.

Light meter   An instrument used in photography for the purpose of measuring light, translating that measurement into an f/stop—shutter speed combination to provide good exposure.

Limelight   Oxy-hydrogen, dubbed "limelight," used first for photography in experiments conducted by L. L. B. Ibbetson in 1839. With it, he succeeded in making a daguerreotype through a microscope with an exposure of five minutes—at a time when 25 minutes was the usual exposure, in full sunlight.

Limning Embellishing with color: a daguerreotypist frequently employed a limner in his studio to tint portraits for the purpose of achieving a "more natural" look, actually one closer to the appearance of a painting.

Link A member of the Linked Ring.

Linked Ring The Linked Ring Brotherhood, an association of photographers formed in England in 1892 by a group lead by George Davison. Its members broke away from the influence of the Photographic Society (of Great Britain) to emphasize and expand an interest in art photography. Annual exhibitions were held from 1893 until 1914, providing a showcase for important new work, including that of James Craig Annan.

Lithoprint stereograph A kind of card stereograph which did not come into great circulation until around 1898. Lithoprint stereos were made both in color and in black and white, and many of those in color were of a humorous vein, or sentimental, of children or of the conventional travel scenes. The humor might be crude, and the color was often garish, as it was in the postcards of the day. Lithoprint stereos are more typical of the early twentieth century than the nineteenth, and therefore any early cards from the 1890s may be valuable, depending on the quality of the original work and the present condition. Other valuable lithoprint stereos include those showing the results of the San Francisco earthquake and fire, the Russo-Japanese War, the Great White Fleet, the Balkan War of 1912–13, the St. Louis Exposition in 1904—and anything on American Indians.

Little Galleries The Little Galleries of the Photo Secession (group of photographers) at 291 Fifth Avenue in New York City, and thus also affectionately known as "291." The Galleries were established in 1905 by Albert Steichen and Alfred Stieglitz for the display of photographs as works of art. In 1907 Stieglitz himself returned to "pure photography" and, to bolster his own views, the Little Galleries began showing other forms of art along with the photographs; the artists included Rodin, Picasso, Matisse, Renoir, Dove, and other innovators.

Logo The insignia by which a photographer or studio indicates its work.

London The London Stereoscopic and Photographic Company, founded in 1854, a popular publisher of thousands of stereoscopic views, including its fine "North American" series; or the London Salon, an annual exhibition of photography organized by the Linked Ring, an organization of pictorialists. This salon provided a model for exhibits of photographs in other countries during the 1890s.

Luminance The light reflected from a subject for photography, a property both of the subject and the lens image and depending upon the intensity of the incident light as well as reflectance of the subject.

Luminous photograph One made to glow at night or in the dark, possibly prepared in any one of a number of ways, usually appearing as an ordinary black and white positive by day.

Luxograph A device for taking photographs by artificial illumination, patented in England in 1878 but only briefly popular in the United States.

M   The abbreviation for mammoth plate. The term originates in the classification of daguerreotype sizes. The daguerreotype mammoth plate ranges in size from 15 by 18 inches to 22 by 25 inches, although most mammoth plates are around 18 by 21 inches.

Macrophotography   The process of enlarging from a negative to produce an unusually large positive.

Magazine camera   A camera capable of storing a number of plates (or cut films) and containing a mechanism for shifting the plate following each exposure. The simplest mechanism dropped the plate to the bottom of the camera after exposure and had a spring to push the next plate forward. The invention of this type of camera, around 1850, is credited to Marcus Sparling.

Magic lantern   A device for projecting a picture through a glass slide onto a screen or wall in a darkened room. The magic lantern show provided parlor entertainment at the same time as the fad for viewing stereographs. The first showing to attract public attention was at the Crystal Palace exhibition in London in 1852. (See also **Lantern slide.**)

Magnesium light   An early system for indoor or nighttime photography. Early in the 1860s a burning magnesium wire was used in experiments to find a satisfactory additional source of light for taking photographs. Following reports of its use in Europe, magnesium was used by Charles Waldeck of Cincinnati to take stereographs underground in the Mammoth Caves of Kentucky. His photographs created considerable interest when they were published by E. and H. Anthony of New York. Magnesium light did not, however, prove satisfactory for general use since it not only produced a very harsh glare but also generated an unpleasant and lingering white smoke.

Mahoganytype   A facetious term: an all-black picture, the result of having forgotten to put the plate in the camera.

Marion   The Marion Company, possibly the largest photographic dealer in England in the middle of the nineteenth century.

Mat   A cardboard frame used to border (isolate, enhance) and protect a photograph.

Matte   An emulsion surface in a photographic paper which is dull and non-reflective, relatively lifeless as opposed to glossy.

Medallion portrait   A head-and-shoulders portrait enhanced by being enclosed in a contrasting circle or oval to produce the effect of a border. This border was often fancifully embellished. The figure itself might be predominantly light against a dark medallion, or vice versa. This was a style of portraiture popular with the carte de visite and continuing through the 1890s and later. Various patented devices were made available to studios to help photographers achieve special effects.

Medium plate   A daguerreotype size of plate, namely the sixth plate, 2¾ by 3¼ inches, abbreviated 1/6 p.

Megalethoscope   A large photographic viewer having a lamp as a source of light and utilizing photographs on thin paper specially mounted on a curved frame to achieve a third-dimensional effect, the invention of Carlo Ponti in the 1860s. A fine example brought $1,200 at auction in 1976.

With camera, tripod, and reflectors, Charles Waldack of Cincinnati and his crew prepare to enter the darkness of Mammoth Cave, in Kentucky. The year is 1866. Waldack's achievement in making subterranean photographs was hailed as a near miracle. Stereographs of the photographer as well as his pictures were published and circulated. Although this stereo purports to show "the gentlemen who conceived and executed the project of photographing the cave," Waldack himself is not identified. (Courtesy of the Library of Congress USZ62-11004.)

Melainotype A kind of photograph produced on sheet metal of the type manufactured in 1856 by William Neff for the making of "photographic pictures on japanned surfaces." Although Neff preferred the term "melainotype," his rival manufacturer, Victor M. Griswold, called his own almost identical plate the "ferrotype plate." Eventually, however, "tintype" became the more familiar term, eclipsing both the others.

Melanograph A collodion positive made directly on black paper by a process introduced by Dr. Giles Langdell of Philadelphia in 1853 and, independently, in England one year later.

Mercury bath In the daguerreotype process, a slightly warmed bath of two to four ounces of highly purified mercury, over which the photographic plate is inverted and fumed to bring out the latent image. The mercury might be heated in a cast iron pot over an alcohol lamp and the plate to be fumed placed face down on a rack over the boiling liquid.

Metamorph A photographic print containing a distorted image achieved by warming the wet film, stretching or otherwise warping and changing it.

Mezzotint A photographic print in which a softened effect has been obtained by interposing a sheet of glass, mica, or possibly a piece of tissue paper between the negative and the printing paper.

Microfilm An exceedingly small photograph or one much reduced, usually on transparent or opaque paper. The microfilm library is a repository for tiny negatives which may be printed and enlarged as needed. The idea for such a library is not new: in 1853 Sir John Herschel proposed the storage of small negatives in a library. The use of microfilm for documentation and libraries to house microfilm was not launched in earnest, however, until around 1938.

Microphotography A nineteenth-century definition was "taking diminished copies of photographs, or photographs of microscopic objects." Today it is the photographic technique of reduction, in which small negative sizes are employed. Photomicrography, on the other hand, is photography through a microscope. During the 1850s there developed something of a fad for viewing tiny photographs so small that they could not be seen with the naked eye. Among the work admired was a photograph no larger than the head of a pin, on which the Ten Commandments had been produced. A sensation was produced in 1867 with the exhibition of a micro-portrait mosaic of all 450 members of the French Chamber of Deputies, at the International Exhibition in Paris. Such microscopic photographs were achieved by using a special collodion which would leave the picture grain-free. Microphotographs were worn as jewelry and often viewed by means of a special lens invented by Lord Stanhope, who died in 1816, long before he could have anticipated its use in photography. Such mounted mini-photographs are called "Stanhopes."

Midget In British terminology, a small size of mount for a photograph. Midgets include the Victorian midget and cabinet midget, each just slightly over 1 by 2 inches, and the promenade and boudoir midgets, each approximately 2 by 3 inches or very slightly less, and the panel midget, over 4 inches by almost 2. At this distance in time, these distinctions appear fairly exquisite.

Miniature camera Any very small camera: one of the first was that invented by Thomas Skaife in 1858 to accommodate plates no more than 1 inch square. In

1860 Adolph Bertsch produced a metal-box camera which was 4 inches square and had a fixed-focus lens. Another early miniature camera was that devised by Charles Piazzi Smyth, who photographed the Great Pyramids of Egypt using sensitized microscope slides. In the 1880s, with cameras using the dry plate, it was possible to produce cameras in very small sizes, and there resulted the fad for the so-called "detective" camera, small enough to be hidden in a waistband, under a buttonhole, in a man's hat, or disguised as a package, a cane, or opera glasses. The owner of a miniature camera which he hid about his person might even violate propriety by taking a lady's picture even though he had not been introduced to her and asked her permission.

Miniature case   An enclosure, usually hinged, especially designed to hold a photograph, which was customarily a portrait, usually a daguerreotype on silvered copper, though sometimes the ambrotype on glass or the ferrotype on metal. In popular use between 1846 and 1865, the miniature case was advertised as "an everlasting keepsake," and was "one of the most important personal art forms to enter the home" according to the leading authority on these cases, Floyd Rinhart. The earliest cases were of leather on a wood frame and closely resembled the cases which had been made previously to contain small painted portraits. Later, cases might be covered with papier mache or paper, or velvet; after 1854 they were almost all made of thermoplastic, a substance invented by Samuel Peck and capable of being molded like gutta percha. These exceedingly popular thermoplastic cases were produced in a wide range of designs, which Rinhart has catalogued as dealing with (1) history and the sentiments of the people, (2) nature, or (3) featuring traditional and mostly geometrical designs. These cases are usually either a very dark brown or black, though some are tan. The velvet cases might be red, green, or blue. Some of the handsomest cases were elaborately decorated, possibly with mother-of-pearl. Miniature cases have been collected for years, with the result that they may not always contain their original photographs. Any identifying slip found under a picture may not refer to the actual photograph in the case. Although some of the earlier cases had spaces for two portraits, after 1850 it was more usual for the case to accommodate just one. American cases generally open after the fashion of a book and are usually around 3 to 4 inches in size. The smallest may be around 1¾ by 2 inches, the largest 7 by 9 inches. The daguerreotype and the ambrotype are protected under glass. Pictures are matted and there is almost invariably a "protector" as well, of paper-thin malleable brass decorated with an embossed border. The major reference work on this subject is *American Miniature Case Art* by Floyd and Marion Rinhart, published in 1969.

Miniature photograph   A particular size of photograph: approximately 1⅛ by 2 inches or smaller. Miniatures on paper, like the similarly small tintypes called gems, were mounted in albums especially designed for them. Such albums were popular beginning in the 1860s. As late as the 1880s the illustration of a book might, rather whimsically to modern eyes, include dozens, even hundreds of these miniatures arranged closely together.

Missouri method   A method for restoring daguerreotypes devised by the Missouri Historical Society and preferred as a method of cleaning by many institutions over the more crude instant-silver-dip method. The Missouri system employs six steps, as follows:

(1) Removing the image from its case and washing it in distilled water for several minutes.

(2) Immersing the plate in a chemical solution of 1,500 cubic centimeters of

distilled water, 70 grams of Thiourea, 80 cubic centimeters of phosphoric acid (85 percent), and 2 cubic centimeters of non-ionic wetting agent. The plate is to be left in this solution until the discoloration in the plate has disappeared.

(3) Removing the plate from its bath and cleansing it by holding it under running water for one minute, then agitating briefly in a mildly soapy water.

(4) Rinsing again in running water, then washing again in distilled water.

(5) Immersing for one minute in 95 percent grain alcohol.

(6) Drying the plate over a small flame.

Modified print One in which the image has been altered, as might be accomplished in the gum-bichromate print. At the opening of the important Photo Secession exhibit held in 1902, Stieglitz vigorously defended the modified print: "It is justifiable to use any means upon a negative or paper to attain the desired end."

Montage A composite picture made up from several photographs or combination of photographs with other objects. The earliest attempts at photographic montage were called composition prints (q.v.). A frequent use of the photographic montage has been to recreate some important public event for which no actual photograph exists. Sometimes it has been used to deceive. A sensation was once caused by the circulation of a purported photograph—actually a montage—showing the Pope dressed in the costume of a Freemason.

Moon photography The moon has always been a fascinating subject for photographers. One of the first photographs of the moon was that taken in 1840 by John W. Draper. In March, 1851, John A. Whipple made a successful photograph of the moon through the telescope at Harvard College.

Motion photography The taking of pictures of objects in motion constituted a major technical problem for those using the slow cameras before the invention of the shutter. During the 1870s Eadweard Muybridge perfected a technique for taking a succession of pictures of animals in motion by using a battery of cameras lined up parallel to the direction of the action. Two other pioneers in motion photography working at the same time and making separate contributions were Thomas Eakins and J. E. Marey. In 1880 Muybridge succeeded in projecting motion pictures from his series of photographs. In the area of still photographs of motion, important contributions were made by professional sports photographers between 1900 and World War I.

Mottling A spotty, granular appearance in a negative or print, possibly—in a print—caused by the texture of the paper stock which is used.

Mount The backing or support for a photographic print; varieties of mounts include those which are plate-sunk, the India-tint, the raised oval, etc.

Mourning mat A mat of dark paper used in mounting a daguerreotype, usually a portrait of someone deceased; however, the dark mat might sometimes be embellished with gilt.

Multiple A multiple photograph is one registering a number of images, each made separately on a single plate, either by means of a camera with a battery of lenses or in succession. The multiple gum print, for example, is a form of gum-bichromate printing in which the image is successively built up on a paper coated with a sensitive pigment by printing, drying, recoating, redeveloping.

Multiplying camera A type of camera with more than one lens, capable, with two or more exposures, of producing a number of pictures from just one pose. In the ferrotype studio, for example, such a camera might produce 16 exposures on a quarter plate. These pictures would then be cut apart with tin-snips following processing. The multiplying camera was also an economic asset in turning out numbers of cartes de visite or cabinet cards from one sitting. The "multiplying box," as it was called, was developed to the point where it was capable of producing anywhere from 50 to 100 pictures at a time. In the time once required to produce a single photograph, the studio was now able to make many. The first multipliers were sold by Simon Wing, originally of Waterville, Maine, under a patent granted to Albert Southworth, according to their contemporary, Edward M. Estabrooke.

Mutoscope "A hand-cranked peep-show device dating back to 1895 in which card photographs mounted on a reel slipped by to recreate an action sequence," according to an article by Andrew H. Eskind which appeared in the photographic magazine *Image* (IMP/GEH, Rochester, New York) in March, 1976. Eskind's article titled "Mutoscopes Old and New" and more flippantly subtitled "She Banked in her Stockings; or, Robbed of her All," reports on the collection and interests of the late Douglas Crockwell. Crockwell's material was exhibited in 1967 at the Museum of Modern Art in New York, and both the *Image* article and the catalogue for the show are good sources of information.

National Daguerrean Gallery A collection of daguerreotypes made by Edward Anthony with his partner J. M. Edwards, consisting of portraits of the members of Congress. The "Gallery" was exhibited until it was destroyed by fire in 1852.

National Photographic Society A membership organization of professional photographers formed in 1868. After some internal squabbles in the 1870s, the then-lagging society was revived in 1880 as the Photographic Association of America.

Naturalism A style of photography concerned with capturing images directly from nature—especially associated with the English photographer P. H. Emerson, who published a book titled *Naturalistic Photography* in 1889. Naturalistic photography repudiated the formalistic "art" photography popular at the time which relied heavily on the formal rules of composition derived from the classical teaching of painting. Whereas "art" photography had been characterized by a sentimental view of peasant life, a use of costumed models to create allegorical scenes, and the production of combination prints (q.v.), Emerson advocated photographing people in their everyday costumes at everyday occupations, in their usual environment.

Natural photography After World War I, a school of photographic thought favoring sharpness of detail along with clarity of image and specifically opposed to the manipulation of the negative for the purpose of obtaining special effects. Photographers associated with this school of thought include Edward Weston, Brett Weston, and Paul Strand.

Negative A developed photographic image in which the lights and shades are reversed. In 1864 J. Towler defined the negative thus: "An actinic impression on glass or waxed paper, in which the lights and shadows are inverted, as also the figures and the different items that form the picture; that is, right becomes left, and left right." The process of photography makes available a simple process for reversing tone values, not only between white and black but in the colors. The negative is mostly used as the intermediary step in the production of the positive print, although negative prints, often blending fact and fantasy, are a special art form. The first image obtained in the history of photography was a negative made by Niepce, possibly around 1816. The first negative to be captured in a camera was obtained by Fox Talbot around 1835. The word "negative" was first used by Sir John Herschel to describe a calotype made on paper rendered translucent by waxing. Today, a print may be a collector's item if it is made directly from the original negative even though the work is not done by the original photographer—provided that this fact is carefully specified.

Negretti & Zambra An English firm founded in 1850, photographers and suppliers of photographic goods. In 1863 Henry Negretti became the first to photograph London from a balloon.

Ninth plate A very small daguerreotype plate size, 2 by 2½ inches, abbreviated to 1/9 p.

Nitrocellulose Nitrocellulose roll film, invented by the Rev. Hannibal Goodwin in 1887 and improved upon by the Eastman firm, the type of roll film in use to this day.

Oil print A type of photographic print achieved by a highly controlled process devised in 1904 by G. E. H. Rawlings. An oil image is produced on a gelatin base, often specifically for the purpose of producing a photograph which will look like a painting. In the oil-pigment process, color may be added when the paper has been sufficiently processed so that the subject shows in gelatin relief.

Opacity The light-stopping power of a negative.

Opal A photograph transferred to opal glass by the carbon process or transferred to an opal previously sensitized.

Opaline A print mounted under glass and then over plush or some similar material which may possibly provide a fancy style of border.

Opalotype A positive made on an opaque white glass, producing what was called an "opal picture" (one on clear glass produces a transparency).

Operating room The "glass room" in the photographic studio where the photographer arranged his light, posed the subject, and operated the camera. This appears to have been the usual nineteenth-century use of the term, although it has at times been applied as well to the darkroom. In *The Ferrotype and How to Make It* (1872) Edward M. Estabrooke makes it clear that "operating room" and "glass room" are the same and has a separate chapter on the darkroom. However, according to Waldack and Neff, in their *Treatise of Photography on Collodion* (1857), the darkroom ". . . is designed to make the operator practically acquainted with the nature and relations of the salts, acids, solvents, and solutions which he employs; so that his operating room shall become a little laboratory, wherein he shall understandingly prepare his chemicals, and when not in working order, correct them . . ."

Ordway-Rand The collection of that name, the most extensive and best-preserved collection of Matthew B. Brady negatives, acquired in the early 1880s by Col. Arnold A. Rand and Gen. Albert Ordway. The collection was offered to Congress without action being taken. It was eventually rediscovered by E. H. Eaton, who with F. T. Miller as editor published the collection in the monumental ten-volume

Photographic History of the Civil War (1911), combining the Brady photographs with those of Alexander Gardner.

Orthochromatic plate   A photographic plate sensitive to all colors but red. The development of this kind of dry plate, chiefly through the work of Dr. Herman W. Vogel at the end of the nineteenth century, prepared the way for the panchromatic emulsion in 1904.

Overmat   A cardboard mount with a window through which a photograph may be viewed.

Oxalotype   A process devised by Sir John Herschel producing, by the use of oxalate of iron and ammonia, a blue picture lacking in clean whites.

Oxymal process   Introduced in 1856 by John Dillwyn Llewelyn, an extension of the wet-collodion process by which plates might be preserved for a longer time than hitherto possible. The collodion plate was treated with a syrup made of a mixture of honey and vinegar to improve its keeping quality.

Ozalid   A white-print process used in the same fashion as the blueprint.

Ozobrome   A system for producing carbon pictures from bromide prints, patented in 1905 by Thomas Manly.

Ozotype   A printing process patented by Thomas Manly in 1899, affording opportunities for great control, and in use until around 1914.

P   Abbreviation for plate, followed by a number, sometimes appearing in a description of a daguerreotype or other type of photograph to indicate the size, as in P 1/6 to indicate the one-sixth plate size. Plate sizes are derived from the size of the photographic plate employed by Daguerre, known as the whole plate, 6½ by 8½ inches. The early plates were cut by hand and therefore may vary slightly from the standard. (See **Plate** for a listing of plate sizes.)

Painterly photograph   A photograph made in direct imitation of some work of art or style of painting, slavishly following the rules conventionally guiding artistic disciplines other than photography. Victorian photographers, for example, were particularly fond of posing models to resemble classical paintings or statuary, finally achieving pictures of such an excess of triteness and sentimentality as to trigger a movement back to naturalism.

Palladium print   A print on paper which has been rendered sensitive with salts of palladium, a substitute introduced during World War I when platinum paper had become scarce, similar in overall effect to the platinotype: the image is a delicate gray. The use of the substitute was finally itself abandoned around 1930.

Palladium toning   An expensive method of toning a photograph, providing various shades of brown.

Panchromatic   Descriptive of a photographic plate sensitive to all the visible rays including red, which had previously been always rendered black. Panchromatic plates did not become commercially available on a large scale until the 1930s, when they were marketed by the Eastman Kodak Company.

Panel   A size of mounted paper photograph, 8½ by 4 inches. The date for the introduction of this particular size seems to be unknown.

Panotype   A collodion photograph made on oil cloth or on black paper, apparently in the 1850s and possibly only in France.

Pantoscope   A wide form of photographic lens; *or*, a scroll or diorama which might be unrolled so that a series of pictures were made to pass before an audience to provide the impression of a changing panoramic view. Popular in the 1850s, the views might be based on photographs: the Pantoscope of California was an illustrated lecture delivered by J. Wesley Jones to accompany his showing of paintings and sketches derived from his collection of about 1,500 daguerreotypes of the western frontier made around 1851. (The paintings were raffled off in 1854; the disposition of the original daguerreotypes is unknown.)

Paper negative   The first paper negative was made by the Englishman W. H. Fox Talbot in 1835. The calotype negative produced by Talbot made a print of an especially soft quality, evocative of mood and thus very much in contrast to the brilliance of the daguerreotype. The calotype was rarely attempted in the United States, where the daguerreotype reigned until the mid-1850s when it was replaced by the negative on glass made by the wet-collodion method. Long after this, in 1885, the Eastman-Walker Rollerslide reintroduced the concept of a paper negative: both sides of the paper were coated with the emulsion to produce a single print from a double negative, thus cancelling out any grainy defects residing in the paper. By 1888, however, other new techniques had again rendered the paper negative obsolete.

Paper photography   A photographic print on paper, rather than on metal or glass. Any American photograph made on paper before 1854 is considered a choice collector's item, since the daguerreotype dominated the field of photography before that time. Although the Langenheim Brothers of Philadelphia made some effort to introduce the calotype around 1849, there was but little response, and by 1854 the wet-collodion method of photography on glass had become so popular that it had outmoded both the daguerreotype and the calotype.

Paper stereo   Sometimes called a "papier" stereograph, or stereogram, this is one in which the view is enhanced by hand-tinted backing paper. Such a stereo might also be perforated, often producing a dramatic effect. A paper stereo, for example, might be both colored and perforated in an effort to depict all the horrors of Hell —the Devil's eyes bright, the flames rising.

Parlor album   A type of family photograph album made with a fancy binding and designed for display in one's home. Such an album might be bound in red velvet or in leather, with gilt lettering, gilt edges, and elaborate clasps. A few contained music boxes that played when the lid was raised.

Parlor photograph   In the late nineteenth century, "parlor photograph" appears to have meant one to be viewed through a stereoscope, that standard item of front-parlor equipment, rather than a picture to be hung on the wall.

Passepartout   A cut-out matting, as may be found under the glass framing a daguerreotype in a miniature case: thus, a type of ornamental frame for a photograph. Or, in printing, any type of ornamental frame appearing on a page; it might be used, for example, to surround a photograph or the text on a page, possibly the title page. The passepartout album contains slots into which photographs may be inserted.

Pearson The Pearson Publishing Company, responsible for *Pearson's Magazine*, which carried off a number of journalistic coups including photographing the New York Stock Exchange in 1907 with a camera hidden up a sleeve.

Pellet process A blueprint process: the true cyanotype, rendering blue lines on a white background when a copy is made of a line drawing. The process produces a positive from a positive.

Pellicle The thin photographic emulsion used to coat a plate or roll film.

Pellielle The term used by Hannibal Goodwin of Newark when applying in 1887 for a patent for his transparent flexible film, which he proposed for use in the roller-camera. Goodwin's idea of flowing a solution of nitrocellulose over a smooth surface such as glass eventually proved essential to the development of the film industry.

Pencil of nature A fanciful term for photography: *The Pencil of Nature* is the title of a book published in six parts by Fox Talbot, 1844-46. It contains the history of his invention of the calotype, along with 24 actual photographs showing architecture, still-life arrangements, and works of art. It is generally thought to be the first book published with photographic illustration.

Permanent photograph A print made by the carbon-print process invented by Alphonse Poitevin in 1859; *or*, the trade name for the reproduction of a photograph by the Woodburytype process. The Woodburytype is especially durable and possesses a brilliance which it retains to an unusual degree.

Phantoscope A late nineteenth-century invention and possibly the first successful apparatus for projecting motion pictures.

Phenkistascope A kind of parlor toy invented in the 1830s, independently by both Plateau and Stampfer. By rotating a number of images placed on a disk, the sensation of viewing motion is produced.

Philadelphia School A well-defined school of photography between 1854 and 1859, centered in Philadelphia, heavily influenced by the "painterly" concept of photography. Photographers associated with this school include Carey Lea, Coleman Sellers, E. L. Wilson and, later, W. T. Purviance and John Moran.

Photochrome The Photochrome Engraving Company of New York, Alfred Stieglitz's firm for the reproduction of many of the finest examples of American and European photography early in the twentieth century.

Photochromscope A type of camera invented in 1891 by the Philadelphian Frederic Eugene Ives, to take three positive transparencies which are then superimposed to create a single three-color image.

Photo-Club de Paris In the 1890s, along with the Linked Ring and Photo Secession, a leader in the movement to view photography as a new art form. The Club's first exhibition was held in January, 1894. The impressive catalogues for its series of exhibitions were folio in size, and each contained numerous photogravures.

Photocomposition A modern process for setting type by photographic means, a term, therefore, not relevant to old photographs.

Photo-crayon A photographic enlargement in which the finishing touches have been supplied by crayon. Crayon embellishments were popular for portrait enlargements especially in the 1870s among those who could afford the additional art work.

Photo-engraving A method for reproducing a photograph. Early attempts were made to produce an etched daguerreotype plate from which paper proofs could be pulled, but without much success. The first photo-mechanical illustrations from the daguerreotype appeared in a German publication in 1840. By 1842 Hippolyte Fizeau had succeeded in having two of his photoetchings appear in the two-volume *Excursions Daguerriennes*. . . . In England, Fox Talbot, disturbed by the way his calotypes faded, experimented to find a method for achieving a permanent picture by using printer's ink. In 1852 he patented a method for etching a plate which he called Photoglypty. In 1858 he patented an improved process, based on aquatint engraving and thus producing half-tones. Other experimenters were Paul Pretsch (photogalvanography, 1854), C. D. Dallas (Dallastype, 1863), and Niepce de St. Victor (heliogravure, 1855). Finally a superior process was conceived by Karl Klic of Vienna in 1879, and this process was licensed for use abroad. In 1890 Klic was working on a rotogravure process for the rotary cylinder presses which were already in use, though credit for its invention is sometimes given to Adolf Brandweiner, also of Vienna.

Photo-finishing The commercial business of processing film for the photographer who does not develop or print his own pictures. This type of enterprise did not come into existence until after the introduction of the Kodak camera by Eastman in 1888.

Photogalvanography An early photo-mechanical process invented by Paul Pretsch in 1854.

Photogen A pyrotechnic light for use in photography patented in 1857 by John Moule. By this means a portrait might be taken in as little as 15 seconds; the sitter, however, had to be screened from the dazzling source of light by a sheet of blue glass.

Photogenic An adjective applied to a good subject for photography, representing the "sum of a series of aesthetic problems." It has been said that to be considered photogenic an individual should be either entirely nondescript, to fit any role required of him, *or* have an enormously vibrant and compelling personality.

Photogenic drawing An early term for photography. Fox Talbot, in 1835, used "photogenic drawing" to describe his experiments with the calotype. After 1841 the term was apparently used only in the general sense, since usually either daguerreotype or calotype was specified.

Photoglypty The Woodbury process. (See **Woodburytype.**)

Photoglyphic engraving A process invented by Fox Talbot and patented by him in 1852, embodying one step in his development of a superior method of half-tone engraving. Adapting the procedures used in the aquatint, he brought out the middle tones by breaking up large areas into a cloud of small dots, using either grains or resin for this.

Photogram A photograph made simply by placing an object or objects on a light-sensitive paper. The earliest experiments of this sort were conducted by Fox

Talbot in the 1830s. According to Laszlo Moholy-Nagy, an exponent of the photogram, this is a "pure" form of photography, capturing the patterned interplay of light on a sheet of sensitized paper without the intervention of apparatus. Photograms may be produced by a moving beam of light or by using a glass which has been painted with a design, or by creating one image over another, for complicated and interesting images comparable to abstract paintings.

Photogrammetry The science of surveying and map-making by means of photography, sometimes aerial photography.

Photograph A suspension of grains of silver or of dyestuff in a gelatin base, capturing a view in a moment of time. (See also **Photography.**)

Photographic enamel A kind of photograph produced by burning the image into porcelain, making it, once annealed, as permanent as a ceramic painting. The process was invented in 1854 by M. Lafon de Camarsac and might be used in a decorative pin or brooch.

Photographic film The modern photographic film, unknown before it was first marketed in 1885 by George Eastman, consisting of a base—a transparent flexible sheet—and an emulsion which consists of a light-sensitive coating.

Photographic hall At the Centennial Exhibition held in Philadelphia in 1876, the site of a wide range of exhibits of photographs collected from various countries and including all known kinds of photographs from daguerreotypes to transparencies. The exhibit was particularly interesting since it both marked the height of attainment for wet-plate photography and in retrospect, the end of its importance since it would soon be outmoded by the dry plate.

Photographic jewelry Jewelry of the type which became popular in the 1860s, incorporating tiny photographs made especially for this purpose. The tintype was favored because of its durability, but any kind of photograph, even one on paper, might be used. The jewelry might be a brooch, pin, locket, stickpin, or similar item.

Photographic outfit The collection of materials and supplies, including the camera as just one item, necessary for the practice of photography. The term is, however, usually applied to the great amount of equipment which the photographer using the wet plate had to haul about with him. Because wet-plate photography required the preparation of the glass plate, its exposure, and development all within a half hour at most (before the plate had a chance to dry), the materials for the entire photographic process, from setting up the tripod to drying the print, had to be carried into the field if the photographer wished to take pictures outside the studio. In *Photography and the American Scene* Robert Taft has furnished a "typical list of equipment carried by an expeditionary photographer of the early seventies." It includes a stereoscopic camera, with one or more pair of lenses, two box cameras with their lenses, two tripods, a "dark tent," and, along with the chemicals including ten pounds of collodion, 36 ounces of silver nitrate, two quarts of alcohol, ten pounds of developer, and 1½ pounds of fixer, nitric acid, and varnish, also scales, weights and trays, and 400 pieces of glass for the negatives. All this was, of course, for a trip of some duration, but the basics were still necessary for a trip which lasted but a day. Some professional photographers, making an extended trip into unknown or unfamiliar territory might hire several porters or even engage a string of wagons, horses, and drivers.

Photographic panorama An extensive over-view of a scene produced by the amalgamation of a number of photographs. One of the earliest was produced by Francis Frith from seven different negatives. Over eight feet long, it was exhibited in 1858. Possibly one of the largest panoramic views produced at the turn of the century was a 35-foot view of the Krupp works, shown in London in 1903.

Photographic parlor Beginning with the daguerrean gallery and continuing throughout the nineteenth century, the photographer's waiting room was designated his parlor. In the larger establishments the waiting room might be elaborately decorated, even by the standards of the day. While awaiting their turn to be photographed, clients might have the pleasure of inspecting examples of the photographer's work in a surrounding of luxury: rugs upon the floor, in the corners potted palms and statuary, perhaps a piano, and overhead singing birds in cages and stuffed animals suspended from the ceiling. Many photographs of these waiting rooms have survived, since they were often used for advertising.

Photographic ring One kind of photographic jewelry. Queen Victoria encouraged the fad for wearing jewelry which incorporated a photograph by herself wearing a signet ring which contained a group of five portraits of members of her family. Each of the photographs was only about one-eighth of an inch, and to be seen properly the ring had to be examined under a magnifying glass.

Photographic Salon The name "Photographic Salon" was chosen by the Linked Ring Society of London for its first exhibition, held in 1893, borrowing the term "salon" to indicate that photography, just as much as painting, was an art in its own right and entitled to as impressive a showing.

Photographic Society A group having the purpose of advancing photography in some way, often from a special point of view. Amateurs did not band together in societies in any great numbers until the 1850s when amateur photography became more popular and the need arose for an exchange of information on the techniques for the new, much more complicated, wet-plate photography. It has been estimated that by 1885 there were possibly about 20 photographic clubs and societies in the United States and by the end of the following decade almost five times as many, evidence then of considerable interest but miniscule compared with the thousands of clubs today.

Photographic Society of London England's oldest and best-known photographic society, founded by Roger Fenton in 1853. Its exhibitions, held annually, greatly encouraged the advance of photography both as a science and art. In the 1880s, however, it was reduced to little more than a debating society, but then revived with a change of name—first the Photographic Society of Great Britain and, after 1894, the Royal Photographic Society—to become today the world's oldest continuously active photographic society.

Photographic Society of Scotland An association established in 1856 with Sir David Brewster as president. It was disbanded in 1867. (See also **Edinburgh Photographic Society.**)

Photographic stamp A miniature photograph, almost invariably a portrait, to be affixed to some personal document. Commemorative stamps of this sort are often produced in limited quantity.

Photography Writing with light, a descriptive term which originated with Sir John Herschel. Niepce had used the word "heliography," and Fox Talbot employed the term "photogenic drawing." Helmut Gernsheim informs us that "photography" is a term which was introduced in 1839 specifically to mean the making of a permanent picture with light. Photography may be defined as the science/art of forming and fixing an image on a surface which has been made sensitive to light. According to J. Towler, "the art of photography comprehends all the operations of taking a picture on a sensitive surface by means of light and chemical reagents."

Photogravure Not itself a photograph, but a reproduction of one, in ink on paper. It is produced by an intaglio process invented by Karl Klic of Vienna around 1880. Following a fairly complicated procedure, an ink residue is left in the recessed portion of a printing plate from which an image is transferred to paper. Photogravure was introduced into England in 1883, but its use was at first limited to large editions because of the expense involved in preparing each plate. Fifteen years later, when the process had been improved to utilize cylinders rather than plates (rotogravure), it came into wide use. Photogravures painstakingly produced by hand may faithfully represent the original. The use of a translucent ink may permit a soft color, and the plate may even be altered by hand, permitting especially subtle effects. The appearance of limited-edition photogravures in the Photo-Secessionist journal *Camera Work* helped to establish the artistic capabilities of this medium. Among the photographers especially admired for their gravures are Edward Steichen, Alfred Stieglitz, J. Craig Annan, Alvin Langon Coburn, Baron Adolph de Meyer, and Gertrude Kasebier.

Photo-journalism A fusion of the visual and the written: reporting a news story partly or even solely by means of photographs. This was a practical possibility only after 1890 and the introduction of the photogravure and halftone. The photo-journalist must possess diverse skills. "Carrying out a magazine assignment is only half of photography. The other half is getting information"—Margaret Bourke-White. Photo-journalism had its beginnings before the days when photographs could be reproduced in the media. Roger Fenton photographed the Crimean War in 1855, but his pictures had to be converted into wood engravings to appear in the *Illustrated London News*. With the slow wet-collodion process he used, it was not possible for Fenton to catch scenes of action, but his pictures of the scenes of battle still brought the war home to the *News*'s readers with a greater urgency than had been possible before. During the American Civil War, Mathew Brady's staff of photographers faced the same problem with the wet plate and, grim-visaged as their photographs are, these pictures are not stop-action. Photo-journalism as we know it today was created by the invention of faster cameras and the introduction of halftone processing. Photo-journalism came into its own after the *New York Daily Graphic* published the first halftone on March 4, 1880.

Photo-jumelle A kind of detective camera, one of the first which was designed to be held at eye-level. The invention of Jules Carpentier in 1892, this camera had two identical lenses, one forming the image on the dry plate and the other on ground glass for viewing. This popular camera, with its fixed focus, was sold with a fixed-focus enlarger.

Photo League of New York Under the influence of work done by photographers associated with the Farm Security Administration in the depression years of the 1930s, the Photo League was formed under the leadership of Aaron Siskind and subsequently produced a number of group documentations, including one titled *Harlem Document*.

Photolithography The transfer of a photograph by means of the lithographer's stone for the purpose of obtaining several impressions (duplicates). The first American patent for a photolithographic process was taken out in 1858 by James A. Cutting and L. H. Bradford. However, few examples of these early halftone reproductions have survived.

Photomechanical process Any process in which, through the action of light upon chemical substances, a printing surface is prepared from which a number of impressions can be made on a printing press—whether the ink is below, on, or above the surface of the plate which is used.

Photomezzotint The reproduction of a photograph produced mechanically by a kind of carbon printing patented by Sir Joseph W. Swan in 1865. The result is similar to the Woodburytype (q.v.).

Photomicrograph A photograph taken through a microscope and therefore not just any small photograph. There has been interest in such photographs from the earliest days, with both Daguerre and Talbot experimenting.

Photo montage A combination print which may be produced by any number of methods, including multiple exposures and pasteups with re-photographing.

Photo-panorama A series of photographs taken from a successive series of positions and thus showing a changing view of scenery, as in the *Panorama of the Hudson*, published in 1906, containing photographs taken from the deck of a Hudson Dayliner as it progressed down the river. This may, incidentally, be the first publication to contain any panoramic views of a river.

Photo relief The Woodburytype (q.v.): a process for photomechanical printing in popular use between 1875 and around 1900.

Photosculpture A process devised in 1861 by M. Willeme of Paris to make dimunitive facsimiles of statues or even of living persons by taking a series of photographs from various angles and shaping plaster or clay after the silhouettes thus produced. His process might possibly have required as many as two dozen photographs of the subject.

Photo Secession An informal association of photographers organized in New York City in 1902 under the leadership of Alfred Stieglitz for the general purpose of promoting a more creative photography. In many ways it was the American counterpart of the Linked Ring Brotherhood which had been formed about a decade earlier in London and had exerted an international influence. Photo Secession became the dominant movement in American photography, holding its own shows and publishing its own journal, *Camera Work* (q.v.), with Stieglitz as editor. In 1905 the movement sponsored the opening of the Little Galleries at 291 Fifth Avenue in New York. Branching out from photography, the journal became a leading advocate of a whole new movement in the arts, art and literature as well as photography, and the Galleries showed not only the work of the greatest photographers of the day but also the work of such leading experimental artists as Rodin, Matisse, Picasso, Rousseau, Renoir, and O'Keefe. Three of the leading photographers among the many associated with Photo Secession were Stieglitz, Edward Steichen, and Alvin Langdon Coburn. The importance of Photo Secession in the history of photography rests both on its having encouraged new heights of artistic endeavor in photography and in having insisted on critical attention to photography as one of the arts. In its journal and in the exhibits it sponsored, the movement proved fairly tolerant of a wide variety of styles of photography, though perhaps it is today most closely identified with the altered print and a vision clouded with sentimentalism as appeared in the work of Clarence White and Gertrude Kasebier, far removed from the radical experimentalism of the avant-garde painters of the same period. By 1910, Stieglitz, working more and more in "pure" photography, had abandoned the Photo-Secessionist movement.

Photo-story A series of photographs with captions, the text intimately tied to the pictures to relate a story. The earliest photo-story was perhaps the photographic interview conducted by Nadar, the father and son who shared the same professional name. The Nadars interviewed the scientist Michel-Eugene Chevreul and published their photographs-cum-text in *Le Journal Illustre* on September 5, 1886. In the United States, the *Illustrated American*, which began publication in February 1890, was one of the first to exploit the possibilities of the photo-story, but soon shifted its emphasis away. *Life* magazine (q.v.) would eventually prove to be the most notable exponent and effective vehicle for the photo-story.

Phototelegraphy A technique for producing at a distant point a photograph readied for printing by a process first put to practical use in 1907 by two publications, *L'Illustration* and *The London Daily Mirror*. The subsequent invention of the vacuum tube made great improvements possible, and in 1925 American Telephone and Telegraph instituted a transcontinental service for transmitting pictures.

Phototint A kind of photographic illustration produced by a process developed by B. J. Edwards, simpler than the heliotype but considered finer in its results.

Phototype A method for photographic reproduction in collotype developed by the French engraver Joubert around 1860 but never advanced commercially.

Photo-xylography The process of rendering a photographic image on a boxwood block as a guide for the wood-engraver.

Photozincography A photomechanical printing process for reproducing an image, developed in England between 1859 and 1862 and used satisfactorily around that time, with great savings, for the making of facsimiles or reductions, particularly of maps. For example, the English Ordnance Survey published both photographs and the photozincograph facsimiles of maps, manuscripts, etc., and in 1862 published a book, *Photozincography and Other Photographic Processes. . . .*

Physionotrace A device invented in 1786 by Gilles-Louis Chretien, for producing a miniature engraved copper plate by simple mechanical means. It is not, properly speaking, an ancestor of the camera, though sometimes referred to as such.

Pictorial photography Also known as pictorialism, photography more concerned with the artistic possibilities of the medium than the mechanics of technique, sometimes in direct imitation of the composition, lighting, and poses of classical painting. Such photography often depicted an admired subject in a lovely setting, for the avowed purpose of moral instruction. According to critics of pictorialism, it frequently means pictures which are simply pretty, and no more than mildly pleasant at their best—or revealing a superficial point of view. Henry Peach Robinson, late nineteenth-century English leader of a school of "salon" photographers, represented the height of pictorialism, with his contrived and elaborate allegorical prints constructed from a number of negatives.

Picture interview The first published combination of an interview and a series of photographs was that conducted by Nadar in Paris in 1886. (See *Photo-story.*)

Pigeon post   During the Siege of Paris, 1870–71, carrier pigeons were used to convey messages between the Delegate Government and Paris; this was one of the first uses of photography for carrying message by air. At first the message was copied out in large characters and then reduced to a plate under three inches in size, from which contact prints were made. Subsequently the photographer Nadar tried to convince the Government to try using microphotography but the reduction method prevailed, except that the messages were then printed on a collodion membrane rather than on paper. The entire experiment failed because too few of the pigeons made it through the lines to complete their mission.

Pigment print   Specifically, a print made on a versatile type of paper which has been made light-sensitive with a coating of a mixture of colloid, a pigment, and potassium bichromate, in popular use between 1895 and 1915. Its great advantage was that it permitted great control during the printing process. For example, a part of the image might be washed away and then the print re-sensitized and exposed under the negative again.

Pigment process   Any one of several printing processes in which the image is formed from a pigment imbedded in the sensitive photographic support, such as the carbon, gum-bichromate, or ozotype processes.

Pinchbeck   The flexible, light, gilt-metal frame used in the assembly of a miniature case for a daguerreotype or other type of small photograph. The substance pinchbeck, the invention of a watchmaker named Christopher Pinchbeck around 1730, is an alloy of copper and zinc in appearance resembling gold and thus a kind of "false gold." In the miniature case, this pinchbeck both helps protect the photograph from damage and from dust and serves a decorative purpose.

Pinhole image   The image which results from light passing through a tiny hole to form a picture on an opposite surface. The earliest reference to this phenomenon may be that in the writings of the Arabian scholar Alhazen, who lived between 965 and 1038 A.D.

Pioneer Amateur Photographic Club   An organization formed in New York in 1883 to serve the needs of amateurs, particularly those working with the newly available dry plate.

Pistol camera   A single-lens miniature camera with a very fast lens and convenient to use, invented in 1856 by Thomas Skaife. *Or*, a hand-held camera with a grip like that of a pistol. Some cameras of this kind were manufactured around 1890 and advertised as "detective" cameras, but it is extremely difficult to imagine their having been used in an unobtrusive fashion.

Place, The   See **American Place, The.**

Plain salted paper   The type of uncoated printing paper which was prepared by the photographer himself for printing. Beginning with Fox Talbot, the calotypist had to adapt ordinary writing paper to his needs by selecting a fine grade and sensitizing it by immersing it in soluble chloride and then floating it in a bath of silver nitrate. This paper was printed by daylight, then toned and fixed. Usually any watermark was cut out of the paper to be used, but not always. Photographs made on plain salted paper have a characteristically soft brown appearance. They are also highly subject to fading. Plain salted paper was made obsolete by the invention of albumen paper, which could be manufactured in quantity.

Plastic photograph The single image composed by re-photographing two identical images slightly out of register for the effect of bas-relief.

Plate A smooth surface of either glass or metal on which the photographic image is recorded. The invention of photographic film and the beginning of its commercial production in 1885 outmoded the dry collodion plate which had in its turn only recently outmoded the wet plate, both of glass. *Or*, "plate" may mean a printed photograph, as in "this book contains 20 plates by Steichen."

Daguerreotype plate sizes are only approximate, since the copper plates were originally cut by hand. "Standard"—actually only approximate—plate sizes are derived from the size of the daguerreotype plate used by Daguerre himself, 8½ by 6½ inches. The various plate sizes are generally given as follows:

Double Whole Plate (8/4 p)	8½ by 13 inches
Whole Plate (4/4 p)	6½ by 8½
Half Plate (½ p)	4½ by 5½
Quarter Plate (¼ p)	3¼ by 4¼
Sixth (Medium) Plate (⅙ p)	2¾ by 3¼
Ninth Plate (1/9 p)	2 by 2½
Sixteenth Plate (1/16 p)	1⅜ by 1⅝

In addition, the "full" plate is about 8 by 10 inches, larger than "whole." The Imperial is any daguerreotype plate larger than "whole."

The quarter-plate and sixth-plate were most popular for the daguerreotype portrait, and the ambrotypes, which were made later, followed the same sizes, since they could then be conveniently fitted into the same kind of cases. So standard had these sizes become that it was the quarter-plate size which was made available to amateur photographers when flexible film was first marketed.

Tintypes were produced in various sizes, including those used for photographs designed for miniature cases, but the tintypes are particularly interesting for their smaller sizes, including those called "gems," sometimes so tiny they might be mounted into jewelry.

Platinotype A highly permanent kind of photographic print made on an uncoated paper rendered light-sensitive with salts of platinum. The platinotype is especially prized for its long tonal scale and its rare delicacy. The platinotype process was invented by an Englishman, William Willis, and patented in 1873. Commercial papers were made available after 1879. Favored for fine prints by many turn-of-the-century "art" photographers, the platinotype continued in popular use until World War I, when platinum became hard to obtain. The manufacture of this type of paper finally ended around 1930. It was apparently the only kind of paper in its day positively guaranteed against fading. One of the leading exponents of platinum printing was Frederick H. Evans. The platinum-and-ferroprussiate print is one which has gone through the developing process for a second time, after being re-sensitized with iron salt solution; the result has a characteristically blue or blue-green tone.

Platinum print Platinum print is the more modern term and has been recently applied to a revival of platinum printing as exemplified by the work of George Tice. (See the previous entry.)

Platinum toning The treating of a print with platinum rather than gold toning. Platinum is said to be capable of as many subtle variations.

Photographing flowers was one of the specialties of Edwin Hale Lincoln of Pittsfield, Massachusetts. This platinum print of the flowers of the Tulip Tree is typical of those he produced for his four-volume folio book titled Wild Flowers of New England, *published in 1904. Using large old-fashioned glass plates, Mr. Lincoln brought his plants indoors to photograph them by natural light with a favorite camera which had no shutter. For interiors, he is said to have opened the lens and then waved a 100-watt bulb with reflector about to "paint" the room evenly with light. All his prints were made on platinum paper until, at the age of 89, he found to his disappointment he could no longer obtain it. (Courtesy of the International Museum of Photography/George Eastman House.)*

Plumbeotype A hand-pulled copy of a daguerreotype rendered on a lithographic stone, produced by a method devised by John Plumbe, after whom the method was named. Plumbe, the mid-nineteenth century proprietor of a chain of daguerrean parlors, in 1847 published *The National Plumbeotype Gallery,* a collection of 27 portraits prepared by his process.

Plumber A wad of cotton which a sitter held inside his cheek to make his face appear wider and therefore, by the standards of the day, more attractive for a daguerreotype portrait.

Pocket camera A camera which is small enough to be carried about conveniently in a man's pocket. The first such camera may have been that offered by the Marion firm in 1884. The original Kodak, since its largest dimension was 6½ inches, was not a pocket camera; the 1895 Kodak, however, only 2¼ by 2⅞ by 3⅞ inches, might qualify.

Point Lobos A site on the coast of California famous for a now-legendary series of photographs taken by Edward Weston over a period of about 20 years beginning in 1929.

Polaroid A camera which produces a positive picture within the camera itself within seconds; the invention of Edwin H. Land in 1947.

Polyartist An early term applied to the photographer (calotypist) who made his prints on paper.

Polyoroma A development from Daguerre's diorama (q.v.) making it possible to show slides by daylight as well as by artificial light.

Polypose A portrait in which the sitter appears in more than one position.

P.O.P. Printing-out paper.

Porcelain picture A photograph made on porcelain by the collodion wet-plate method. That such photographs were not unusual is seen from the fact that prizes were sometimes offered at fairs for the best in this type of work. Such photographs may date back to around 1860.

Porcelain process A method for adding color to a photograph on glass.

Posing chair A chair of the type used in the glass room (q.v.) of a studio. According to Edward Estabrooke, in *The Ferrotype* . . . , first published in 1872, "Posing chairs are now in general use and are in great variety. In selecting, choose one of the most graceful design and best finish. A great revolution in the style and finish of these useful chairs was made, I think, in 1866, by the introduction at that date of 'Sarony's Universal Rest and Posing Chair.' Mr. Sarony sold immense numbers of them, until they indeed became universal in use. The most popular posing chairs are now made in imitation of the shape of the Sarony chair, with which most photographers are already familiar." It was usual for the posing chair to be elaborately carved and massive in appearance.

Positive A registering of light and dark in which the values are not reversed as they are in the negative. Thus, the tonal values appear as they are in nature. The first positive was produced by Niepce in the 1820s. Although in the positive light and shade appear "natural" to the observer, it should be noted that in some positives, most notably the daguerreotype and ferrotype, the delineations are reversed right and left. The ambrotype, which is a negative viewed as a positive, does not exhibit the same reversal.

Positive printing paper The first paper used for printing was common writing paper prepared for photography by being sensitized, and was known as plain salted paper. Albumenized paper represented the first major improvement, since it was capable of being mass produced, and displayed greater detail.

Postcard The photographic postcard became popular in Germany around 1884 and migrated to England where, after 1901, the Rotary Photographic Company helped build interest into a collecting fad. Such postcards remained enormously popular in both England and the United States until around 1914 and even later. During this period some persons had postcards made up to their special individual taste; such photographic cards may be particularly valuable today.

Postcard aesthetic Following the pioneering work in outdoor photography in the West, including the work of T. H. O'Sullivan, C. E. Watkins, A. J. Russell, W. H. Jackson, and E. Muyrbridge, among others, a spate of professionally competent but on the whole unimaginative photographers sold their pictures for use on postcards. According to Weston J. Naef, writing in *Era of Exploration*, it would appear that these photographers expected that the grandeur of nature might make up for any technical deficiencies. Hence, "postcard aesthetic" is a derogatory term.

Postmortem photography A popular form of photography almost from the beginning, when registering the appearance of the dead seemed an appropriate form of mourning. One of the most admired and widely circulated of these photographs was one of Edward VII in profile. Many postmortem portraits were, however, of infants and children whose short lives had not included having their pictures taken before their decease.

Praxinoscope An optical toy, introduced in 1877 by Emile Reynaud, creating an illusion of movement through the use of 12 mirrors arranged inside a drum which is rotated. This toy is considered an antecedent of the motion picture. Developed from the zootrope, the praxinoscope produced a brighter picture and a smoother sense of action.

Preserver A gilded, flexible metal frame used in the assembly of a miniature case (q.v.) after 1850. This preserver, or protector, is made of paper-thin malleable brass in the form of a rectangular frame with embossed border and wraps around the entire assembly. It may serve the dual purpose of enhancing the picture and helping to lock the glass, the mat, and the photograph together into the case. The preserver may be called "pinchbeck," from the type of metal used, a kind of false gold.

Print To print: produce a positive picture by the transmission of light through a negative placed directly upon a sensitized surface; *or*, the result of producing a photographic image in the final, usually positive, state.

Printing-out paper Paper capable of producing a photographic image; historically, the term may refer to the paper which the photographer himself prepared for his own use.

Printing service The commercial enterprise of developing and printing photographs. According to Helmut Gernsheim's *The History of Photography*, the first printing service ("in permanent ink for photographers") was that offered by the firm of Alfred Pumphrey of Birmingham, England, around 1877.

Process In photography, to process is to follow the sequence of steps by which light-sensitive materials are made to produce the photographic image.

Process work The business of touching up a halftone plate made from a photograph for the purpose of its reproduction.

Promenade A photograph which is a variation of the cabinet card: a smaller photograph is mounted on a card only slightly smaller than the standard. The promenade card was introduced around 1874 but it does not appear to have become especially popular. One of the great appeals of the cabinet cards was that they were uniform in size and therefore easily exchanged and fitted into a standard type of album.

Psychic photography "Spirit" photography, a general term covering various aspects of the registration of the images of psychic phenomena, including portraits of ghosts, pictures of "thoughts" or other apparitions, portraits of visions said to have been seen only by psychic persons, and images said to have been achieved without the agency of a camera. The term also applies to trick photography.

Publics This is the term which the cabinet photographer J. M. Mora applied to his collection of portraits of celebrities, many of whom were in some manner associated with the theater. Mora was so successful with his "publics" that he is said to have sold 35,000 copies of one alone, a portrait of the actress Maud Branscombe.

Pure photography Photography for its own sake. As explained by Peter Henry Emerson in his *Naturalistic Photography* (1889), "pure" photography should function as an art independent of painting and be based on the greatest possible "simplicity of means." He advocated a truthfulness of vision, with no faking and no posing, with free and original composition following after nature, to obtain a photographic image which, of course, would not be altered with retouching. Pure photography is exemplified in the work of James Craig Annan and that of other members of the (British) Linked Ring Brotherhood, formed in 1892,

Quarter plate Abbreviated 1/4 p, a daguerreotype size 3¼ by 4¼ inches. The quarter plate, along with the sixth plate, was a popular size for both the daguerreotype and the ambrotype, for fitting into a miniature case. This is the size also familiar, much later, as one of the most popular sizes for film for amateur use.

Quick Also called "quickstuff," slang for accelerator, a chemical addition used in the daguerreotype process to reduce exposure time, introduced around 1840, thus within a year of the introduction of the daguerreotype. Bromine and chlorine were used, in addition to the original iodine, to fume a daguerreotype plate before it was exposed in the camera. The use of quick made portraiture possible, since the subject did not have to hold his pose so long. Wolcott's *American Mixture* was one of the most popular of the commercial brands.

Rapid rectilinear lens A type of lens introduced in 1866 by J. H. Dallmeyer and —separately—by Adolph Steinheil, having a maximum aperture of $f/8$. This type of lens was much later used on the early Kodak cameras and remained in popular use until well into the twentieth century.

Rayograph A photograph of the type made by Man Ray in 1922 by placing an object to be photographed—three-dimensional or opaque—directly on light-sensitive paper, and thus a twentieth-century development of one of the earliest techniques used by Fox Talbot in his experiments to produce the calotype.

Reflected light   Any light which bounces off a subject for photography. Reflection is a property of the subject and may be stated as a percentage: black velvet, for example, reflects only 2 percent of the light which falls on it. Incident light, on the other hand, is that falling upon a subject.

Reflex camera   A type of camera which incorporates a mirror affixed to the camera base to reflect the image onto a ground glass at the top of the camera, thus permitting the photographer to observe his subject up to the second of taking the picture. It was the introduction of this type of camera which removed from the photographer the necessity of having to drape a black focusing cloth over his head and the camera in order to take the picture. Thomas Sutton patented such a camera in 1861, yet none was manufactured for sale until 1884.

Reichenbach patent   A patent issued in 1889 for a method of creating a transparent flexible film of nitrocellulose, similar to the Goodwin patent (q.v.), and providing the formula for the first successful manufacture, by Eastman, of such film.

Relief printing   A photo-engraving process by which a halftone is achieved by breaking up a single photographic image into small dots; these dots may be produced by photographing through a screen.

Relievo ambrotype   An ambrotype mounted by a method devised in Glasgow in 1845 and introduced in England in 1857: the background of the photograph is scraped away and then the photograph is mounted slightly away from a white backing, to produce a slight shadow and thus put the picture into relief.

Reloading   The introduction of new film into the camera, or, before the days of film, a new plate. A breakthrough in the development of the camera occurred at the end of 1891 when the Eastman Company introduced a new kind of Kodak which for the first time made it possible to load film in daylight.

Rembrandt lighting   A style for lighting a photographic portrait after the manner of a classical painting, i.e., one by Rembrandt. The style was made popular by A. S. Adam-Salomon, a Frenchman trained as a sculptor, William Kuntz, and others. The sitter would be placed against a relatively plain background to emphasize the features of his face, and with the use of movable platforms and reflector screens, a new subtlety of light and shading might be achieved. With the profile characteristically back-lit, Rembrandt lighting became especially popular for cabinet photography. The technique was, however, often mishandled and the effect rendered over-dramatic. Examples of this lighting used to good effect are found in the work of W. J. Baker of Buffalo, New York, and of William Notman of Montreal.

Rest   See **Headrest.**

Reticulation   A defect in a print: the wrinkled aspect of the surface of a processed emulsion which may result from temperature changes or certain chemical actions.

Retouching   Changing a negative in such a way as to alter or modify a line, a texture, or value. Retouching has been the common practice of many portrait photographers seeking to "improve" the appearance of the person sitting and thus make the picture more acceptable. In a cabinet photograph, for example, retouching was routine. Yet there have always been purists who object to this practice. Retouching, it has been pointed out, can hardly be considered integral to the process of "drawing with light." During the 1850s some amateur societies refused to admit retouched photographs for exhibition or, if it was permitted at all, required that the original negative be exhibited alongside the altered print. Retouching has, however, been particularly useful to those photographers who believe that a photograph should if possible resemble a painting. In discussing the photography of Lewis Carroll, Helmut Gernsheim has pointed out that it did not seem to occur to him that retouching "is not fair to either art," photography or painting. "The mind of the artist is cramped by the photograph, and the truth of the photograph is violated by the paint."

Revenue stamp   See **Tax stamp.**

Reversal   The transposition from left to right and vice versa characteristic of a positive which is made directly, as may be observed in the daguerreotype or ferrotype. A right-left reversal is sometimes corrected by re-photographing the picture. This would probably be true for any daguerreotype showing an outdoor scene in which a sign reads properly rather than backwards. In portraits, however, apparently few persons objected to seeing their picture reversed, since this was the way they saw themselves customarily in the mirror. The term "reversal" in modern use also means the process of converting a negative image into a positive.

Rinhart   Floyd and Marion Rinhart, collectors of old photographs and the co-authors of numerous books and articles on a variety of aspects of nineteenth-century photography. Their work includes *American Daguerreian Art* (1967), and *American Miniature Case Art* (1969). There is also *America's Affluent Age* (1971), on American life from 1840 to 1860 and illustrated primarily from daguerreotypes of the period. In a reference book or catalogue, the name Rinhart followed by a number refers to the number assigned to a miniature case style in the Rinharts' definitive work on these cases.

Ripening   A process used in the preparation of the emulsion for a dry plate. The efficacy of the ripening process for increasing the sensitivity of the plate was discovered by the Englishman Charles Bennett in 1878 and by Sir Charles Swan. This discovery was shortly followed, in America, by the successful experiments conducted by George Eastman.

Rogues gallery   A slang expression for a collection of portraits, sometimes of mean characters. In England the expression originated in the instructions issued by Scotland Yard in 1862 that prison governors should have the prisoners photographed for purposes of identification. However, the *American Journal of Photography* has supplied evidence that as early as 1859 the New York Police Department was already keeping a file of photographs, according to William Welling.

Roller-slide   A device for inserting the light-sensitive material—on glass, paper, or, later, film—into the camera. The first such slides, which were produced around 1856, were made in a variety of sizes for attachment to different sizes of cameras. Originally it was simply a box, but in 1885 the Eastman Company introduced a major improvement, the roll-holder, also a box-like container but fitted with two spools and an external winding key.

Roll-film camera   The modern type of camera, which contains a device for winding film off one spool onto another.

Roll-holder   A camera device invented in 1884 by William H. Walker, a camera manufacturer who left his own business to work for George Eastman. The roll-holder is sometimes cited, after the invention of film, as the most important contribution to the development of modern photography. In his biography of George Eastman, Carl W. Ackerman has summed up its function: It was "a light-weight mahogany frame which could be fitted to the back of any standard camera on the market. A continuous roll of the new film could be fastened to spools, revolved by means of a clock key in the outside. This mechanism took the place of, or could be used interchangeably with, the glass-plate holder, and had many advantages, including the convenience of carrying sufficient film for several exposures, making the weight less and eliminating both the danger of glass-plate breakage and the necessity of carrying a burdensome pack of plates in the field. The paper film strip supplied with these roll-holders usually contained twenty-four exposures." Taft has attributed the great increase in the number of amateur photographers to the introduction of the roll-holder as well as film.

Rotogravure   The reproduction of a photograph achieved by an adaptation of the photogravure process (q.v.) to the rotary cylinder press. This adaptation made possible the rapid printing of large editions containing copies of photographs. Commercially introduced in 1895, the rotogravure process was quickly accepted for general newspaper use.

Royal Photographic Society   An organization founded in 1853, which changed its name in 1874 to the Photographic Society of London, and again in 1894 to the Royal Photographic Society of Great Britain. Its first president was Sir Charles Eastlake. Ability in at least one aspect of photography is a prerequisite for individual membership.

Royal Polytechnic Institution   The first photographic studio to be established in England, on Regency Street in London, in 1841. Daguerreotype portraits produced by this pioneer firm are usually enclosed in a case clearly marked with the firm's name. The proprietor, Richard Beard, is not, however, likely to have been the photographer.

S   An abbreviation for stereograph (q.v.) sometimes used in catalogues.

Sabattier effect   See **Edge reversal.**

Salon print   A photograph made in imitation of a painting, both in sentiment and composition, often by posing figures against a fanciful allegorical background. Such prints, popular at the end of the nineteenth century, were frequently framed, hung, and exhibited after the manner of salon paintings, hence the name. One of the leading exponents of salon printing was Henry Peach Robinson, who felt strongly that "no possible amount of scientific truth will in itself make a picture . . . the truth that is wanted is artistic truth."

Salted paper   Paper made sensitive for printing by being immersed in a soluble chloride and then floated in a bath of silver nitrate. Plain writing paper was used, and therefore it is sometimes described as "plain salted." The calotypist had to prepare his own paper for printing and used what he found available, sometimes though not always cutting out the watermarked portion. The salt-paper print has a characteristically soft finish, and the photograph is usually softly defined and somewhat lacking in detail.

Scale   A sequential arrangement from light to dark, or the relative size of either an object or an image; *or*, to scale, to make an image larger or smaller than it appears in the negative.

Scovill The Scovill Manufacturing Company of Waterbury, Connecticut, long-time nineteenth-century manufacturer of photographic equipment beginning with the daguerreotype plate and the miniature case, and thus to a great extent instrumental in the growth of interest in photography in the United States. By the 1880s the company had become one of the world's largest producers of cameras, photographic supplies, and equipment in a competitive market.

Screen In mid-nineteenth century photography, the type of screen—movable vertical surface—used to provide background for a portrait. As a mid-century manual explained, "Screens with graduated tints, shading off from one color to another . . . are to be highly recommended to an artistic operator. Other screens again represent landscapes, castles, shipping, city scenery, etc. . . ." The romantic backdrops of the sort provided by these screens were almost universally used for cabinet-card portraits. With screens, the merchant or his clerk, the matron or young girl might be pictured standing beside a waterfall, gazing at mountains, or standing proudly at seaside with a yacht at anchor in the distance.

Sensitometry The study of the properties of light-sensitive materials, given impetus in 1890 by publication of the work of F. Hurter and V. C. Driffield which introduced a new system for calculating the rapidity of different kinds of plates.

Sentimental The sentimental is a specific kind of stereograph produced in profusion in the 1890s by commercial photographers willing to capitalize on the public's appetite for the humorous, sometimes mawkish, and occasionally even naughty photograph. Recently sentimentals have acquired a new value, as it is realized that they may reveal little-known social customs as well as the popular tastes of the nineties.

Sepia toning Any one of a number of different processes with the purpose of converting a black silver print image to a brownish one.

Series print One produced from the same negative as a vintage (original) print but, because of a lapse of time and other factors, inevitably differing at least slightly.

Serum process A method devised around 1856 for preparing plain paper for printing, using serum of milk and resulting in a purplish picture.

Shadow picture A photograph made simply by laying an object, such as a leaf, directly on sensitized paper which is then exposed to light.

Sheet-metal photograph The tintype (ferrotype).

Shutter A shield between the light-sensitive material in a camera and the front of the lens, controlling the time light is admitted to the camera and allowing adjustment to the speed of movement of the subject being photographed. The earliest cameras had no shutters. Photographers managed the exposure time simply by removing the shutter cap and then replacing it, sometimes counting down the seconds, sometimes regulating exposure time with a watch or clock. With the invention, in the 1870s, of a high-speed dry plate which was capable of a shorter exposure time, cameras began to require shutters which could move more quickly than the human hand and be entirely accurate in timing. It was the introduction of the high-speed shutter which made it possible to take the camera off its tripod and hold it in the hand.

Silk photograph A photographic image made directly on silk fabric. There was a vogue for such photographs around 1856, but because of the perishability of the medium, few examples have survived.

Silver bromide   The designation of the most popular type of printing paper in use from 1880 on.

Silver chloride print   A print on the kind of plain salted paper used by Fox Talbot for the calotype.

Silver-copper plate   The daguerreotype plate.

Silver halide   The combination of silver with halogen elements to create a light-sensitive emulsion such as is used in securing an image in photography.

Silver intensification   A method for restoring a faded calotype by supplementing the silver already present in the image. Such a method may be found demonstrated by Eugene Ostroff of the Smithsonian Institution in the Time/Life book *Caring for Photographs.*

Silver nitrate   One of a number of chemicals which are light-sensitive and the one with which the early experimenters developed the first practical method of photography.

Silver print   The earliest kind of print on paper, the calotype, which was made on plain salted paper (q.v.). The image is characteristically of a pleasingly soft brownish (not silver) tone.

Single lens reflex   A type of camera in which both the viewing and focusing are accomplished through one lens: at the instant of exposure the position of a mirror is changed to permit the recording of the image; abbreviated S.L.R. William Sutton of England patented such a camera in the 1860s, but it was not marketed successfully until 1884.

Sixteenth plate   A very small daguerreotype size, rarely used, about 1⅜ by 1⅝ inches. Abbreviated 1/16 p.

Sixth plate   A daguerreotype plate size, 2¾ by 3¼ inches, also called the medium plate, and abbreviated 1/6 p.

Sky Shade   A device worked out originally by Eadweard Muybridge in 1867 for reducing the light from the sky, which caused overexposure, and making it possible to photograph the sky and clouds at the same time as the rest of the landscape. However, it should also be pointed out that Muybridge's 1872 Yosemite landscapes, much admired for their cloud effects, were probably made by combining two separate negatives.

Slide   A transparency; a photographic print on glass for projection onto a screen for viewing. A slide is a single image, as distinguished from the stereopticon print, though the latter may sometimes be called a slide. Glass slides, either in black and white or colored, each about 4 by 4 inches, provided a popular parlor entertainment from the late nineteenth century up to around 1920, furnishing a look at distant and exotic views or news events. These glass slides, susceptible to breaking and cracking, were marketed often in sets within their own neat wooden box.

Sliding box   A simple type of camera popular between 1840 and 1865 in England, consisting of two open-ended boxes telescoped into each other to focus, lacking a shutter, and requiring the support, therefore, of a table or tripod.

Slow film   Film of relatively less sensitivity to light.

Slow lens A lens limited to large f/numbers and therefore not capable of admitting a great deal of light into the camera.

Snapshot A popular term indicating an "instantaneous" photograph obtained with a hand-held camera. The 1911 *Encyclopedia of Photography* states: "Unfortunately, it suggests a random or unconsidered operation into which a large element of chance enters; whereas the mere fact that the actual exposure given was a short one does not imply that no thought, study, or observation was devoted to the subject." The term "snapshot" is said to have been invented around 1840 by Sir John Herschel but did not come into its present use until the advent of Eastman's Kodak camera, its great popularity and the ensuing fad for amateur photography from the 1890s on.

Society for Photographing Relics The Society for Photographing the Relics of Old London, founded in 1874 in an effort to preserve London's oldest inn, the Oxford Arms; it ceased its activity in 1886. As part of its 12-year campaign to save both the inn and other historic buildings from destruction, the Society issued sets of carbon prints to subscribers along with accompanying historical notes. The photographic work was done by Henry Dixon and J. Boole.

Soft Focus Controversy Sir William Newton, a miniature painter, was one of the first to suggest that a photographic image might be rendered slightly out of focus for a soft and flattering effect in a portrait. At the meeting of the Photographic Society of London held in 1853, there was such a storm of controversy over Sir William's suggestion that he later retracted.

Solar camera The early sun-operated enlarger. One of the most popular of these solar cameras was that introduced by D. W. Woodward in 1857. Enlarging in the mid-nineteenth century presented special problems since the printing paper was excessively slow and hours of full sunshine were usually required.

Solarized print A photographic print containing a reversal of tones such as may occur from overexposure. A partial reversal (the Sabattier effect) may take place if a negative is exposed to a darkroom light which is excessively strong.

Souvenir album A photographic album containing ten or more commercial photographs, usually showing some vacation resort or great city. Such albums were particularly popular from 1890 to around 1910; they might be bound as a book, have a binding after the manner of the fanciful family albums, or fold out accordian style.

Speed The relative light sensitivity of photographic material or of the camera's lens.

Spy camera A detective camera (q.v.).

Sphereotype A kind of collodion positive made on glass with, according to M. A. Root, "certain peculiarities in the method and mounting the picture," devised by one Albert Bisbee, a "heliographic artist" of Columbus, Ohio, in 1856.

Spherical vignette A photograph rounded in form by being pressed over an object such as a convex paperweight or any oval surface and itself then encased with convex glass.

Spirit photography The deliberate introduction of an extraneous, not-fully-exposed image into a picture, a so-called "ghost." Around 1880 there was a fad among photographers of the sentimental school for bringing a figure, frequently draped in a sheet, into a picture for only a short portion of the whole exposure time, to achieve a fuzzy effect designed to mystify, or possibly amuse.

Spotting   Not the same as retouching (q.v.), but the correction of physical defects in a negative, such as light spots, air bells, or watermarks. It may be accomplished with a special spotting solution. The resultant print is called touched up.

Stained glass print   Some experiments were conducted to make prints in color on stained glass during the 1850s, at the same time that other experiments were being made to photograph directly onto leather or silk.

Stanhope   An optical novelty named after Charles Stanhope, who devised a tiny magnifying glass to permit the viewing of miniature photographs such as might be inserted into jewelry or used for other decorative purposes. "Stanhopes" are sometimes depictions of famous scenes, portraits of the members of one's own family, or a page reduced from the Bible.

To quote from George Gilbert's *Collecting Photographica: The Images and Equipment of the First Hundred Years of Photography* (1976): "The Stanhope is named after Lord Stanhope, an English scientist (1753-1816) who conceived the tiny glass-rod lens on which a film positive barely ⅛ inch across could be cemented. After a hole has been drilled through a ring or a letter opener (or even the base of the bowl of a man's pipe and the cover of a cigarette holder, both of which are in the author's collection), it is possible to insert the glass rod with its image. The tiny image is quite easy to see in a magnified view through the aperture in the ring or other carrier of the hidden lens. Images range from the Eiffel Tower of Paris to the Tomb of David in Jerusalem. Watch-fob charms concealed 'fancy' photos: bathing beauties. Collectors find Stanhopes by checking jewelry trays at antique shops and in the flea markets for the telltale ⅛-inch-wide aperture on both sides of jewelry items. Silver or gold charms in the shapes of tiny telescopes and folding cameras almost invariably conceal a Stanhope. Ivory items and especially desk ornaments are often found with the tiny hidden image. Held close to the eye, the astonishing magnification of the lens makes it possible to read captions under as many as eight separate photographs reduced to microscopic dimensions . . ."

Stannotype   A modification of the Woodburytype (q.v.), introduced in 1879 but apparently never put to wide use.

Stereo   The stereograph or stereogram, one of a pair of photographic prints designed to be viewed in tandem, side by side, to produce the effect of depth. The word "stereograph" was coined by Oliver Wendell Holmes. As early as the 1830s Sir Charles Wheatstone had experimented with binocular effect in viewing dissimilar figures of geometric forms which he was able to make appear solid by viewing through his stereoscope, a special instrument devised for this purpose. In 1841 he tried using photographs, both daguerreotypes and calotypes, but the former reflected too much light and the latter lacked sufficient detail. Much later, following the introduction of the collodion print on paper and on glass, the stereograph came into its own. Special stereographic cameras were invented so that the two pictures might be taken simultaneously with twin lenses at a distance apart of about 2¼ inches, the distance between human eyes, thus simulating human vision.

In 1851 at the Crystal Palace Exhibition, Queen Victoria helped give impetus to the growing interest in stereopticon viewing by admiring a small box-like stereoscope which used card-mounted photographs. With the collodion process, such cards could be reproduced in quantity and thus sold cheaply. By 1859 stereopticon prints were being marketed in huge quantities by studios which purchased their negatives from commercial photographers, to whom they might even assign special subjects. Photographers now had a whole new market for their views of scenic wonders. In the United States the craze for stereopticon viewing was initially launched by the Langenheim Brothers of Philadelphia with their albumen negatives printed on glass (hyalotypes). Among the early major makers and vendors of views were E. and H. T. Anthony, George Stacy, and D. Appleton, all of New York. Later publishers included Underwood and Underwood, Langenheim, and the London Stereoscopic Company, among many. Stereographs may be dated by their size. The smaller cards, 3 by 7 inches, popular in Europe beginning in 1854, were introduced into the United States around 1859. The slightly larger size, 4 by 7 inches, also known earlier in Europe, did not become current in the United States until 1870. Stereopticon prints brought to the Victorian parlor all the delights of distant natural wonders, foreign cities, historic monuments, art and statuary, and fascinating archaeological subjects. For tracing the appearance of new views as they were issued, collectors frequently find it helpful to consult the *Philadelphia Photographer*, a journal which from the appearance of its first issue in 1864 published lists of the new releases. The standard book on the subject of stereos is William Culp Darrah's *Stereo Views: A History of Stereographs in America and Their Collection*, published in 1964.

Stereoscope   A device employing twin images for viewing, to create an illusion of depth. The use of the stereoscope for looking at drawings preceded the invention of photography. Credit for inventing the first practical stereoscope goes to Sir Charles Wheatstone; its most familiar form is that invented by Dr. Oliver Wendell Holmes in 1861, with the sliding viewholder added by Joseph L. Bates, also of Boston, in 1864. A history of the stereoscope is contained in Harold F. Jenkins' *Two Points of View/The History of the Parlor Stereoscope*, published in 1957.

Stereoscopic camera   A camera with twin lenses capable of taking two pictures simultaneously from standpoints corresponding to the space between the human eyes; these pictures are then mounted to be viewed in such manner that the two images blend, giving a sensation of depth.

Stereotype   A print producd by the stereotype process of printing, in which a solid metal plate cast from a mold is used rather than the actual type. Prints in color are produced by using magenta (minus green), cyan (minus red), and yellow (minus blue). The process was devised simultaneously and separately in 1869 by Louis Ducos du Hauron and Charles Cros, but it was not until 1935 that subtractive color film (Kodachrome) was made commercially available.

Straight photography   The production of an unaltered print taken from an unretouched negative which has been "produced by normal development, during which no control is possible"—Robert Demachy. The straight print and the salon print represent opposite poles of aesthetics in photography.

Stripping   The process of separating exposed and developed film from its supporting paper, a procedure invented by George Eastman and patented by him in 1884. General acceptance did not come, however, until George Eastman marketed his first Kodak, in 1888. The following year the Kodak converted to rollfilm, though Eastman continued to manufacture his stripping film until 1891.

Stripping film   As stated by Carl W. Ackerman in his biography of George Eastman: "The 'stripping film' which was to be used in [Eastman's] new system of photography comprised a paper base, a layer of collodion, a sensitized gelatine emulsion, and a soluble layer of gelatine between the paper and the collodion, so that, after exposure and development, this soluble layer could be softened by warm water and the paper base separated from the negative and the latter then printed. The broad claims to this stripping film appear in the patent to Eastman . . . Thus photographic film in a continuous strip was originated" (page 47). The "new system of photography" was initially called "a new paper dry plate" and when announced by the Eastman Dry Plate & Film Company of Rochester in 1884, it was promised that "the exposures being made upon a continuous strip which is afterwards cut up and developed, the resulting negatives [are] indistinguishable from those made upon glass."

Stroboscope   A kind of parlor toy invented in 1832, in which a sensation of viewing motion is achieved by rapidly rotating a number of pictures set upon a disk. This machine is sometimes called the predecessor to the motion picture.

Studio portrait   A commercially made portrait. The studio portrait had its antecedents in the carte de visite and the cabinet card. It is larger than either and is generally framed rather than mounted. Generally considered the routine product of bread-and-butter work, with some notable exceptions producd by the most prestigious studios, the studio portrait is beginning to be more appreciated.

Study   Between 1880 and 1890 the "study" meant an arty photograph, often sentimental, which was prized as a decorative work to be hung on the wall. The study, for example, might portray a pathetic scene of leave-taking. Studies were almost invariably intended to be inspirational in character.

Subtractive color process   A system of color photography by which a color is formed by its absorption of its complementary color from white light.

Sun painting   An early term meaning photography: a photograph taken through the action of the sun. Both daguerreotypes and calotypes are types of sun paintings. Picture-taking had to be limited to the days the sun was shining, and studios had to be designed for maximum light. The skylight remained one of the most essential parts of the studio until around 1870.

Sun picture   See the previous entry.

Sure card   A slang expression used by professional photographers for the carte de visite (card photograph) of a popular figure sure to have a lively sale. Since the sure card could prove such a money-maker for the studio, to speed its production sometimes dozens of negatives might be produced at one sitting through the use of the multiple-lens camera.

Swelled-gelatin method   A system of making photo-relief plates. It was much in use after 1875 and especially popular for reproducing photographs for book illustration and even for reproducing cheaper copies of otherwise expensive books. In retrospect, this process appears to have been both fairly uncertain and time-consuming, since it was developed before zinc and copper etching came into use.

Sympathetic photograph   One made on a paper coated with a 10 percent solution of gelatin, floated on 10 percent potassium bichromate, and dried in the dark; when printed, the faint image will change color with changes in the atmosphere.

Sympathetic writing   The application of nitrate of silver to white paper to produce writing that is invisible until exposed to light, and thus a rudimentary form of photography.

Tableau vivant   A posed photograph of a kind especially popular at the end of the nineteenth century. Itself a kind of theater, it was not, however, related to the stage. Amateurs were often willing to pose for a photographer to commemorate some special event or illustrate a maxim. Such "living scenes" might be comic and as such provided the material for popular stereographs.

Taft   Robert Taft, author of *Photography and the American Scene* published in 1938, the first authoritative work on its subject. Taft's history covers the years 1839 to 1889.

Talbotype   Another name for the calotype (q.v.) invented by Fox Talbot. Just as the photograph on silvered copper was called a daguerreotype after its inventor, friends of Talbot apparently felt that it would be appropriate to name his invention of the photograph on paper after him. Furthermore, his invention remained closely identified with him, since he not only patented his process but kept close control over its use by other photographers. However, the name "calotype" has proved more durable.

Tannin process   An early attempt to produce a dry plate by a process introduced in 1861 by the Englishman Major Charles Russell. In a modification of the technique used to produce the wet plate, Russell's plate was first bathed in a tannic acid solution and then dried before use. The problem of the tendency of the collodion not to bond around the edge of the plate was solved by bordering the plate with adhesive; the plate might then be stored for up to six weeks. Such plates were used by amateurs during the 1860s for still-life work.

Tax stamp   Between September 1864 and August 1866 the U.S. Government required a stamp for commercial photographs. Thus the presence of a stamp on the back of a photograph helps establish its date. The stamp was not required, however, for especially tiny photographs or for photographs which were copies of works of art.

Telephoto lens   A type of lens which was introduced in 1891, providing a high magnification compared with the ordinary camera lens.

Thaumatrope   A device by which cards were manipulated by strings to convey a sense of motion and thus a predecessor of the motion pictures; invented in 1825.

Thermoplastic   A substance invented and patented by Samuel Peck in 1854 for the manufacture of an extremely durable miniature case which was often molded into a fanciful design. Thermoplastic was the first plastic product to be mass-produced in the United States. Resembling gutta percha and similarly durable, it is, however, a composition substance rather than taken from nature, as gutta percha is from the tree.

Thirty-five mm.   35 millimeter, the width of the standard flexible roll film used for motion pictures; a kind of film used in still cameras beginning around 1912.

Time exposure   The exposure in the camera of photographic materials with the shutter set to remain open for a period at the will of the photographer, usually longer than the camera's automatic settings. Before the invention of the shutter, the exposure was achieved by the removal of the lens cap, and therefore all exposures were, in a sense, time exposures.

Time-exposure table   A chart detailing the exposures appropriate to varying conditions. One of the earliest was published in the March 1840 issue of the *American Repertory of Arts, Sciences, and Manufactures.*

Tint   A light color applied to a photograph. In daguerreotypes, ambrotypes, and tintypes this color was usually limited to a pink blush applied to the cheeks of a portrait. "Tinting" may mean simply the application of flesh tones, whereas "coloring" may be the use of several colors.

Tintype   A photograph, usually a portrait, produced by the collodion process directly on japanned iron; despite its name it contains no tin but possibly was so-called because of its grey, tinny appearance. "Tintype" was the popular name for the ferrotype (q.v.). Cheaply and quickly produced and usually small in size, tintypes were keepsakes which could be carried about in the pocket or exchanged by mail and were fairly indestructible, though they were likely, however, to be scratched or bent. Tintypes in the small "gem" size helped make possible the craze for photographic jewelry. Their use even extended to their being displayed on tombstones. The tintype is a particularly American phenomenon, popular from the mid-1850s to around 1870. In 1860 D. F. Maltby produced, on a tintype, the first medal bearing the portrait of a presidential candidate after the fashion of a modern campaign button.

Tombstone portrait   A picture of the deceased, usually a tintype, mounted on his tombstone. A number of different patents for methods of accomplishing this were granted.

Tone   The color of a photographic image, or a range of distinguishable shades of grey.

Toning   The process of imparting a pleasing color to a print before, during, or after the fixing. By applying a chemical to a photographic print, its overall color (tone) may be altered. Frequently toning, as in gold toning, is used to warm the color of the print from cold blacks and greys to a more gentle brown. Insufficient toning may result in a print which is an anemic sepia, whereas too much can mean densely dark areas lacking in detail.

Topographical photograph   As distinct from a landscape photograph, it is one which shows the configuration of a scene in nature, because it is of specific geological interest, possibly a mountain or a gulch.

Tourograph   An early type of camera using the dry plate, specifically designed for amateur use; marketed around 1900.

Transparency   A lantern slide or other kind of positive photograph designed to be viewed by looking through it. Although color film for making the familiar modern transparencies was not introduced until 1935, the idea of viewing a photograph as a transparency was not new in the nineteenth century. One of the wonders of the 1876 Philadelphia Centennial Exhibition, for example, was a series of huge transparencies, some three feet wide and almost as high, showing scenic views of the West.

Tripod   A three-legged stand essential for holding the camera steady before the invention of the camera shutter.

Twin-lens camera A camera specially constructed to take stereoscopic pictures; *or*, a kind of reflex camera employing two lenses, one for viewing and the second for directing the image. The latter type was first made by R. & J. Beck to order in 1880, according to Gernsheim's *History of Photography*.

Two-Ninety-One 291, the gallery located at 291 Fifth Avenue in New York City, founded in 1905 by Alfred Stieglitz and Edward Steichen and associated with the Photo Secession movement. *291* is also the title of a monthly magazine founded by Paul Haviland, Alfred Stieglitz, Marie Ernst Mayer, and others in 1915, devoted to modern art and satire.

Underexposure The result of admitting too little light into the camera to form a pale image, resulting in a "thin" negative and a dense, dark positive.

Underwood set A set of stereographs manufactured and sold by the firm of Underwood & Underwood, marketed in sets of from around 50 to 100, neatly packaged in their own wooden box.

Union case A composition—plastic—miniature case for holding a small portrait photograph, usually either a daguerreotype or ambrotype, though possibly tintype or even paper photograph. This type of case was extremely popular in the 1850s and 1860s. It was customarily hinged and usually contained a single picture, though there might sometimes be two facing each other. The Union case was placed on the market in 1854 after the resolution of a patent controversy between Samuel Peck and another inventor. The case is sometimes assumed to be made of gutta percha, but its chief components are wood flour and shellac. Among the companies which manufactured this type of case were the Scovill Manufacturing Company, the Clifford Ambrotype Company, Swain and Mead, and Littlefield, Parsons, & Co.

Uranium printing A process similar to the platinotype, based on the sensitivity of salts of uranium to light. Around 1856 X. J. Burnett of England worked out and patented such a process for the production of a "permanent" photograph. The Worthlytype, which was produced nine years later, was the leading commercial embodiment of this process.

Uranium toning A process using the salts of uranium which, depending upon the exact mixture of chemicals used, might produce a print in color from brownish black to red to an image of pure black.

Value In photography, the presence of black in any amount, rated on a scale ranging from close to white to grey to the deepest black.

Varnished print A print which has been varnished as the final step in processing. This was routine procedure with some paper photography, such as the carte de visite.

Vienna Camera Club Said to have been one of the first organizations anywhere to hold an exhibition of photographs intended to be judged as art, in 1891.

View In photography, an outdoor scene.

View album The type of commercially published photographic album popular from around 1885 on, containing pictures usually of one place or event.

View camera A type of camera lacking automatic focusing, equipped with a viewing screen to enable the photographer to check directly for composition, focus, sharpness of detail, etc.

Vignette According to *The Silver Sunbeam* edition of 1864, "a vignette is a picture of a portrait, consisting of the head and part of the bust, of an oval shape, in the middle of the card, surrounded by a sort of halo, or shading off gradually into the white background." The "card" is the carte de visite. A few years later, in 1872, Edward N. Estabrooke was describing the method of achieving a vignette: "The plan generally adopted . . . is to cut an oval or other suitable shaped opening in the center of a sheet of white card-board, the edge of the opening to be serrated or toothed, so as to cause the ground to blend softly with the portions of the figure and drapery. The card-board is commonly placed on a frame (made and sold by stock dealers for this purpose), and being placed between the sitter and the camera, at a sufficient distance from the camera to cause the proper softening of the outline, the exposure is made as usual, and upon development the card-board will be found to have blended beautifully with the white background, softening the edges where it covers the clothing and drapery of the sitter." Both vignettes and medallions, which similarly created a border, were in great vogue at the end of the nineteenth century, to the extent that it was only well into the twentieth century before the general public became reconciled to the idea of a portrait without either border or frame.

Vintage print One made by the photographer himself or under his direct supervision, usually soon after the picture was taken; *not*, therefore, any print made much later or one made by someone else from the same negative. One collector has said that the vintage print "has the unexplainable magic of presence."

Voightlander A camera of German manufacture, which in the 1840s was the most widely used daguerreotype camera, according to Henry H. Snelling. When it was first introduced the Voightlander dramatically shortened the exposure time from minutes, in full sunlight, to as little as forty seconds.

Vortograph A purely abstract form of photography devised in 1917 by Alvin Langdon Coburn and showing the influence of cubism.

Wax process Or, waxed-paper process: a modification of the calotype procedures devised by Fox Talbot; it was the invention of Gustave Le Gray in 1851. The paper for a negative was immersed in wax until it was thoroughly impregnated, then dried and sensitized. The resulting paper, which was transparent, could be kept in its dry condition for up to two weeks, was fairly sturdy for use in the camera, and got rid of some of the graininess inherent in the paper negative. The wax process was praised at the time as the "simplest of all the processes for taking negatives on paper." Photographers including Edinburgh's Thomas Keith used it to achieve unusually fine detail. However, its popularity lasted no more than six years, since the calotype itself was already on the way to being outmoded by the wet-collodion process.

Wet-collodion print A print resulting from the use of a glass plate coated with collodion by the photographer, sensitized with silver nitrate, placed in the camera while still wet, and requiring immediate development. The inventor of the wet-collodion plate (collodion wet plate), Frederick Scott Archer, published the details of his new process in 1851. From shortly after this initial announcement to the 1880s, the wet process was that in most general use. Professional photographers liked the speediness of the process, which was made available without patent restrictions. Amateur photographers greeted it with instant enthusiasm as well, despite the fact that the wet process required considerable dexterity in dampening, exposing, and developing the plate in one continuous action. The photographer also needed considerable strength of purpose to arrange the transportation of the bulky equipment and portable darkroom required to venture into the field. But the negative produced has a fineness of detail which delighted amateurs and professionals alike and eventually led to a new use of the camera to document important events as well as the daily lives of all kinds of people. The wet-collodion print is generally made on albumen paper, introduced by Blanquart-Evrard in 1850 and which remained in standard use until around 1890. The wet-collodion process was gradually outmoded by the introduction of the dry collodion plate around 1880. Some of the most magnificent prints made by the wet-collodion process were those of Western scenery made around 1870 by photographers such as William H. Jackson, whose pictures helped convince Congress to establish the Yellowstone area as a national park. The wet-collodion process was used for the ambrotype, the tintype (ferrotype), the carte de visite, and the cabinet card. Because it was possible for a photographer to wash a glass plate clean and use it again, it is surmised that, in many cases, only truly excellent photographs have survived, the poor ones having been erased.

Wilderness photography A school of photography which arose in England around 1855-59, represented, for example, by the photographs of Wales taken by Roger Fenton. In America, however, "wilderness" photography may refer to the work of the western photographers before 1880.

What-Is-It-Wagon A mobile darkroom of the sort used by Mathew B. Brady's staff for the development of wet-plate photographs made in the field during the Civil War. The presence of this strange piece of wartime equipment is said to have roused the curiosity of the soldiers, hence the name.

Whole plate Abbreviated ¼ p, the largest standard size of daguerreotype plate, 6½ by 8½ inches. The name is taken from the size of plate which Daguerre himself used. Half-plate, sixth-plate, and other smaller plate designations are derived from this basic size. Plates larger than the standard could be produced only by an especially skilled operator. Plate sizes may not be entirely precise, since initially at least they were cut by hand.

Woodburygravure Not the same as Woodburytype; the name was applied to a process developed in 1891 for transferring the Woodburytype directly onto the printed page so cleverly that it has the appearance of having been printed there.

Woodburytype The earliest form of photo-mechanical print, distinguished by its continuous halftones and therefore remarkably close to the original photograph from which it was taken. This process, patented in 1864 by the Englishman Walter B. Woodbury, used the original negative to form a relief of bichromated gelatin which could then be processed to produce a run of over 30,000 prints from a single mold. The American rights to the Woodburytype were acquired in 1870 by John Carbutt of Philadelphia. At the time a great improvement over other available methods of photographic reproduction, the Woodburytype was used extensively for book illustrations even into the 1890s, despite the fact that each print had to be mounted. Slightly purplish in color and lacking any grain, the Woodburytype is admired for its brilliance and sharpness of detail. Beaumont Newhall has said that there is no finer process for reproducing photographs than the "now unfortunately obsolete" Woodburytype. The prints, which retain their lustre and clarity, are of renewed interest today, when so many other photographic prints from the nineteenth century are fading.

Working solution   Photographic chemicals mixed ready for use.

Wothlytype   A method of printing, devised around 1864, using paper coated with collodion containing nitrates of uranium and silver.

X-ray   Following the 1895 discovery of the X-ray by Wilhelm Conrad Roentgen, X-ray photography was taken up as a novelty—resulting in the production of some unusual and even lovely pictures.

Yellow mount   One of the earliest mounts for stereoscopic views published before 1870 and therefore especially valuable.

Zinc photography   A method for the reproduction of photographs for use as illustrations, invented by a Parisian lithographer in 1859. After 1880 it was in extensive use in the United States, particularly for the reproducton of drawings and maps.

Zoetrope   One of the predecessors of the motion picture; a type of action toy consisting of a rotating drum employing a succession of pictures on lithograph strips viewed through slits.

Zone system   A method devised by the modern photographer Ansel Adams to place areas of subject brightness on an exposure scale and then develop the negative in accordance with this placement.

Zoogyroscope   Or zoopraxiscope; a projection lantern containing photographs on a glass wheel which is rotated to produce the sensation of viewing motion; the invention of Eadweard Muybridge and sometimes called the first true motion picture machine.

Zoopraxographical Hall   An elaborate building constructed for the 1893 Chicago World's Fair, where Eadweard Muybridge gave demonstrations of his action photography and lectured on his photographs of animals in motion.

Value in Old Photographs

The pages which follow contain information on some of the prices which have been paid for various photographs offered for sale by dealers and at auction houses dealing in photographic materials during the 1976 and 1977 season. The auction sales reported were generally limited to the sales of photographica, and all the dealers were specialists in such materials. Allowance should naturally be made for any price trends which may have been noted since that time. The prices paid for photographic materials generally have been following a swift upward trend for a number of years.

Even the most careful catalogue description cannot always convey the full impact of a photographic image, and therefore at least some of the prices for items as described are bound to seem somewhat capricious to those of us not privileged to have seen the items when they were offered for sale. It may be difficult to understand why one lot at auction containing four cartes de visite went for $32, whereas what appears to have been a very similar assortment, also of just four, went for only $11. The first may have contained a charming portrait of a young lady much more graceful than any of the stiff figures in the second lot, but we would have had to be present at inspection time before the auction to observe this. On the other hand, it is not too difficult to understand why a photograph of a western scene with the signature of one of the well-known photographers of the early West should command $300 whereas the work of some unknown brings no more than $30.

There is a danger in trying to arrive at a general statement of values from just a few examples. The prices paid for specific items as reported here are intended as no more than *examples* of the price the genre may be expected to command. It will be more realistic to compare price levels in general than to be guided by any specific price paid for a single item.

Collecting photographic images is a highly personal hobby, and individual matters of taste play an important part, often influencing price.

The price paid at some particular auction for an item may well be escalated by the competition of the moment between two avid collectors of the same type of material. Or, the price may have held at rock bottom simply because of the chance absence of anyone interested in acquiring this one particular item.

However, it will be more likely that, overall, the prices paid at any auction will faithfully reflect the market. Auction sales are heavily frequented by dealers who, naturally, must pay a fair price to be able to find a market subsequently for the item at retail, and therefore at auction we find a fairly consistent scale established for a whole range of various kinds of photographs and for the works of a large number of individual photographers.

One factor which should also be taken into account is that a catalogue description may establish the provenance of any item and therefore help establish its value. Such catalogue descriptions are carefully worded after research by the experts employed by the house. It may thus be pointed out for the first time that a photograph is a rare example of a long-outmoded technique, or one of the earliest examples of a new process. Or that it might be the work of some imaginative photographer well ahead of his time. Or that it might be the product of a hitherto unknown and unappreciated photographer. Or perhaps that the image is one which is in an unusually fine state of preservation. Any of this might help escalate—or even create—value.

A warning should be sounded. The published price may be, in many instances, considerably higher than that a private individual might be able to realize if he were to offer a similar photograph for sale in the local market. The exception might be, of course, the unusually lovely photograph, the newly discovered example of the work of a well-known photographer, the collection which has been built around some subject of social significance. Two examples of the same nineteenth-century photograph are rarely offered for sale in precisely the same condition, and certainly never are two photographs offered for sale on two different occasions to precisely the same market. Such variables add spice to the trade. For the collector, they provide a challenge which keeps him eager for the news of the next auction, eager to open the next catalogue as it arrives in the mail, and always hoping, meanwhile, to make some marvelous discovery—at a beautiful price—at some out-of-the-way shop or tucked in among the otherwise routine images of a private collection offered for sale.

Seeking an expert appraisal may be the only way to determine the value of some item for tax purposes or for possible sale. If you know of no photographic expert in your own area who is qualified as an appraiser of old photographs, you might be able to locate such a person through a reputable dealer in old books, an antique dealer, or any local representative of the American Society of Appraisers. Any appraisal of old photographs will, of course, cost you approximately as much as the appraisal of other works of art or other antiques such as old jewelry, china, or furniture.

Although we all may dream of making a rare discovery, in an unexpected place, of some photographic treasure by a photographer no one has yet heard about, the chances are that the exciting new image is most likely to turn up just where it is most expected: in the collection of a person sufficiently knowledgeable about photography to have been able to trust his own judgment and who had the funds to back it up, in the collection made by some person highly competent in one area of photography (perhaps the editor of a photographic journal, for example), or in the collection made by one of the associates of a well-known photographer.

Probably one of the fields relatively unmined to date is that of photography in Canada, where there were apparently relatively fewer photographers operating before 1870 than in the United States. Books published in Canada illustrated from photographs or even with photographs are particularly sought.

Even though most family collections of old photographs will probably yield little of interest to persons outside the family, ambrotypes and the earlier daguerreotypes might be examined carefully to see if there is among the merely competent images some which are truly excellent, or enclosed in an unusual case. Among the photographs on paper, it is often the scene itself, the type of process used, or some other detail of specific interest relative to photographic history which may make the photograph valuable rather than the quality of the image alone.

The subject of a photograph on paper may make it especially interesting even when the photographer is unknown. A small collection of less than ten portraits of leaders of various American western Indian tribes has sold for several hundred dollars. The combination of Indian subject with a name photographer seems almost irresistible. An original print by Karl Moon of an Indian, possibly from around 1910, sold at auction, along with a second print, for $475. A single mounted platinum print, copyrighted 1898 as noted in the negative, by F. A. Rinehart, went for $70. Three silver prints by Lee Moorehouse, made around

1900, have gone for $325 as a lot. Even photographs which are relatively poor and by unknowns seem to have a market these days if they document some aspect of Indian life which has now disappeared. And, of course, Curtis photographs consistently bring some of the highest prices at auction.

Transportation is another subject which seems to fascinate collectors. At one auction $70 was paid for a single large mounted photograph showing a train loaded with 30 stagecoaches, probably from around 1868. At another auction an 1876 photograph, described as rare and showing a group of 100 men with various tools, "probably the crew that helped build the transcontinental" railroad, brought $150. A single view of a locomotive made around the turn of the century could be worth more than $10, as might any well-made photograph showing some aspect of motor transportation at around the same time.

Sports is another good subject. An early boxing scene, thought to have been made around 1886, with neither the photographer nor the place identified, has brought $70 at auction. A large collection of over 50 photographs made in the 1920s showing baseball players, some of the prints from a photo service, has brought $45. Cricket is among the most interesting subjects.

There is a special market for early photographs showing Black family life. Even photographs which are limited aesthetically have brought good prices. On the other hand, that perennially popular subject, Niagara Falls, which has continued to attract photographers, amateur and professional, right through the nineteenth century into the twentieth—is apparently still in demand. An original print in the original oak frame, from around 1885, might be worth well over $100. Scarcity and demand are the important factors here.

Sometimes the photograph tells us much more today about local customs than the photographer could ever have dreamed when he took his picture. A fine large view of the 60 members of a police force somewhere out West has brought $85 at auction; most of the men, although not all, are in uniform, and each has his number in his hat—either a bowler or a rakish stetson.

There are photographs which have a fairly ghoulish attraction. They might be from a collection depicting the Spanish American War and include several grisly scenes; $100 has been paid for such a collection of only 16 prints. Just half that amount, $50, was paid at auction for another lot, in this case a single print, showing a group of about 100 persons, mostly Japanese, gathered about the casket of a child, possibly

With the destruction of the Maine in Havana Harbor on February 15, 1898, war between the United States and Spain appeared to become inevitable. The peacefulness of this scene has its own poignancy. The print was presented in 1951 to the Library of Congress by the heirs of General Hugh L. Scott, who was himself primarily famous as an Indian fighter. (Courtesy of the Library of Congress USZ62-11020.)

around 1900; neither the precise location nor the photographer are identified.

About all that can be said about photographs showing well-known personalities is that there is a good likelihood that they may be valuable. Just how valuable depends upon many factors aside from the subject. Within months of each other two photographs of General U. S. Grant appeared in the auction market; one showing Grant on Lookout Mountain in 1863 sold for $25, whereas the second, of Imperial size made around 1863, mounted and in the original mahogany frame, identified by a tag as by Gurney and retouched as was the common practice, was bought for $800. A single photograph of Mark Twain, signed by him, dated 1879—spotted but otherwise good—has brought $90. Subjects as diverse as Chester A. Arthur and Louis Armstrong bring strong prices. A collection of 53 almost entirely hitherto unpublished photographs of John F. Kennedy and his family around 1954, including a number of charming ones of the young Jacqueline Kennedy, brought $6,000 at Sotheby Parke Bernet.

Many of the most valued portraits are those made by the well-known photographers, and the reader is referred to the sections on nineteenth- and twentieth-century photographers, where some of the prices recently paid for examples of their work have been noted where the information was available.

Condition, in an old photograph, can be of varying importance in assessing value. The older photographs, on metal or on glass, almost invariably have some defects due to the passage of time. Any reputable dealer in old photographs carefully spells out in his catalogue any aspect of an image which makes it less than "fine," no matter how minor the defect. Since the photograph made on paper is frequently to be found unblemished by time, it is especially important that any slight blemish should be mentioned. If the photograph is unmounted, there may be some tears or creases, perhaps just at the corners. Sometimes the mount itself is spotted or foxed. Occasionally the entire picture is faded. Even if the subject of the photograph is important enough to outweigh any minor defects in the image, these defects should still be described. In addition, the catalogue should comment, if it seems necessary, on the photograph's overall quality: dark, light-struck in one corner, etc.

The catalogues and price lists issued by the following dealers in photographic materials have been particularly helpful in supplying reliable information as reported on the pages which follow: the auction houses of Sotheby Parke Bernet, Inc. (980 Madison Avenue, New York,

New York 10021), Swann Galleries, Inc. (104 East 25th Street, New York, New York 10010), the California Book Auction Company (224 McAllister Street, San Francisco, California 94102), and Plandome Book Auctions (113 Glen Head Road, Glen Head, New York 11545), as well as the Witkin Gallery, Inc. (41 East 57th Street, Room 802, New York, New York 10022), The Photo Album (835 No. La Cienega Boulevard, Los Angeles, California 90069), Allen and Hilary Weiner (392 Central Park West, New York, New York 10025), Charles B. Wood III, Inc., (South Woodstock, Connecticut 06267), Zita Books (Box 123 Ansonia Station, New York, New York 10023), and Daguerreian Era, run by Tom and Elinor Burnside (Pawlet, Vermont 05761). There are, of course, many more fine dealers, and a growing number of them, too.

We hope that the following information detailing the value of a wide range of kinds of old photographs will encourage more owners of old photographs to appreciate their own family collections. In particular we hope that some inkling of the possible value of the nineteenth-century images may lead more people to take the proper steps to preserve what is an irreplaceable and priceless part of our heritage.

PLEASE NOTE: Listed here are only works for which a value has recently been established by public sale or auction. It should not be assumed that these listings establish any kind of norm. Nor should it be assumed that the most significant or valuable works of any individual photographer have necessarily been included.

All prices quoted are for images in very good to fine condition unless otherwise indicated.

The Mirror of Nature

Daguerreotypes constitute the earliest form of photography in America. For this reason alone they would be especially honored by collectors. However, they also provide us with an honest view of people as they were then. When the images are of persons who were important in national affairs, they may be of special value to the historian. Equally important, daguerreotype portraits are often lovely enough to be treasured for themselves.

It will be found that a great many daguerreotypes, unless the surface

This scratched, oxidized, and spotted daguerreotype proved to contain important information for the New England restoration at Old Sturbridge Village in Massachusetts. The Thompson Bank, one of its exhibits, has been restored to its appearance in the picture, probably made around 1845. Note the reversal in the lettering of the sign. (Courtesy of Old Sturbridge Village.)

A badly scarred daguerreotype of Fenno House, Old Sturbridge Village, Massachusetts, shows the milk cans lined up along the front of the house. (Courtesy of Old Sturbridge Village.)

The wear in the daguerreotypes contrasts with the clarity of the modern print made from an old glass plate. This particular plate furnishes a wealth of detail and shows an old-fashioned coach still in use at the beginning of the twentieth century. (Courtesy of Old Sturbridge Village.)

of the picture is badly scarred, are offered for sale at ⟨
quick survey of the daguerreotypes offered for sale at a ⟨
ket by a number of different dealers or presented at a ⟨
offering antiques and curios may make it appear that th
mum going price, with $30 to $50 not unusual. However, the wise collector of old photographs should not assume that therefore any daguerreotype must be worth that much. At one auction, which was
nationally advertised, a number of images which had been described in
the catalogue as "lightly spotted, otherwise excellent," and all in cases
identified by Rinhart, brought bids no higher than $7 to $10 or $11.

Up to $75 may on occasion be rather routinely paid for a daguerreo-
type portrait which is especially striking, conveying the appealing personality of the sitter, or for one which includes an interesting prop
to designate the sitter's occupation, particularly if other than the par-
son's Bible, or any portrait showing unusual skill in the photographer.
In daguerreotypes valued at several hundreds of dollars the fine quality
of the image is important; the daguerreotype is capable of such a fineness of detail that the beauty of a really lovely image is only made
further apparent by examination through a magnifying glass. What can
perhaps best be called the emotional content of the picture is also important: a bright confrontation with the camera is characteristic of
daguerreotype portraits, and in many of them it is this "straight-forward
look" which helps us recognize these sitters as real people. Everything
is sharply in focus, the sitter looks directly at us, and the resulting
daguerreotype is the "straight" photograph in its purity.

Since the daguerreotype portrait is almost always to be found in its
own case, price may be influenced to a considerable extent by the rarity
of the case and its condition. The daguerreotype case is customarily
identified by reference to the Rinharts' *American Miniature Case Art*,
the standard work on the subject. If the case is one of the more common
types, it may not necessarily add much to the value of the image. Even
a fairly interesting case, if it is worn or broken, may not add value. Any
daguerreotype found simply enclosed in its brass mat and preserver and
lacking any case at all would probably have to be fairly unusual to overcome this deficiency. It is worth pointing out here, as before, that any
printed information found tucked into the back of a miniature case may
not always necessarily refer to the daguerreotype at hand. Daguerreotypes, and ambrotypes too, have frequently been moved from one case
to another by a dealer more interested in presenting an attractive package than in the proper identification of the image.

The daguerreotype was introduced into the United States in September, 1839, and subsequently flourished particularly from 1845 to around 1855. The 1845 date represents the rise of the professional studio for making daguerreotype portraits, and the second date, 1855, the introduction of the wet-collodion method of photography and the beginning of the short fad for the ambrotype. The very earliest of the daguerreotypes made in this country have, of course, an antiquarian value apart from any aesthetic interest. One clue to identifying the earliest is that they are of a silvery appearance without that brown cast which was produced by gold toning. During the first year of experimentation in this country, portraits were still extremely difficult because the exposure time was almost unbearably long for the sitter, and for this reason some of the earliest pictures attempted were of outdoor scenes, on bright sunny days. Most of the earliest daguerreotypes—those which could be properly identified as to date—have already, for the most part, been acquired by museums.

Of special interest to the historian are those portraits which were made by one of the big-city studios and may be positively identified as to subject. Since each daguerreotype portrait is unique, it is always possible that some newly surfacing one showing one of the great and famous men of the day may give us a new glimpse into his character and personality. Yet almost any daguerreotype portrait has something to tell us about our ancestors, famous or humble. It may show us the shy young girl, in her elaborate side curls; the young man stiffly holding his beaver hat; the formally-posed newlyweds; the widow holding out the mourning portrait so that it faces the camera; the old man who probably could remember the American revolution; or the death portrait of the old lady in her lace cap. The love for our children is revealed in the large numbers of portraits which were made, even though the taking of a child's picture presented quite a problem to the photographer of the day. The exposure time was too long for an active child, and there are many surviving images in which the mother who holds the child in her lap is in sharp focus, whereas the wriggling child has hands or head which appear fuzzy. Many photographers apparently tried to solve their problem by catching the child heavy-lidded, about to drop off to sleep; and, of course, there is that touching portrait of a child, taken of the dead infant.

The daguerreotype did not lend itself to the identification of the photographer on the plate itself. It is therefore sometimes extremely difficult to be sure of his identity. If the seal has never been broken, and the daguerreotype never, therefore, lifted out of its original case, then it is possible that the name appearing on the case or inside is that of the studio responsible for the image, though the photograph need not necessarily be the work of the individual photographer who operated the studio. A "Brady studio" photograph need not be by Brady, for example. There are only a few experts who are qualified to identify the photographer from a daguerreotype image and even they are frequently reticent about venturing an opinion. Although each daguerreotype is a unique image and therefore the same one is not to be found twice, one of several taken at a single sitting may, however, be identified within its series.

Since most daguerreotypes were portraits, usually of the fourth-plate or sixth-plate size, any larger plate may be of special interest. Likewise, any landscape, often made on the larger plate, is of interest, since few photographers cared to venture their equipment out of doors. Although there were relatively few amateur photographers, some of these did take their cameras outside, producing some of the most interesting pictures of all.

Every daguerreotype should be carefully examined for any of the following defects which would tend to lower its value:

—Hairline scratches in the plate, or any other marks or abrasions, no matter how minute.

—Spotting, as from chemicals that might have been used in a faulty attempt to clean the plate.

—Tarnish along the edges of the plate, although this may be relatively unimportant if not affecting the major area of the image.

—Any scars or swashes through the image caused by a poor attempt to clean the plate.

—If there is a case, look for these defects: a broken seal; a worn or broken case, or one which has been awkwardly repaired; or one which is clearly just half of the original double case.

Among the various factors which may contribute value to the daguerreotype are the following:

—The presence of that extraordinary sharpness of detail which is one of the glories of this particular photographic medium.

—That "expression of a fleeting instant"—an intimate quality of facial expression which makes you feel that you know this subject.

—A portrait subject who is a member of the military, a Black, or an Indian.

—A portrait of a deceased person. Although portraits of dead infants were common enough, the portraits of mature or elderly deceased people are more unusual.

—A sharp focus, with no wobbling of the head, hands, or feet apparent, as might be characteristic of the portrait of a child.

—A pose which is not the straightforward American look, especially one which has been varied by some pleasurable asymmetry, not often to be found in the daguerreotype.

—Nudes are among the most unusual daguerreotypes, but they do exist. When they come on the market, nudes bring some of the highest prices.

—An interesting background, especially one which has been altered or modulated in some way, as with the addition of a screen.

—Any imaginative use of side-lighting for a more dramatic effect.

—The introduction of an interesting prop, such as a book, a vase of flowers, or an elaborately carved chair. In the case of a child's portrait, the prop might be a baby carriage or even the family dog.

—The use of a prop to indicate the subject's occupation or hobby, possibly a sextant or the apparatus used by the chemist (or daguerreotypist). Such "occupational" daguerreotypes are of special interest to the social historian.

—A grouping of more than three people in a single picture—or even better, four—especially if the group can be identified as having some relationship other than the family tie.

—In a portrait, an outdoor setting or a setting devised in the studio to give the impression of an outdoor setting—most unusual.

The following short list of some of the higher prices paid recently for daguerreotypes illustrates many of the above points. This list is offered to assist the reader in defining what may be most important in evaluating any daguerreotype rather than as a guide to be taken literally in establishing prices. Each unique image furnished by the daguerreotype must be seen to be evaluated properly. Furthermore, any image's historical interest may influence value to a considerable extent, as may also the exigencies of the market on any one particular day.

For the definitions of plate sizes as noted below and elsewhere, please see **Plate** in the glossary.

—Far outdistancing the prices of other daguerreotypes offered at the same auction sale, a half-plate portrait of the admired lion-tamer Isaac Van Amburgh, showing him in costume with his leopard by his side. $500

—A sixth-plate maternal portrait, in which the head of the child is sharp, the image enclosed in a fine leather case but with the cover loose. $40

—The picture of a town hall in Connecticut, a sixth plate with very sharp detail, enclosed in a lovely leather case with "lush green velvet pad, also fine." $275

—A slightly tarnished sixth plate, a "lovely, heavily gold-toned" portrait of a "curly haired youth with new sidewhiskers and a 'blue' shirt-front." $30

—A sixth plate of a lady, with depth to the background, the portrait heavily gold-toned, the plate cleaned and in excellent condition. $50

—A half plate "superbly executed," showing a woman of serene demeanor, the portrait by J. Gurney of New York, in a damaged leather case. $225

—A realistically hand-colored sixth-plate portrait of a lady, by Claudet of Regent Street. $100

—A sixth-plate portrait showing two young girls with their dog, the photographer unknown. $50

—An unusually fine vignette portrait, a sixth plate, tinted, and handsomely framed in a scalloped brass mat. $65

—A quarter plate of a girl standing, with a basket of flowers alongside. The photographer is unknown, but possibly British. In an unadorned case in fine condition, the image is catalogued as "of museum quality." $65

—A fine sixth-plate portrait made by R. H. Vance, identified by the dealer as a leading photographer in San Francisco in the 1850s. $60

—A sixth-plate portrait of a man, with inky blacks and bright whites, and with the logo of the J. H. Whitehurst Galleries of New York embossed on the leather pad of a worn case, with "Whitehurst" stamped on the brass mat. $35

—A pair of sixth-plate images of a little girl, both tarnished, and in a case requiring some repair. $35

—A quarter-plate portrait of a seated young boy, produced by Brady's Gallery, with the original seal; the plate and the leather case both in very fine condition. $145

—A quarter-plate portrait of a freckled young man, by Alexander

Deckers. A student under Frederick Langenheim, Deckers served as an administrator with the Langenheims until 1849 and after that entered into a partnership with Victor Piard. $50

—An unusual grouping of eight men, a fine image, a half plate, with the photographer unknown. $250

—A grouping of four men, the half-plate image heavily gold-toned and the plate cleaned, the photographer unknown; in a "gorgeous, green leather case." $100

—In the horizontal format, a sixth-plate portrait of three children in which the faces of the children have been tinted; in a full leather case. $45

—A tinted sixth-plate portrait of a young girl, the plate in fine condition, and the coloring employing both reds and greens with a "subtle blue background." $35

—An early sixth-plate portrait of a little boy, the image found behind a mat made of paper. $45

Ambrotypes

Antique dealers and dealers in old and rare books who do not regularly deal in old photographs sometimes err, even today, in mistaking the ambrotype for the daguerreotype, since both types of images are most frequently found in the one-fourth or sixth-plate sizes and enclosed in miniature cases. They err in pricing the ambrotype as though it were a daguerreotype, of course, rather than the other way around. Those who know old photographs are aware that the ambrotype is worth roughly one fourth the value of the daguerreotype, sometimes less.

The daguerreotype was America's introduction to photography and was made from 1839 to the mid-1850s and sometimes later, whereas the ambrotype followed the daguerreotype as the popular means of portraiture, and remained popular for only a brief period of six years. Thus, most ambrotypes were made in the late 1850s. By the time of the Civil War, the tintype had already become exceedingly popular and, furthermore, the ambrotype had been outmoded by the positive on paper made from the wet-collodion negative on glass, as exemplified by the carte de visite. Although it is possible to date most ambrotypes with a greater accuracy than is generally possible with other types of photographs, this is probably one of its few major attractions for the collector of photographica.

Yet the ambrotype can have legitimate appeal for the collector of Americana whose funds are limited. Although little appreciated when fine daguerreotypes were more accessible than they are today, the ambrotype must be accepted now as an important photographic medium representing the few years that it flourished (1854–1860). The ambrotype portraits made during those years show us the face of America, the way in which people wished to present themselves socially, and the clothes they wore. Thousands upon thousands of these portraits were made, and many of them are still to be found and may be acquired at prices which are often miniscule compared with the prices usually commanded by other types of old photographs.

It is still possible to pick up an ambrotype portrait for as little as one dollar, even enclosed in a case, although the case might be in poor condition or not very lovely or interesting. The image, however, may be fine, or need only the insertion of a new backing or the repair of its varnishing to present a new and attractive appearance. The collector should be on the lookout for any portraits made of persons known in public life during the years just before the Civil War. The ambrotype portrait of an important person is especially valued since the ambrotype was "everyman's" means of portraiture, more than the daguerreotype had been, and therefore it was relatively uncommon for people of prestige to go to the ambrotype studio to have their picture taken.

The introduction of collodion set off a wave of amateur photography, in spite of the difficulties inherent in preparing the wet plate for each new image one wanted to record, so we are fortunate now in having a number of outdoor pictures as well as studio portraits produced by this method. We may not be able to identify the photographer, but frequently the scene is highly recognizable. Certain subjects attracted the photographers more than others. Among the subjects considered highly suitable for photography were scenes in the White Mountains and views of Niagara Falls. Two hundred dollars was recently paid at an important auction for a half plate showing five men standing together offering a toast, with the almost inevitable Niagara Falls in the background. This particular image was enclosed in a brown thermoplastic case. There are, of course, other and diverse scenes, such as village streets, horse-drawn vehicles, people seated outdoors, and blacksmith shops. There can be a great fascination in scouting for these heavy glass

plates which record a way of life which was soon to be swept away
with industrialization, the war, and an accelerating western expansion.

Generally speaking, the outdoor scenes are worth considerably more
than the portraits. A whole-plate view of Niagara Falls, made around
1855, presented in a case of design not mentioned in Rinhart, has brought
as much as $400 at a New York City auction. The auction house Sotheby
Parke Bernet was able to attest that it was probably the work of a Canadian photographer, Saul Davis. At an auction of photographic materials
held by the California Book Auction Company, most ambrotypes sold for
$20 and under; however, there were several exceptions, including one
outdoor scene made around 1857 showing seven people in front of a two-
story house. This sold for $55. Another outdoor scene went for a bid of
$75. This was a photograph made around 1858, showing two men in a
horse-drawn cart. In each of these cases price might have been influenced by the importance of photographic evidence in the history of the
West. Photographic records made of the developing West have an historic importance that photographs made in the East during the same
period rarely match.

The following additional examples of the relatively high prices paid
for other ambrotypes may presage generally higher prices for ambrotypes, particularly outdoor scenes, and a growing appreciation for the
work of those generally anonymous photographers who turned out the
portraits. Many of these photographers, we can assume, were former
daguerreotypists who chose to learn and practice the new collodion technique rather than be phased out completely by the advancing technology
of their craft.

—A portrait definitely identified as of George Peabody of Boston, the
image finely tinted, in a contemporary elaborate gilt frame measuring
over 14 by 12 inches. $180

—A half-plate portrait of two young girls, charmingly posed, the image
in fine condition and enclosed in a full leather case. $75

—In a tiny oval frame scarcely more than two inches long, a portrait of
a man of about thirty years, seated in front of a pedestal and a flowered
curtain with a table nearby on which has been placed a vase of flowers.
                                                                  $42.50

—A "lovely image" of a couple posed in their garden, the picture 6 by
slightly over 5 inches, enclosed in a passepartout mount with the paper
seal "almost intact." $85

—A quarter-plate portrait of a young man, the image very sharply detailed, with the reverse varnished and one spot needing repair. $25

—A sixth plate, the photographer unknown, showing a family at the beach. The detail is sharp, although the picture is fairly dark, the emulsion varnished and painted. $20

—By C. C. Schoonmaker of Troy, a sixth-plate portrait of a mother and child, with "nice side-lighting and inky blacks," in a Union case by S. Peck & Co. $45

—By J. Douglas of Glasgow, a quarter plate of a man, "sharp and contrasty," hand-colored, with the "varnish barely cracking" on the back, and not varnished on the emulsion side. $25

Many of the same criteria which help established value in the daguerreotype also apply to the ambrotype, but there are special considerations as well, some of which may be listed as follows:

—The image should be fairly sharp and contrasty, since this was not always necessarily the case with the ambrotype.

—Both the glass plate and its backing should be in fine condition, although often the appearance of an ambrotype may be dramatically improved simply by substituting a new backing for the old.

—Hand-tinting which shows a delicacy of touch or provides a realistic appearance to a portrait increases value, although by itself hand-tinting does not add to the value of the ambrotype, since such tinting was generally the rule.

—If the ambrotype is enclosed in a case, it is an advantage to have the original seal intact.

—If the ambrotype is a portrait, a gracefulness in the pose or some other compelling or unusual aspect increases value, since on the whole ambrotypes were turned out at a fast clip for a mass market with scant attention paid to posing.

—More interesting than the portrait of a single individual is the picture of several people in a group, particularly if the picture has a folksy or humorous aspect, such as a group of men seated around a table drinking or several children with a dog.

The Lowly Tintype

To many serious collectors of old photographs, the notion that anyone might be interested in collecting tintypes might seem laughable. The "dead grey" surface of the medium and the garishness of a great deal of the tinting, the very speed with which these photographs were so routinely produced—some by itinerant photographers with studios set up in tents—and the fact that they were so cheap: all these facts seem to rule out the possibility of their having any artistic interest. It is true that tintypes, generally, lack artistic merit. Yet the tintype, an American invention and a uniquely American phenomenon from its first appearance in 1856 through the Civil War and into the 1870s—and beyond—has something special to tell us about the American life of that period.

One has only to think for a moment of the role which the tintype played during the Civil War, when another name for the tintype was "lettertype" because of the frequency with which these light, small, and durable photographs were sent through the mails. V. M. Griswold, inventor of the tintype, probably spoke the truth when he stated: "Every soldier (God bless them!) and every soldier's lassie, had to have one or more pictures, and every father, mother, brother, and sister who remained at home had to have such a souvenir of the departing one—departing upon an errand involving such fearful results, and such uncertainty of a future return to reunite the broken chain of family ties and family loves. Many of these little momentoes are all that remain to thousands of sorrowing hearts, to bring up once more the beloved features of those who sleep 'the sleep that knows no waking,' upon many a Southern battle-field, wearing on their bosoms similar momentoes of loved ones at home, whose smiles will greet them no more on this side of the grave.

"Most of these pictures were Ferrotypes . . . which cost but a few cents, and which, but for the discovery of such a process, could never have had an existence in such quantities; their cheapness and means of rapid production only making such universal ownership possible. . . . I know that it has been fashionable, and quite common, to sneer at and ridicule the Ferrotype as an inferior picture, and I do not intend to argue against that assumption; but I venture the assertion, that none of its rivals have given so much pleasure and gratification to so many people of all classes, and none of them can be produced with such directness, certainty, and rapidity; all elements of cheapness and extended usefulness and popularity."

These comments appeared in 1872 in the first edition of *The Ferrotype and How to Make It,* by Edward M. Estabrooke. The overall purpose of Estabrooke's book was to urge ferrotypists to take the fullest advantage of the artistic capabilities inherent in their medium.

From the very beginning, photography had been praised for the uncompromisingly truthfulness of the image. And it had been excoriated just as severely by the traditional artists and by other critics for the uncompromising ugliness of its relentlessly probing vision. In an era which was becoming increasingly sensitive to the possibilities of the photograph as a means of creative expression, the tintype seemed crude.

Yet Estabrooke, although he was fighting a losing battle, pointed out that the tintype, or ferrotype, was, like other forms of photography "quite as willing to heighten artistically the beauty of a Scott-Siddons as to exaggerate the ugliness of a Caliban—to hide in shadows the disagreeable, and to smooth down the projections and wrinkles, as [it might be] to force them with relentless exaggeration upon our attention." A few pages later he added: "Photography takes the human form, sitting bolt upright, without effort to soften or improve. Art comes in, and behold! the pose is changed from rigidity to ease; the light is tempered and made to fall with softening effect upon the features; draperies are employed to give depth of shadow and brilliancy of effect, and the resulting portrait, instead of being barely tolerable—because of likeness to the original—is praised and valued highly, and secures for the skillful operator the gratitude as well as the patronage of all concerned." Estabrooke included in his book two examples of the well-made ferrotype portrait which must win our admiration. Surprising as it may seem, there were societies of tintypists formed not only to discuss sales techniques and technology but the fine points of the aesthetics of their art as well.

Still, most of us today know the tintype by the albums laden with those tiny stiff portraits of frightened-looking people or by the collection of portraits we may occasionally come across of men in various types of uniforms. It may therefore come as news that some fairly high prices have been paid for a few outstanding works in this medium.

For example, each lot judged worth between $40 and $50: a full-length portrait of a young athlete, in whole-plate size, matted and framed, showing him leaning jauntily on his bat, around 1870; another whole plate, framed in a case, of a melancholy youth wearing his Civil War uniform;

and, two portraits together, each of sixth-plate size, one showing a blacksmith in his leather apron and the second a shoemaker seated at his bench, one portrait lacking its case and the other with a damaged case; another pair of ferrotypes, one a tinted horizontal quarter plate, showing three men seated about a table, each holding up a Union case which he is displaying for the camera, the other, a portrait. Another pair of portraits presumably of dead infants, sixth plates which had been tinted and each in a floral case, brought $30. One of the portraits had been treated with a chemical overlay to heighten the somewhat ethereal effect. However, on the other hand, it is not at all uncommon to find a group of as many as 30 portraits offered as a single lot and being sold for no more than $20. At auction, an album containing 45 tintype portraits has sold for $17. As a single lot, 20 tintypes all in their paper frames have sold for a mere $15. And a lot of 25 pictures of women dressed in a fascinating array of bonnets was probably a bargain at $7.

There are many shops and flea markets where a collection of tintypes may be picked up for around 25¢ each, even today. Collections which have already been sorted out by subject and any collections of tintypes all in paper frames are usually sold for more. A collector interested in concentrating on one particular subject in the tintype—such as just portraits of young women, or of children, or men in uniform, or various styles of clothing—would probably be wise to purchase and sort through the piles of tintypes which are sometimes offered as a single lot at a bargain rate.

In searching for valuable images in tintypes, it is worthwhile, however, to look for the really effective photograph, whatever the subject. It is there. It is often found in the larger size, half-plate or even whole-plate size. And it is often not a portrait but rather the picture of a group or of an outdoor scene, almost invariably with people. The following five tintypes sold as a single lot at auction for $37.50: two women seated on the grass under an open umbrella; a family group including the dog, posed in front of an elaborately painted backdrop; a teenager wearing a sailor suit and holding both binoculars and a pistol; three men in an open buggy; and a portrait of a young man.

Tintypes, if they have not been carefully preserved in an album or in miniature cases, are often found in damaged condition. They are frequently lightly scratched and may sometimes be bent. With the passage of time, some have darkened considerably around the edges. If enclosed within a paper frame, as many were, this frame may be either soiled or considerably foxed. All of these conditions must be considered defects.

However, they may at times become relatively unimportant if the image has some interest, shows artistry on the part of the photographer, or reveals to us some interesting aspect of nineteenth-century life.

Two of the most fascinating kinds of tintypes are those "gems" of tiny size which were set into jewelry—lockets, breastpins, and medallions—and those which were used in campaign buttons. These images were put to a special use and are priced with reference to considerations outside the field of photography.

Card Photographs

Collecting cartes de visite was a popular fad which swept the United States, as well as all of Europe, in the year 1859. These cards originated in France, where the design for them had been patented by the enterprising photographer Disderi in 1854. Collecting cards continued to be fashionable through the Civil War years in this country, to the extent that the card portrait became the standard kind of studio portrait for those years until replaced by the similiar but slightly larger cabinet card in the late 1860s and early 1870s. Among the cards most highly prized today are those showing Civil War soldiers and those, much more rare, showing Civil War scenes. Among the types of cards which were popularly collected on both sides of the Atlantic were those showing members of European royalty and those depicting the leading European statesmen of the day. Among the legions of public figures who were willing to pose for their portrait on a carte de visite and authorized the distribution of copies, none were more adept at striking a good pose than the actors and actresses who found themselves as much at ease before a camera lens and a single photographer as before a large audience. Recognizing the great publicity value in these cards, they frequently posed in the costumes for current or especially popular roles. Any large collection of cartes de visite can read like a roster of "Who Was Who" in the world of power and politics and the theater. Albums containing cartes de visite are usually arranged with the "publics"—cards showing the great men of the day, the kings and queens and the leading political figures admired in one's family —first, followed by the portraits of the members of the family.

These cards made collecting photographs open to just about everyone.

The British royal family was reported to be as enthusiastic about collecting them as everyone else.

The carte de visite, 2½ by 4¼ inches, has a mounted photograph which has been made on a paper of "superior quality, well-albumenized, possessing a heavy gloss, white, and free from spots." It was thus sufficiently durable so that the cards might be sorted and re-sorted and shuffled about in a collection, sent through the mails and exchanged, left out on the table, or stored fairly carelessly. The cards were routinely toned and often varnished for even greater durability. Sometimes the image was colored, and then the varnishing process might be necessary to help retain the color. They were made to be handled and exposed to the light.

These cards are often found in a condition which may be described as from fairly good to truly excellent. There may sometimes be a slight soiling; sometimes they are lightly foxed. Occasionally the image will be found starting to peel from its mount, and when this starts to happen there may also be some marginal tears. However, such relatively small defects may be outweighed by the importance of the style of presentation or the unusualness of the subject, as well as the rarity of the card.

According to N. G. Burgess's *Photograph Manual*, a work popular in the 1860s, "the visiting portraits" are "full-length miniatures of the human face and form . . . generally taken in a standing position, with a landscape background, or one made with panel paper, or a plain background having a small portion of a curtain in view. Some have a pedestal, or a pillar or column represented, with the subject resting the hand gracefully upon the one or the other." In addition, a variety of other props might be introduced by the photographer. He might embellish the little scene with an ornamental chair, an urn made of wood or plaster of Paris, or any article of drawing room furniture provided it were sufficiently elegant. The panel paper to which reference is made is a kind of wallpaper which has been pasted to a screen so that it might be employed as a movable background.

Diverting as some of these fancy backgrounds may be, the excitement in collecting cards lay in accumulating an assortment of the most popular portraits. Collecting cartes de visite before 1870 was somewhat analogous to the fad for collecting postcards 40 years later, or, much later, baseball cards. Many collectors boasted that they had thousands of cards and it seems improbable that more than a few of these collectors were particularly interested in the quality of any of the separate images, although it is true that among the most sought-after cards there were some of outstanding merit from the "best" studios. One result of this collecting fever is that there are still plenty of routinely made, relatively uninteresting cards on today's market for which there is little demand.

At auction, a collection of about 80 portraits of babies and small children has brought lazy bids of $8, $9, $10. A collection of up to 100 cards portraying men of various ages is bid in at about the same amount, though an equal number of cards showing women, young and old, may be considered worth $15, possibly because of the greater variety of the clothing. An assortment of 60 cards, hand-colored, showing the native costumes of Holland, Switzerland, and France, is likely to go for a bid of no more than $14. Cards showing scenes throughout Great Britain or views of England, mostly of cathedrals, frequently are sold at auction for no more than 30¢ or 40¢ per card. Many dealers are now pricing cards at 50¢ to $1.

Some examples of cards sold by the lot at auction include the following:

—10 views of various American scenes. $19
—14 portraits of "American reformers and diplomats." $35
—9 publics of actresses, made around 1870. $17
—7 cards of curiosities including midgets and side-show performers.
                                                                   $22.50
—61 scenes in Europe, including architecture and ruins. $20
—73 "sentimentals" mostly either depicting children or made specifically for children, including many with a religious theme. $11
—15 cards, in good condition, including the portraits of kings and national leaders. $37.50
—14 portraits of authors and illustrators. $35
—60 portraits, mostly from lithographs, or engravings rather than direct portraits. $27.50
—54 portraits of famous people, almost all from engravings, paintings, or lithographs. $30
—A set of 13 cards, portraits of Union and Confederate soldiers. $27.50
—Portraits of 14 Union soldiers and generals. $32.50
—6 portraits of contemporaries of Abraham Lincoln and one card of a Lincoln portrait. $32.50

—A collection of 13 cartes de visite, a curious assortment of Union and Confederate soldiers, including some Confederate officers, and a photograph of Confederate flags. $80
—Two cards attributed to Brady, probably made in 1863, showing Confederate soldiers in front of a barn, and with cannons and trenches in the background. $80

Cartes de visite, cabinet cards, and old mounted photographs—many of us have these in our family collections. Some are charming, others chiefly notable for the details of costume shown. The photography is often routine. There is growing interest in collecting these late-nineteenth century photographs by subject, or for the name of the studio. The gentleman above has been identified as H. W. Herrick, wood-engraver and artist, an exhibition of whose work was recently shown by the Manchester (N. H.) Historic Society. The photographer, who is unknown, appears to have had some talent.

—"Quite a rare lot" of cards related to the South, including a portrait of Robert E. Lee.　　　　　　　　$65

—A set of two portraits of Mary Todd Lincoln, made by E. Anthony and by M. Brady; lightly foxed, otherwise good.　　　　　　$32.50

—From Brady's National Portrait Gallery, a single card titled "Edwin Booth and Daughter" and published by E. and H. T. Anthony.　$22.50

—An album containing a modest 22 cards, including some from negatives by Brady, and all of persons prominent around 1861.　　　$40

—An album bound in green morocco, containing 100 cartes de visite of various Victorian personalities, including cards by Disderi, Sarony, Silvy.
$150

—Another 100, similar in content, also from the best known studios.
$225

—An album of important Civil War personalities containing about 160 cards, most from Brady's Gallery or that operated by Gurney, both in New York City. The album is gilt-decorated morocco and the cards are window-mounted and with pencilled identifications.　　　$550

Six uncut cartes de visite by A. Calavas, studio portraits of nudes made in the 1870s in Paris for a sample album, have, as a single lot, brought $80.

Many cards are considered more valuable because they are of important people during the American Civil War or because they were made by one of the most admired photographic studios of the day.

There are a few cards individually rare enough to command a high price, such as the portrait of Samuel Morse by Sarony which recently brought $70 at auction.

For people who collect photographs, cartes de visite showing a photographer's rig, his horse and van perhaps, or the steps leading up to his studio under the overhanging sign, seem to have a special attraction. Such an "occupational card" may bring anywhere from $35 to over $100 at auction.

Sorting through a great many cards and albums of cards may occasionally prove rewarding. Amid the many duplicates and dull pictures there may be a treasure or two: sold at auction at Sotheby Parke Bernet in New York, two albums including 185 cards by Brady—an almost complete representation of the Union Senators and Congressmen, many of the cards signed by the subject either on the carte itself or in the album, including Lincoln's portrait, signed by him below—brought $2,800.

For the beginning collector, the name of the game is recognition. At flea markets, church sales, privately held "tag" or garage sales, and in out-of-the-way shops one may still find tables of cards for the customer to sort through. Since the worthwhile card is one of a well-known public personality, the ability to recognize the important faces of the period can pay off. A study of illustrated history books helps. More immediately useful may be the *Dictionary of American Portraits* (1967) compiled by Hayward and Blanche Cirker and published by Dover. When cards can sometimes be found priced as low as 15¢ each, the recognition game can become a worthwhile hobby as well as a fascinating one.

Cabinet Cards

The cabinet card, which is slightly larger than the carte de visite— about 4½ by 6½ inches to accommodate the mounting of a slightly smaller photograph—was introduced around 1866 as a fashionable new variation on the earlier carte de visite. An aggressive promotion on the part of the studios issuing these new cards had the effect of enlarging the fad for collecting cards and of encouraging the production of albums as a means of storing these cards and displaying them as well.

Since they were produced in vast numbers and were highly durable, cabinet cards are still available in quantity. Some individual cards of especially attractive, interesting, or odd subjects may be worth $5 to $10. These cards are more frequently, however, to be found at prices no higher than 50¢, at small shops and flea markets, for example. The collector himself sorts through them to find the interesting ones. A good working knowledge of American history may help in identifying the subjects of importance, and a familiarity with the social customs of the 1870s can help in spotting those cards which may be truly unusual. Cabinet cards are rarely offered at important photographic auctions, and when they are it is usually in huge lots. One of the highest prices paid recently at auction for a collection of cards was for an album containing about 40 portraits of American authors and statesmen, and it achieved a bid of $200. The cards were all window-mounted in an album of calf binding, many of them identified as to subject, and several of the cards were signed. The same sum of $200 has been paid for a single cabinet card, a portrait of the author George Sand by the photographer Nadar, but this is truly a great exception in the general price range.

Collectors of cabinet cards are sometimes more interested in an aspect of the card other than the image itself. Since retouching was customary with these portrait cards, there are collectors who are primarily interested in the various special effects which were achieved by different photographers. After around 1875 cabinet cards were sometimes produced by one of the photo-mechanical processes which had by that time become available. These processes included the Woodburytype and the Artotype, producing "permanent" photographs which may now be separately collected. The backs of the cabinet cards were customarily lavishly decorated with advertising for the studio, in a style invented by Disderi for the earlier carte de visite. These marvelously embellished ads appeal to some collectors, who are as interested in the styles of advertising and the location of the studio as in the image. Two of the large and prestigious studios whose work is collected are J. M. Mora and Napoleon Sarony, both noted for the quality of their portraits.

Lantern Slides

Lantern slides—images on glass to be projected for viewing—seem, to date, to have stirred little interest in the collectors of photographic materials. However, as a demonstration of what really interested the American public in the 50 years between 1870 and 1920 they may have few parallels. Lantern slides show us: the scenic West; exotic views abroad; the streets of San Francisco, New York, and other American cities before the automobile; disasters which excited the imagination; the Navy, the Army, and the posturing and the actual events of war. Among the producers of these lantern slides were Sears Roebuck, Underwood & Underwood, the Scovill Manufacturing Company, Eastman Kodak, and the Keystone View Company, as well as the New York Motion Picture Company and such institutions as the American Social Hygiene Association. Slides showing courting couples in a series of poses were made to be shown during the playing of a specific song. Slides were offered in a series of comic cartoons, as well, sure to arouse appreciative laughter each time they were shown. A boxed series of slides was offered, pictures and text together, for the handy presentation of a lecture on hygiene, physical fitness, or good personal relationships.

With the lantern slide, stay-at-homes could enjoy the sights which would greet the well-heeled traveler. Views of Samoa, Alaska, Japan, and Italy were all popular. There was also a good market for the handsomely boxed set of American views, especially those of California or Yosemite, particularly if some of the views were colored.

The lantern slide is a photograph enclosed within glass, the edges usually sealed with a paper tape although sometimes it is framed in wood. The standard size is 3¼ by 4 inches. A set of slides was sold in a fitted oak box with a removable top and two clasps and a hook. There might also be included a compartmented wooden sliding apparatus for inserting each slide into the lantern. A complete set as issued, still in its original box, is most highly valued. Slides still packed in their own neat box are frequently found in excellent condition, and the collector need not settle for slides which have suffered damage. Damage may include spotting or cracked, chipped, or scratched glass. Sometimes the paper seal is starting to peel off, and sometimes it is lacking. Just slight damage to a few slides in a complete set might not, however, affect the value of the set too seriously.

A complete set of 50 views might bring, at an important auction, anywhere from $35 to $65. Also at auction, individual slides of particular interest have been purchased for between $2 and $5. However, at flea markets and out-of-the-way shops, it is undoubtedly still possible to purchase fascinating slides for a great deal less.

Stereographs

The stereograph, or stereogram as it has also sometimes been called, was first produced commercially around 1850. Initially made on either glass or paper and later almost overwhelmingly on paper, or "board," the stereograph remained popular for decades, well into the twentieth century.

The stereograph is a pairing of two photographs which have been taken simultaneously through twin lenses, usually set in one camera, just 2¼ inches apart so as to approximate human vision by duplicating the distance between the eyes. When viewed through the stereopticon, the effect can be stunningly realistic. The three-dimensional single picture

which the viewer sees is capable of exaggerating depth and distance for
such dramatic results that a feeling of vertigo may result. A single one
of the pair of photographs might also, of course, be reproduced separately
without the special effect.

During the last half of the nineteenth century, gathering in the parlor
to look at a series of stereographs, handing the stereopticon back and
forth with each new view, had all the attraction that watching television
has today. The ingenuity of the stereo publishers in producing fascinating material seemed almost limitless. In a time when travel for pleasure
was a privilege restricted to the very rich, stereos brought home the antiquities of ancient Greece and Rome, the streets of Paris and London,
the magnificence of cathedrals, works of art, the Alps, peasant costume,
the wonders of the American West, and, later on, a feeling of how it might
have been to be present at important historic events. The market seemed
able to absorb thousands of these stereos offering a window on the world.
Eventually the stereo publishers expanded their business into the publication of the instructive lecture, the humorous anecdote, even the naughty
picture.

The earliest stereos, produced before the Civil War, now have an antiquarian value quite aside from any aesthetic value they may possess.
These earliest may be identified not only by subject and costume, as well
as publisher, but by the fact that they were made on a relatively thin
stock. It was only in the early 1860s that the more familiar heavy board
began to be used. At first the corners of the stereo card were square and
only later were they rounded off. The color of the card also helps to date
it. Those produced before 1861 were generally of a light color, varying
from white to cream or grey. When the heavy board began to be used, it
was grey and of a dull appearance. Then, somewhere between 1860 and
1863 some cards began to appear in a light yellow color, and, following
the Civil War, cards blossomed out into a variety of shades—pink, violet,
green, blue, and even purple or red. Very late, after 1890, the cards,
which by then had again reverted to grey, were curved to increase the
illusion of depth. Early in the twentieth century some cards of a deep
charcoal color were also produced.

Among all the various types of old photographs which are collected,
stereographs join the carte de visite and the cabinet card in being both
photograph and published material. The Langenheim firm in Philadelphia
was one of the first in America to enter the field of producing stereographs. Their interest began with the glass slides they called hyalotypes
and expanded to unmounted twin pictures on paper. Early Langenheim

stereos are always identified with the firm's name. In 1855 this same firm also became the first to market as one a whole set of views of the same or related subjects. The Langenheim brothers also pioneered in being the first to assign their own photographer to go out into the field and take pictures to order for stereos they thought would prove popular. Among the especially popular views produced by Langenheim are those showing Niagara Falls and views of the White Mountains, today worth possibly $10 apiece. Although the glass stereo views may be offered for less, $20 is not an unusual price for an early view, and a view such as that of Mt. Washington with the Langenheim imprint and a handwritten caption has brought $70 at auction.

Another early trade series of special interest to collectors of stereos is that issued by the book publishing firm of D. Appleton & Co. of New York. Their stereographs were produced in fairly limited quantity. During this same initial period the photographic studio of E. Anthony, in 1859, also began to market its own stereos. The later Anthony views of the Civil War, bearing the Brady credit line, are among those especially valued today. Collecting Anthony views has the advantage that not only is each view labelled and thus identified, but there is also generally a descriptive line or two. Among the leading foreign producers of stereographs were Ferrier of France and the London Stereoscopic Company. The latter produced a number of views of American scenes, including the sights to be seen in New York City. If in fine condition, a single stereograph from the London "North American" series may be worth up to $15. The Canadian firm of Notman also produced stereographs, and one of its earliest views, on a cream-colored mount, may, if in good condition, be worth a similar amount. Other Canadian publishers included Climo's and Ellison.

Among the most enduringly popular cards were those showing Niagara Falls. Two of the best known photographers of the Falls were Platt D. Babbitt and J. McPherson. Other well-entrenched subjects were the Brooklyn Bridge, the architectural triumphs of Europe, the ruins of antiquity, and statuary, including the monuments erected to the heroes of the Civil War. Those who did not own an example of the genre sculpture of John Rogers might at least view it on a stereogram. Disasters such as floods, fires, and wrecks sold stereographs in the nineteenth century the way they sell newspapers today. The extremely lifelike pictures of public personalities, including actresses, were popular also. The Philadelphia Centennial celebration in 1876 caused an outpouring of stereographs as did the Alaska gold rush.

There are many stereo cards which we might classify today as oddities.

They include those showing a "departed one" with an attempt made at adding a three-dimensional effect to what was originally an ordinary photograph by inserting the photograph within an actual wreath and then re-photographing with the dual lens. Also, today we find the "comic" scenes which we may no longer find amusing, and a portrayal of the events leading to a wedding, from the first encounter through the proposal, to the boudoir. One odd series of cards, copyrighted in 1868 by Charles H. Shute & Son, purported to show actual whaling scenes but was actually a fairly crude set-up from models. Even photographs of flat religious paintings were made into stereographs, but these display a lack of understanding of the stereo process.

In a field of many competitors, the firm of Kilburn Brothers in Littleton, New Hampshire, emerged, around 1873, as the largest producer of stereo cards in the world. Having started with its local views of the White Mountains—which are now the most valued cards issued by this company—and in 1875 changing its name to Benjamin Kilburn & Co., by 1905 this single firm was publishing over five million cards annually.

Contrary to what might possibly be expected, stereo cards which were colored are not necessarily more valuable than those not tinted. Similarly, the lithoprint stereo of later date is not especially valued. The lithoprint stereo became popular beginning in 1898. On the other hand, the "tissue"—which is often colored—is highly esteemed. One reason for its value is that it is so fragile that few have endured and it has therefore become relatively scarce. The "tissue" is a stereograph which is viewed by looking through the picture rather than by seeing the picture by reflected light. It therefore anticipated our modern transparency. Possibly the first tissues were imported from France at some time between 1865 and 1875. Such cards include those called "diableries." Designed to fascinate and horrify, these pictures of the Devil and of the tortures of the damned in Hell are backed with red-tinted paper or are colored red, and, in addition, there are pin-prick perforations to simulate the whites of eyes, etc. Using the same technique for a bizarre effect are the fairly gaudy theater scenes also imported from France at around the same time. One of these is probably worth at least $3, possibly much more.

William Culp Darrah, author of *Stereo Views: A History of Stereographs in America and their Collection* (privately published in 1964), states there are basically four different types of collections of stereos. The general collection, which can be fairly eclectic, is one which becomes more important the larger it grows. Even though such a collection might start with as few as 100 cards, it could easily grow into thousands upon thousands. To begin such a collection, he suggests the purchase, from a reputable dealer, of a large representative assortment covering a wide range of many types of cards. From this beginning, he says, the collector can specialize should he eventually decide to do so. With a bit of luck, many interesting individual cards may still be picked up for about 25¢, and sometimes the purchase of a great many cards will eventually turn up one which is truly rare and thus valuable. Darrah estimates that a rare card might be one in 1,000, although he admits it might possibly be only one in 10,000.

After the general collection, there is the collection by subject. There is no end to the possible subjects. Just a few of the possibilities are the portraits of famous people, or cards showing dolls, Masonic materials, Catholica, the White Mountains, the circus. A third category is geography: cards showing a particular city, state, or foreign country, or even one particular feature of history. Lastly, one might collect the work of an individual photographer or publisher. Such a collection can prove the most difficult of all, since it is the general practice to sort these cards by subject rather than source.

So many stereographic prints are to be found in such fine condition that the collector need not accept those which are damaged, unless, of course, the particular subject or the early date provides a compelling reason. The earliest prints made on paper may be somewhat faded. Some are lightly rubbed. Sometimes prints are soiled from excessive use or improper storing. The paper may be foxed, or the photographic emulsion may be slightly cracked. Occasionally a card may have some slight surface tears.

It is worth noting that the date of the stereo on glass is extremely important. One made in the twentieth century may be worth 25¢ or nothing at all. However, a set of three views of Niagara Falls made by S. Mason in 1858, in size 6¾ by 3¼ inches, brought $37.50 at auction, even though the glass had some fine cracks and the image was spotted. A group of four tinted glass stereos of Niagara Falls, by F. Langenheim, each still in the Langenheim firm's original mount with title, credit line, and the date (1856), brought $275 at an auction conducted by Sotheby Parke Bernet in New York.

Also at auction, the following lots of American views have commanded over $50: a collection of 20 views of *Alaska*, including 9 from the Keystone series of 1898; a set of 24 stereographs depicting the life of *Blacks*, made around 1900, including scenes in the cotton fields, children, and a Black regiment in training; 21 cards of *Blacks*, with "racial humor" printed in the margin; 18 views of *Boston* from the "America Illustrated"

These faces reveal the ordeal endured by settlers who have just escaped an Indian massacre. In 1862, Chief Little Crow led an uprising in the upper Minnesota River Valley to protest the failure of the Government to honor Indian claims. This picture is one of the stereographs issued by J. E. Whitney in his series titled "Gems of Minnesota Scenery." (Courtesy of the Library of Congress USZ62-11024.)

A photograph made in 1886 by C. S. Fly of Tombstone, Arizona, shows a captive white boy in Geronimo's camp. The photograph only recently became known. (Courtesy of the Photo Album Gallery, Los Angeles, California.)

series; a large collection of 84 views of the Philadelphia *Centennial Exhibition* of 1876; a set of stereo cards 4 by 7 inches or even larger showing mountain scenes in *Colorado*, the cards thought to date from around 1880; 40 cards of *Massachusetts*, showing various historical sites, possibly dating from 1880; 11 views of *Michigan*, including residences, with both printed and handwritten captions; 28 views of *Ausable Chasm*, four with the revenue stamp affixed; a single "well-composed" view showing the lower falls at Trenton in *Oneida County*, New York; 16 views of *Yosemite* by C. E. Watkins, all with printed captions and most in good condition; a group of just 7 cards also by *Watkins*, from the 1860s; a group of 38 *Yosemite* cards dating from around 1900.

Stereo cards which are likely to be more valuable are: cards depicting Indian life or showing early views of western scenery; scenes from the Civil War, especially if from the photographs made by the team headed by Mathew B. Brady; stereographs which depict Blacks; and views derived from photographs taken by the men associated with either government surveys of the West or the building of the railroads. A fine portrait or a card in very fine condition will naturally be prized. Beyond that, at least from the evidence of the activity in the market, it would be unwise to attempt to generalize further.

Stereographs showing foreign views, so popular for parlor viewing with the Victorians whose opportunities for travel were limited, today often attract the beginning collector. Since they are usually offered for sale already sorted by country, this may make finding particular cards relatively easy. At auction, the following sets of cards sorted by subject have all sold at over $50 for the lot: issued by the firm of Underwood & Underwood, the boxed set published to resemble a handsomely bound pair of books, collections showing scenes in *Burma, China, Egypt, Japan, Mexico*, the *Philippines*, all offered separately at auction; also, 45 views by *Francis Frith* showing Egypt and the Holy Land, including 8 signed in the negative; a collection of various views all of *English cathedrals* produced at various times over the last half of the nineteenth century; 29 views of various scenes in *Europe*, all backed with hand-tinted papers, some perforated; 31 views made by *Hippolyte Jouvin*, most from the Vue Instantee series c. 1870; 22 "scenes animees" of *France*, all with hand-tinted backing papers; 60 views of *Germany* produced between 1850 and 1880; 50 views of Japan, including three hand-tinted, most in very fine condition, made around 1900; 16 views of Scottish scenery attributed to *George Washington Wilson*, somewhat faded; 75 cards from the *Spanish-American War* in Cuba, made by either James M. Davis or W. B. Kilburn.

The Photograph Album

In American homes of some standing during the late nineteenth century, the photograph album—elaborately bound in velvet, perhaps, and with brass clasps—was as characteristic of the style of the day as the elaborately carved and fringed furniture, the potted fern standing in the corner, and the sculpture by John Rogers. At that time the album provided entertainment for an evening at home, it was a reminder of friends and relatives whose pictures were there but who lived too far away to visit frequently, and it also provided a solemn review of one's ancestry, at least back to those persons still living in the 1850s. There were elderly men and women who had been born back in the eighteenth century who had consented to sit before the camera, often returning the stare of the uncapped lens with their own self-conscious stare.

The notion of hanging a photograph on the wall had not yet occurred, and the thought of "art" photography would have seemed outlandish to those who prized the technique of photography as a means of recording reality. The daguerreotype and the ambrotype had been cherished for their honesty, but each of these forms of photography was delicate enough so that it had to be protected under glass. The arrival of photographs on paper, produced by the wet-collodion method invented in the early 1850s, released a flood of portraits, first the carte de visite and then later the cabinet card. These mementoes on stiff cardboard were at first simply collected by the fistful, as collectors enthusiastically exchanged portraits of relatives including young people, men in uniform, newlyweds, successful men, the old, and the deceased. By the early 1860s, however, the idea of an album as a means of saving and preserving photographs had already become popular. Albums were designed to be the suitably large and elaborate repositories for a family collection which might number hundreds of pictures, and, of course, as an appropriately ornate addition to the parlor furnishings. An album might be bound in velvet, calf, or morocco and decorated with mother-of-pearl. A few concealed music boxes which would commence to play when the front cover was lifted. By 1876 at least one firm had begun to market an album which contained stereo cards and a fold-out pair of lenses for viewing the cards.

Most albums held card photographs which were inserted into pages which were fitted with recessed pockets to hold the pictures. There might be two of the larger cards to a page, often inserted back-to-back so that each side of the page displayed pictures. Or, many tiny tintypes might be displayed on a single page. If the photographs were the larger ones on paper, the album would constitute a record of a family's enthusiasms, by including "publics"—portraits made and sold by the big studios, showing persons prominent in public life, from actresses to the members of the nobility. A visitor to the family, by turning the pages of the album, might come to know how this family felt about politics and world affairs. If the album also included the pictures of art or of foreign scenes (as it might after the 1870s) the visitor might also begin to understand the family's taste in a number of other areas as well.

We may become excited when we learn that one dealer in photographica has priced at over $3,000 a set of seven albums containing photographs—more than 750 albumen prints—collected on a trip around the world made in 1877, and we might wonder if among our own family collection of albums there might be one or two worth at least a fourth, or even a tenth of that. It is possible, but perhaps unlikely. This particular set of albums had the following advantages: the photographs were each mounted separately, on single leaves rather than back to back; the collection included both unusual views and those made by photographers who are now eagerly collected; included were 11 large Yosemite views, possibly by Muybridge, an unusual picture of a scene from the Madras famine of 1876, a number of folding panoramic views of cities, and some views of scenes in China which may have been taken by John Thomson; the seven volumes were uniformly bound in quarter green morocco.

It is more likely that any albums we own date from around the turn of the century—or later—and represent the activities of one or two camera buffs in the family. As Gail Buckland has pointed out in *Reality Recorded/Early Documentary Photography* (1974) published by the Graphic Society, the photographs preserved in a family album are usually of two types: the simple and straightfoward "snapshot" taken quickly for the photographer's own pleasure; and the image which can be said to be "created" rather than "snatched." In the latter instance, the photographer is "thinking in terms of communicating part of what he feels about the occasion, the place, or the person. He considers composition, time and movement and tries to give a comprehensible form to his perceptions." Although this may, in retrospect, be imputing greater care and discretion to the photographer than he was actually exercising, still the

Demonstrating that a stylish picture need not be dull, this portrait of the actress Anna Held was made by Aime Dupont of Fifth Avenue, New York, around 1900. (Courtesy of the Library of Congress USZ62-11046.)

distinction between the two kinds of photographs is an important one. A great many family albums contain, of course, a mixture of the two kinds of pictures, and it is the fortunate family that has had at least some part of its history recorded by the truly artistic and thoughtful photographer. Albums consisting entirely of photographs of the snapshot variety do not interest collectors—unless, perhaps, the pictures happen to be the unique record of some newsworthy events important not only within the family but for the world at large.

The work of the really careful photographer is exemplified in the section of *Reality Recorded* devoted to the work of Colonel Henry Wood (1834–1919), which is the concluding section of this book based on an exhibit of documentary photography held in 1972 at the Victoria and Albert Museum in London. Colonel Wood became interested in photography in 1860. He used the wet-plate method of the day, which required elaborate and painstaking preparation of each plate before it was placed in the camera, and then immediate development. Not only were his pictures carefully composed, they were as thoughtfully arranged later in the family album. He was successful with his "straight" photography, as Gail Buckland points out, because he "put creative, psychological and emotional energies into his photographs." In other words, he was a family photographer of unusual talent and great dedication as well as technical ability. Today, his affection for his subjects still shines through his photographs, inviting us to enjoy the scenes which so clearly delighted him. We are additionally fortunate in that his family passed through scenes, both in India and elsewhere, which seem strange and even glamorous to us today. We see his wife strangely deflated, having shed her crinoline underskirt to go mountain climbing, the children playing games or play-acting for the benefit of the camera, and we are admitted to the crowded interior of their Victorian home. Additional interest is provided by the fact that a number of Colonel Wood's pictures are composed in clever montage. His photographs give us considerable insight into how he and his family lived, the photographs are interesting in themselves, and his documentary is both amusing and enlightening.

The sad truth of the matter is that probably few of the family albums tucked away in trunks and boxes in the attic could qualify as amusing, or technically excellent, or, in most cases, particularly enlightening for a general public. This does not mean that they are not delightful to own, since they provide a sense of family history available only through photography. The type of album which would also be of some interest to the social historian might be one containing the pictures of men who were famous—or infamous—ranging from a general in the Civil War to the brothers Frank and Jesse James. A family album can also have a specific interest for the community where the family lived and thus be of great value to a local historical society or museum.

Occasionally there is an album which is valuable as the record of a public project, such as the building of a railroad or highway, an airfield, or dam; or of an occupation or way of life now gone, such as that of the blacksmith or itinerant photographer; or of customs and fashions peculiar to the nineteenth century. One album which recently came into the market consisted of a collection of over 400 photographs of gravestones and memorials, all assembled before 1883 and apparently the work of one photographer. Because of its rather technical interest, this album was valued by a dealer at $125. Another album, valued at $65, contained 34 prints showing the progress of the construction of New York City's Fourth Avenue subway between 1913 and 1917, each photograph carefully identified. The historic interest of this particular album was clearly apparent.

Among the albums most likely to have some monetary value are those in which the photographs possess some continuity and the photographer has clearly had a story he wished to tell. It helps if both the photographer and the place are definitely identified. The date or at least the approximate date should be established. In general, those albums which were compiled before 1870 are the more valuable, although many albums of a later date include photographs from an earlier period. An interesting or unusual subject may be more important than the date, however, and of course a truly lovely image or collection of such images will always be admired. There are undoubtedly many photographs of high merit yet to be discovered still tucked away in albums along with more routine work.

It is hard to make sense out of the bald reports of an auction in which a number of albums were offered and brought in widely differing bids. The following three lots were sold at a single auction:

—Together, *three* family albums, mostly containing studio photographs and including a number of handsome portraits, but with the bindings of all three albums definitely shabby, the albums undated but possibly from around 1910. $15

—A collection of *eleven* personal albums, mostly records compiled from trips taken abroad some time early in the twentieth century, the photographs of various places, various dates. $130

—*Two* albums containing 75 and 300 photographs respectively, most of

them professional studio views, many showing Italy and other European
countries, possibly from around 1875. $180

Without being able to know what else may have been involved, we
can see that the earlier albums, with their professional photographs, are
apparently of more interest than an entirely personal family album. Those
family albums which were made up between 1890 and around 1910 rarely
sell at auction for more than $20 unless they contain some unusual ma-
terial such as the report of a trip to some little-explored land. The album
which depicts a potpourri of events which time has robbed of their meaning, or one in which the photographs are uniformly undistinguished, may
have no takers. A high price of $65 has been paid for a single album of-
fered at auction which contained 60 cartes de visite and a goodly number
of tintypes as well as some cabinet cards, including the portraits of celebrities, all mounted within imitation wood covers decorated with heavy
metal clasps. Yet many albums more handsomely bound in morocco or calf
and containing up to several hundred cabinet cards have frequently sold
for one-third of that amount. Albums which, from the catalogue description alone, appear to be remarkably similar may sell for widely different
amounts, over $60 or under $20. Each album had 20 boards and thus
about the same number of photographs. The bindings were similar. Without personally examining these two albums, we cannot really know why
one should be worth more, the other less.

The album containing early Kodak prints is in a class by itself. It is
not surprising to find $160 paid at auction for a single personal album
with its 188 photographs taken with the historic Kodak No. 2. The images,
in this particular case, included 75 taken on a tour made through Japan,
and there were explanatory hand-written captions to accompany the pictures. The album itself was a quarto (large) portfolio with a half binding
of black morocco, and it was believed to date from around 1893.

Fortunately, the pictures taken with the first two Kodak cameras issued by the Eastman Company are easy to identify by their shape and
size. Kodak No. 1, put on the market in 1888, was outfitted with film and
came from the factory already loaded for 100 negatives. The exposed
film had to be returned to the factory for processing. The prints, which
were returned along with the camera, which had been once more loaded,
were circular and a scant 2½ inches in diameter. Each was separately
mounted within a gilt-edged chocolate-colored frame. In the Kodak No.
2, which was put on the market the following year, the image was enlarged to a circle 3½ inches in diameter.

It was only in the 1890s that the modern type of family album, with its multitude of pictures, including snapshots, became possible, following upon the sale of cameras advertised as "No work: You push the button, we do the rest." Before the Kodak, there were few amateur photographers with the time, patience, skill, and money to produce enough work to merit its being mounted in an album. This fact helps explain the popularity of the commercially produced albums which were sold in great numbers at the end of the nineteenth century. A great many of these were travel albums, although others were organized around a theme, such as the English royal family or an exhibition of science or art. There was also the album fairly arbitrarily arranged around an artificial theme, such as one produced by the firm of Mora, which contained the photographs of society belles each dressed in the costume of a different nationality.

The album format may include contents of a widely varying nature, as the following kinds of publications and personal collections, all listed by one house under the heading of "album," attest.

—*Skating Troupe*: an album of 20 photographs inserted within bordered frames, showing both male and female skaters, one of the women fetchingly attired in tights, apparently a professional troupe but unidentified as to country, possibly dating from the 1880s. $35

—*Concord, Massachusetts*: A collection of 33 original photographs of various Revolutionary War sites, apparently made in the late nineteenth century, along with a few other scenes and some portraits, the 6 by 8 inch photographs mounted in a white-board oblong folio album. $55

—*Costume des Pays*: A folding type of album, with 12 mounted photographs in color, possibly dating from 1895. $27.50

—*Early Minnesota*: In all, 50 photographs published by Witney's Gallery of St. Paul, each window-mounted, the album mounted in brown morocco with the original brass clasps, perhaps dating from the 1860s. $425

—*Rocky Mountains*: A collection of 46 mounted photochrome views designated as "superb" by the auction house, all published around 1903 by the Detroit Photographic Company. $200

—*Biplanes*: A collection of 230 photographs, including views of biplanes on takeoff; the year is 1919 and the photographs are excellent. $15

Looking over the reports of the prices paid for various kinds of albums offered in the market, it can be readily seen that without the opportunity to examine each and to compare, it is close to impossible to generalize

The ultimate snapshot: Here is George Eastman, on the deck of the S. S. Gallia in 1890, aiming his own Kodak at the photographer, who is Fred Church. This picture provides a fine example of the excellence possible with the early Kodak. In addition, our knowledge that the man in the picture is Eastman, the inventor and promoter of this particular camera which was to revolutionize photography, makes this an important photograph. The pose, concentrating on the camera, adds yet another dimension. (Courtesy of the International Museum of Photography/ George Eastman House.)

concerning value. Presented at auction recently were two albums each containing a collection of cartes de visite. The first, probably made up around 1861, contained 50 portraits of various notables, many of them English. With its fine morocco binding and brass clasps, it commanded $500 in the auction rooms of Sotheby Parke Bernet. The second, offered at another auction house, brought only $8. Dating from the Civil War period, it contained the portraits of 80 different young women, mostly by New England photographers. This binding was also morocco, with eight white glass bosses and two metal clasps, and all edges were gilt. The house had estimated that it would bring $100. Perhaps the right bidder was simply not in the room, or perhaps a lucky bidder was. Or, the first album may have contained at least a few rare and unusual photographs.

There is one special type of album which deserves separate mention. This is the college or school annual. Apart from the merit of its photography, the annual may be of special interest to the institution itself or to its alumni, or it may contain a rare photograph of some person who later achieved prominence. However, any class book published before 1860 is sure to be of interest and thus worth perhaps up to $70 or even $100, whether it contains mounted or inserted photographs, cartes de visite or tintypes. The later annuals, with pictures and text printed together, are worth much less.

It is possible that in the future the photograph album may represent one of the more lively areas in collecting. There are still many albums in the possession of the original families, their contents assumed to be of a limited interest. Undoubtedly we have yet to discover many excellent photographers and many fine images tucked away.

Published Material

In recent years we have seen a rapidly growing interest in a variety of kinds of publications which have significance for the history of photography. These publications include books about photographic processes with examples of early photography contained as illustrations, books by photographers, books about individual photographers and their work, the early photographic journals, and all kinds of ephemera. One example of ephemera is the advertising brochure for the photographic parlor specializing in the daguerreotype or ambrotype. Another, produced more than a century later, and thus fairly recent, is the handsome poster illustrated with a dramatic montage produced on the occasion of a museum or gallery exhibit of old photographs—or even for the work of a modern master.

Many nineteenth-century books of interest to the photographic historian are now considered worth $100 or more. It is no longer unusual to find, removed from the original book, early illustrations produced by some now outmoded process such as the Woodburytype; if truly lovely, these may be worth $100 by themselves. Sun pictures of the kind which furnished the earliest book illustrations or the photogravures made by the members of the Photo-Secessionist movement may be valued at several hundreds.

Prestigious auction houses which have traditionally offered rare and scarce books or paintings and antique furniture are now regularly scheduling auctions especially for the sale of photographic materials, which may include both books of antiquarian interest and rare images, along with antique cameras and other types of equipment, such as stereopticons and other old viewing instruments. Most of the material which is offered at auction is derived from the first hundred years of photography, or up to around 1940. But in photography there is a surprisingly swift process of aging and sometimes the term "vintage print" is applied rather broadly, covering anything from material produced in the early twentieth century to the earliest work, say from the 1950s, of a photographer who is still actively exhibiting. Fortunately for the collector who wants to learn more about value as determined in the market, the lively bidding at these auctions is followed by the publication of the list of prices realized. Both the catalogues describing the items offered at auction and the list of the prices paid are available at a moderate fee. The list must, however, be separately requested.

The current interest in all manner of photographic publications is sending more people back to examine their own bookshelves with a new eye. They may now find that they own hitherto unsuspected treasures. These may include books which they once collected because of their value in some other area. Sometimes they include books picked up on impulse, possibly simply because they seemed rather quaint. There is beyond doubt still a great amount of photographic material to be mined. Dealers complain that they cannot find enough photographic material to satisfy the potential market. It is one of the favorite laments of the dealers in old and rare books that they can find so little material for stock: "If I had it"—with a shrug and a sigh—"I certainly could sell it." The same complaint comes from the proprietors of those shops which make no more pretentious claim than that they sell 'just plain junque."

Published material of interest to the photographic historian ranges from the odd and unusual item to the rare book worth thousands of dollars. Among the different kinds of publications now being sought are the early instruction manuals. In the first decade of photography in the United States there were few manuals published. After the initial circulation of information on how to make a daguerroeotype and a flurry of interest on the part of persons with some training in chemistry, it seemed to be the general impression that daguerreotypy took no great skill. This is no doubt derived from the fact that in the early 1840s some itinerant peddlers added making daguerreotype portraits to their various offerings. The traveling phrenologist, for example, might offer a daguerreotype portrait as something of a "come-on." Not only would he provide you with a reading of your character derived from his analysis of the meaning of the shape of your skull, he would throw in the magic of your portrait as something of a bonus. There did seem to be little skill required.

Beginning around 1844 and 1845, however, the establishment of the studio for making the daguerreotype portrait, the advent of skilled operators, and the patronage of the powerful and wealthy began to lift photography to a level where more than mere competence came to be required. There arose the beginning of a demand for the instruction book. In 1850 we find Levi L. Hill, in his book on the making of daguerreotypes, explaining "most of those who embark in this beautiful branch of industry are like a traveller without a guide. A few days' instructions (so-called) send them out through the country in swarms; and a few days' trial of their skill either sends them back again, Jack-and-Jill-like, tumbling down the hill of science, or convinces them that, if they succeed at all, it must be by the efforts of their own unaided genius."

During the 1850s the collodion process swiftly supplanted the daguerreotype, and it was a scant twelve years later that N. G. Burgess, in his photographic manual, was, in turn, pointing out that compared with the collodion process the making of a daguerreotype must be considered a fairly simple matter requiring scarcely more than a rudimentary knowledge of chemistry. From the date of the introduction of wet-plate photography the instruction manual would be a popular item and enjoy a steady market.

Early manuals are now collected by both those who are interested in the history of photography and by the collectors of old and rare books. The edition may be important. The first edition of a book by an English photographer, published in London, may be worth five times the first American edition. However, important as the first edition may be, in the case of manuals, a later and revised edition may also be valuable, especially if it contains new information, as was frequently the case. Burgess's own manual, mentioned above, went into many editions, and the eighth, published in 1862 and containing a treatise on the method of making cartes de visite as well as stereoscopic pictures, has recently sold for $50 at auction in New York.

Collectors find of equal interest those manuals published by the makers of photographic equipment; sometimes these are just a few pages in length. A Scovill catalogue issued in 1886, consisting of an 86-page itemized list of prices along with just 21 pages on "How to Make Photographs," has brought $60 at auction. Yet it is still possible to find nineteenth-century catalogues, manufacturer's books of hints, and manuals of instruction for specific items for as little as $3–$10. Among the "sleepers" still to be found on the back shelves are the manuals for various kinds of cameras; pamphlets on the chemistry of photography and other fairly technical materials, such as works on photographic optics and on color photography; and early twentieth-century dictionaries of photography. These last may be especially interesting because of their illustrations. Advice to the ambitious on how to make money from their camera is another type of item still to be found rather frequently. One example is *How to Make $10 a Day with Your Kodak.*

Incidentally, if one's interest is in the instructions for making a photograph by an early process, it may be unnecessary to scout for the original instruction manual, since a number of these manuals are now available in reprint. For example, the first edition (1872) of *The Ferrotype and How to Make It* by Edward M. Estabrooke, with its two tinted ferrotype portraits mounted inside the covers, has sold at auction for $160, whereas the facsimile published in 1972 by Morgan & Morgan costs only around $9. The great attraction of the original is, of course, in the sample photographs. Substantial value is added to any manual by the presence of an original photograph. The brief 128-page *Art and Practice of Silver Printing* by H. P. Robinson, published in London in 1881, with its original mounted photograph as frontispiece, may be worth close to $100.

The view album—"Gems of . . ."—"Best Views of . . ."—"Illustrated Guide to . . ."—so often found in any old family collection of photographs, is another kind of printed material of new interest today. Usually printed either on heavy paper or boards or with the photographs inserted into windows, and often with a panoramic fold-out, these albums are frequently discovered with the mailing envelope still present, unused. Sometimes depending on factors quite extrinsic to the merit of the photographs, a view album may be worth anything from truly nothing to $10–$20 or even $50. Those published before 1910 are more valuable, as are those from the most respected studios and publishing houses. In some instances it may be possible to identify the photographer, and this can add to the interest. Before the days when the traveler could take along his own camera and produce snapshots of the scenes which interested him, the view album served as the momento of any trip. It was the standard souvenir of a trip abroad, and was displayed in the parlor to be shown to guests. Similarly, there was a big business in the United States of publishing albums covering such favorite scenery as the White Mountains, Niagara Falls, the Rockies, and the California Coast. The most popular albums were those showing vacation areas and those extolling the virtues and beauties of the large cities. Eventually even relatively small communities would follow suit, producing their own albums showing Main Street, the Fourth of July parade, the historic sights. Many of these albums were bound in fancy covers, enlivened with pictorial effects or made of leather, even laced and tasselled. Frequently the condition of the cover as well as the nature of the contents helps establish price.

The earliest of the published albums contain original photographs; later albums may be illustrated with Albertypes or halftone reproductions. In subject, the view albums covered the world: Darjeeling, Ottawa,

George Barker, known for his photographs of Florida, made this particular picture in 1886 showing strong moonlight on St. John's River, ferry boats, and the masts of sailing ships. Barker was one of many late-nineteenth century photographers who worked in various communities and succeeded in registering the spirit of a place which time has now altered. Such photographs can only become more precious with the passage of time. (Courtesy of the Library of Congress USZ62-10925.)

Hawaii, the Overland Trail in 1903, a suburb of Boston, Alaska, Italian architecture and ruins. The quality of the photographs ranges from poor to superb. The published view album represents one of the areas where the collector with a small investment of money and a large one of time may build a fascinating collection around any number of ideas. This is also an arena in which a knowledgeable scout might turn up a fairly valuable item, such as one of the Scovill publications depicting Italian cities; several of these albums have sold at auction for $75.

Manuals of instruction and view albums scarcely exhaust the possibilities in collecting published materials. There is, for example, an exceedingly broad range of ephemera to be collected. The catalogues issued by the manufacturers of photographic equipment have been mentioned: Many of those published in the early part of the twentieth century bring $10 or more, though only rarely are they considered worth more than $25.

The advertising broadside issued by the photographer or the photographic parlor may be an interesting collector's item. A "primitive and yet decorative piece" touting a daguerrian studio, undated, about 13 inches square, and with some light staining, has been priced by a dealer at $85, and $55 was paid at auction for a broadside advertisement for Frederick's Photographic Temple of Art in New York City, listing all the various photographic processes available from this establishment. This latter, also, was lightly stained. Another broadside, somewhat larger, thought to be from the 1870s, in generally good condition, and advertising a photographic studio in a tiny town in Maine, was judged worth $45. A broadside for ambrotypes and melainotypes—torn and repaired—was bought for $65. The handsomely printed business card for Gurney's Premium Daguerrian Gallery on Broadway in New York has sold for $35.

Another example of ephemera is the city directory which provides the names of the local photographers, with their specialties and the addresses of their studios. Such a directory was offered as a photographic item— the *Boston Almanac for the Year 1859* along with a second directory for the year 1863—and sold for $30 at auction. These particular directories contained both the usual listing of photographers and numerous advertisements for photographic supplies.

There are also those books intended for the instruction of the young which contain a section on optics and sometimes specifically on photography. One example is *The Fairyland of Science* by Anabella B. Buckley, published in 1881 and containing a section titled "Sunbeams, and the Work They Do." Offered at auction under photography rather than as a children's book, it has brought $20.

Moved out of their usual category and placed under the new heading of photographic items, some books gain interest. Early works on chemistry, not especially interesting as textbooks, may attract attention for a chapter on photography, especially if illustrated. Similarly, any handbook on the science of optics gains in interest if it is noted that it contains information on photographic processes. An illustrated biography may be attractive to collectors of photography. One such biography is the first edition copy of *Life and Inventions of Thomas Edison* by W.K.L. and Antonia Dickson, published in 1894, with photographs of the early Kinetoscope films; the book is now worth over $100.

Similarly, magazines of general interest are sometimes found to contain photographs by well-known and highly respected photographers, and articles about them or sometimes even by them. Those illustrations which depict some particular photographic process may be of interest. These may include wood-engravings depicting persons sitting for their portrait, the daguerreotypist at work in his operating room, the studio where daguerreotypes were processed, or even the fancifully decorated parlor where the photographer's clients were soothed with such ameneties as singing birds in cages, classical statuary, draperies, and rugs. The wood-engravings themselves are sometimes derived from photographs, laboriously copied out with the burin. Such engravings from *Frank Leslie's Illustrated Newspaper* have regularly brought about $12 each at auction.

Then there are, of course, those journals especially devoted to photography. The first issue is always important. Volume I, No. 1 of *The Photographic Times*, published in New York, together with the first issue of *The Photographic Journal* of Philadelphia brought almost $30 at a New York auction. Any early issue, or even later ones, should be checked for contents, since there is always the possibility of some truly seminal article.

The variety of names of these photographic journals may be fairly confusing. Names were changed and amalgamations took place. The first journal to be published dealing exclusively with the subject of photography was *The Daguerrian Journal . . .* , a fortnightly established in 1850 by S. D. Humphrey of New York. With one slight interruption in publication it continued as *Humphrey's Journal of Photography* until 1870. In January, 1851, H. H. Snelling brought out the first issue of his *Photographic Art Journal*. This journal persisted, under several changes of name, until 1867 when it merged with *Humphrey's*. For a comprehensive list of the publications issued in the United States and several European countries during the 1850s and 1860s, the reader is referred to *The History of Photography* by Helmut Gernsheim.

Collectors are showing growing interest in various kinds of local histories illustrated with photographs. Frequently such histories have a story to tell us which cannot be found elsewhere, and they often provide not only new insights into the way things were in days past but sometimes provide information that corrects misinformation contained in legend or even the printed word. One such photographic history of the "early days in Minneapolis," published in 1890, sold recently at auction for $90. Other local histories may be priced much lower, depending on both their scarcity and the demand.

The illustrated catalogues of manufacturing establishments often fascinate those collectors who combine an interest in photography with that in a particular product, whether it may be hats, shoes, or locomotives. For example, the Baldwin (Locomotive) Illustrated Catalogue for 1881, with 16 photographs, has been sold at auction for $65.

Even those compendiums of information on some aspect of history of a particular area or based on some single historic event can be of some interest, though often, unfortunately, they are poorly printed. There were a number of histories of World War I, for example, published shortly after the war's end, which were derived from newspaper photographs. Some of these may now be worth up to $25. Even the lowly cigarette company giveaways may be valuable. An album of 265 tiny photographs, all of them showing zeppelins, mounted together in a single book published in Dresden in 1933, has brought $90 at auction.

Sometimes we may be lucky enough to find an odd or truly unusual publication which is of interest because of its photography. It might be a book of photographs privately published by the photographer himself in a very small edition. One such volume, a book of 30 photographs published by an amateur photographer in Philadelphia in 1869, has brought $130 at auction. His pictures were the images created by the turning of a lathe, and there was an introduction explaining how he had made these interesting photographs.

The following list of some of the publications of value in the history of photography is more of a sampling than a comprehensive list of the most historically important books. There are wide variations in both rarity and price. Many readers would certainly want to add to the author's list. However, those books and journals which have been included, we can probably all agree, should be on anyone's list and are among those we should all be on the lookout for. A few of these works are so rare that a dealer in photographic materials might consider himself privileged to hold a copy in his hands just once in his lifetime. Other material may still

This interior shot of a cigar factory by Frances Johnston is particularly interesting for the number of individual portraits it contains. (Courtesy of the Library of Congress USZ62-47559.)

In the cigar factory the photographer found subjects of appealing beauty. c. 1910. (Courtesy of the Library of Congress USZ62-47087.)

be comparatively easy to find. The industrious collector should, however, be alert to the chance of locating any item on the following list, remote as the possibility in some cases may seem. There is always the chance that, armed with knowledge, we may recognize one of the great treasures of photography in some unexpected place.

Important Publications on Photography, by Photographers, With Important Photographic Illustration

A Selected List

The following list is representative of the kind of books and periodicals which are highly valued today. The non-appearance of any particular publication does not mean, of course, that it may not be valuable. Drawing upon information from the 1975–76 market, it has been possible, in many instances, to indicate price. When there is no price indicated, this simply means that, to the author's knowledge, the book or journal was not offered for sale by any of the sources checked. Date of publication indicates the date of the first edition, unless otherwise specified. It is assumed that any copy offered for sale was in from good to fine condition.

Abbott, Berenice
Changing New York, 1939.
With the dust jacket, a first-edition copy has brought at auction $50–$90.
Twenty Photographs by Eugene Atget, 1956
A portfolio of 20 silver prints by Abbott from the original Atget negatives, limited to 100 copies, has brought $3,000 at auction.
Adams, Ansel
Parmelian Prints of the High Sierras, 1929.
This is Adams' first portfolio, executed by him for the Sierra Club, with which he would be long associated.
Taos Pueblo, 1930.
Adams' first book of photographs, with text by Mary Austin.
Making a Photograph, 1935.
Published in London, this is Adams' first technical book and has a foreword by Edward Weston; it may be worth around $40.
Born Free and Equal, 1944.
A report on the conditions of life for Japanese-Americans interned at Manzanar Camp during World War II.

My Camera in the National Parks, 1950.
With its 30 reproductions, a copy signed on the flyleaf might sell for $150 or more.
This Is the American Earth, 1960.
With Nancy Newhall, 83 photogravures, more than half by Adams, the others by numerous other well-known photographers; worth around $50 from a dealer.
What Majestic Word . . . , 1963.
A Sierra Club publication, limited to 250 copies, signed, and with the 15 original photographs, has brought $4,900 at auction.

Album Photographique
The first number of this French journal appeared in 1851, and so many copies were sold that its publisher, Blanquart-Evrard, thought it wise to enlarge his printing plant. The *Album* contained single prints of architectural subjects and landscapes in the romantic style. It lead the way to the subsequent illustration of books with photographs.

Amateur Photographer
A London publication which after 1908 incorporated the earlier *Photographic News* (q.v.). Issues of the *Amateur Photographer*, of interest both for its articles and its many ads for photographic equipment, may occasionally be picked up for a dollar, although a run of eight volumes, 1901–08, in fair condition only, has sold at auction for $100.

American Amateur Photographer
A journal edited by Alfred Stieglitz between 1893 and 1896, notable for its fine examples of a range of styles.

American Annual of Photography
A journal published in New York beginning in 1887, it was profusely illustrated with examples of the work of various prominent photographers, including both original photographs and photogravures. It was also a source of information about various types of photographic equipment. Individual annuals from as late as the 1930s may be worth between $5 and $15, and the earlier issues may be worth up to $35.

American Journal of Photography
This monthly publication was founded in 1852 by Charles A. Seely, and in 1861 it absorbed the *Photographic and Fine Art Journal*. Its last issue was for September, 1867, when it was combined with *Humphrey's Journal of Photography*. Among its most interesting articles were those, beginning in 1861, which described the difficulties of the photographer attempting to take pictures of battlefront activities during the Civil War.

American Repertory of Arts, Sciences and Manufactures, Volumes I and II
Two volumes, published in New York in 1840 and 1841, containing early articles on the daguerreotype, now worth, together, $90.

Anderson, A. J.
The ABC of Artistic Photography in Theory and Practice, 1910. Of the 20 illustrations, four are photogravures by Steichen, Stieglitz, and Coburn. A third edition of this work has been offered by a dealer for $400.

Anderson, Paul L.
Pictorial Landscape—Photography, 1914.
By one of the leading advocates of the pictorial style, this book may be worth around $30.

Anderson, Sherwood
Home Town, 1940.
Utilizes the photographs from the files of the Farm Security Administration; in hardcover may be worth $40.

Annan, Thomas
Old Glasgow, 1877.
An album of 40 carbon prints published for the City of Glasgow Improvement Trust, each of the photographs, *separately,* may now be worth $300-$400.
Old Closes and Streets, a Series of Photogravures, 1868–1869, 1900.
Published by T. R. Annan & Sons, it contains 50 gravures, is bound in full red cloth, gilt-embossed, and has the arms of the City of Glasgow; this volume has been offered for sale by dealers at $2,500–$3,000.
The Old Country Houses of the Old Glasgow Gentry, 1878.
Illustrated with 100 Woodburytypes, the second edition, limited to 225 copies.

Annuaire General de la Photographie
Eleven volumes, from the first year, 1892, through 1905; some with mounted photographs offered as a single lot have sold at auction for $210

Anthony, E. and H.T.
New Catalogue of Stereoscopes and Views . . . , n.d.
Although they may be undated, any of the catalogues issued by this firm are sure to command interest.

Anthony's Annual
This was the international annual of *Anthony's Photographic Bulletin.* The first issue of the *Bulletin* appeared in 1870. Both the *Bulletin* and the *Annual* were important in stimulating and enlarging the public interest in collecting stereographs. Single copies of the *Annual* have brought as much as $25 at auction.

Arago, Francois
"Le Daguerreotype," in *Comptes Rendus.* Academie des Sciences, Vol. IX, July-December 1839.
This is the first disclosure of Daguerre's new process, by the man who was most instrumental in convincing the French Chamber of Deputies to secure the rights to the process. A dealer has asked $750 for a fine copy of the volume containing Arago's 17-page report.

Archer, F. Scott
Manual of the Collodion Photographic Process, 1851.
Both the first edition and the second, which appeared in 1854, are among the great rarities of photographic literature.

Art in Photography
The special summer issue of *The Studio* for 1905, edited by Charles Holme, this work with more than 100 mounted reproductions of the work of Hill, Robinson, Coburn, Steichen, Stieglitz, and others, sells for more than $100.

Art Journal
The issue of July, 1851 (new series), of this British journal contained one of the first published descriptions of the method for making collodion positives. However, *The Chemist* for March, 1851, had contained an earlier article, by F. Scott Archer. A bound copy of the *Journal* for the year 1851 may be worth $50.

Art Union
This British monthly journal of the fine arts contained, in its issue of June, 1846, a specimen photograph by Fox Talbot to illustrate an article on the Talbotype. The public interest was so great that several negatives had to be used successively for an edition which ran to 7,000 copies.

Atget, Eugene
Atget: Photographe de Paris, n.d.
This is the earliest publication of Atget's work, containing 96 gravures, in New York around 1930; there is a preface by P. MacOrlan. A copy has sold for $280.

Atkins, Anna

Photographs of British Algae, n.d.

Possibly produced during the year 1843, this may be the first book ever to be illustrated with photographs, antedating Fox Talbot's *The Pencil of Nature.* Anna Atkin's technique was the cyanotype, a process which would be virtually ignored for the next 30 years.

Autograph Etchings by American Artists . . . , 1859

Containing 12 cliché-verres and possibly first publication of this technique in the United States, a copy has sold for $325.

Barnard, George N.

Photographic Views of Sherman's Campaign, 1866.

This is a 30-page pamphlet with an accompanying set of 61 photographs of Imperial size made from the original negatives. This work is extremely rare. If removed from the collection, a single gold-toned albumen print, 10 by 14 inches, on the original card mount, may be worth $150 to $350. A generally good copy of *Photographic Views,* the "prints in rich, luxuriant state," has been priced at $14,500.

Barraud, William

Men and Women of the Day, 1888–89.

Illustrated with Barraud's own photographs, this is a two-volume work bearing the sub-title "A Picture Gallery of Contemporary Portraiture."

Bayard, Hippolyte

Lo Duca "Bayard", 1943.

This limited-edition monograph, with 48 halftone reproductions of Bayard's photographs, may be worth over $150.

Beato, Felice A.

Photographic Views of Japan, 1868.

With a text by James Murray, this work was published in Yokohama.

Bede, Cuthbert (Edward Bradley)

Photographic Pleasures, 1855.

One of the first books to caricature photography, this book, published in London, contained 24 cartoons by Bradley. A copy of the first edition might be worth $150.

Bedford, Francis

The Holy Land, Egypt, Constantinople, Athens . . . , 1866.

With a text by W. M. Thompson, this work contains 48 photographs from a trip made by Bedford to the Holy Land in 1862 in the company of the Prince of Wales and his party. A copy has recently sold at auction for $110.

Bennett, Charles

In the March 29, 1879, issue of the *British Journal of Photography,* an article by Bennett appeared describing his new process of ripening a dry-plate gelatin emulsion by cooking, an important forward step at the time.

Bierstadt: Harroun and Bierstadt, Photographers

Gems of American Scenery, c. 1878.

Scenes from the White Mountains; 24 stereo plates with a built-in viewer and a double-page litho map, valued at around $750.

Bigelow, Jacob

The Useful Arts, 1840.

This is a two-volume work which contains 27 pages on the daguerreotype and photogenic drawing. It has been called a fine example of "American photographic incunabulum"; the first edition may be worth more than $100.

Bisbee, Albert
History and Practice of Daguerreotyping, 1853.
This early history was published in Dayton, Ohio.
Bisson Freres
Monographie de Notre Dame . . . , c. 1853–57.
With 80 plates after the manner of calotypes but apparently actually from glass
negatives, "a spectacular rarity," priced by a dealer at $8,500.
Blanquart-Evrard, Louis Desire
Traite de photographie sur papier, 1851.
Blanquart-Evrard was one of the earliest, if not the first, of the photographic pub-
lishers.
Les origines de la photographie, 1869.
Bourke-White, Margaret
Eyes on Russia, 1931
The first edition with its 40 plates is worth at least $30.
You Have Seen Their Faces, 1937.
This documentary on the conditions in the South has photographs by Bourke-White
and a text by Erskine Caldwell. A poor copy has been judged worth $75.
Bourne, Samuel
Views in Kashmir, 1865.
This is the large folio edition, containing 25 mounted photographs made during
Bourne's second Himalayan expedition the previous year. A copy has sold at auc-
tion for $625.
Bradford, William
The Arctic Regions, 1873.
This is the chronicle of a trip made by ship up the coast of Greenland in 1869.
The text is by Bradford and the photographs are credited to Dunmore and Crit-
cherson, although some of the photographs were probably by Bradford himself.
There are 129 original mounted photographs, of various sizes, showing icebergs,
Eskimos, etc. One copy has sold at auction for $4,500.
Brady, Mathew B.
The Gallery of Illustrious Americans, 1850.
Containing 12 lithographic portraits after the original daguerreotypes, and thus
a good example of photographic ephemera.
A Photographic History. See **Miller.**
Brandt, Bill
*Shadow of Light,*1966.
Here is a good example of how swiftly even a recent book can join the list of col-
lectibles—worth $50.
Brassai
Paris de Nuit, 1933.
With text by Paul Morand, worth over $300.
Camera in Paris, 1949.
Fiesta in Seville, 1956.
With its 140 photographs, this has sold for $30. The first edition, in French
(1954), is worth somewhat more.
Braun, Adolphe
L'Alsace Photographie, 1859.
A two-volume work, containing 120 topographical photographs.
Catalogue general des photographies, 1887.
In leather, a copy has sold for $120.

British Journal of Photography

A journal in continuous publication from 1860 to the present, the *Journal* made its first appearance as a wall calendar, then was enlarged to a memo-book, and finally appeared in larger size. There is also the *British Journal Photographic Almanac,* published annually since 1869. (See also **Journal of the Photographic Society of London.**)

Burbank, W. H.

Photographic Printing Methods, 1887.

With its original bromide print by W. D. Halmes and a frontispiece gravure by E. Edwards, a dealer might price this at $75.

Burgess, N. G.

The Ambrotype Manual . . . , 1856

This manual went into many editions, with the fourth retitled *The Photograph and Ambrotype Manual,* and the eighth, published in 1862, *Photograph Manual . . . Cartes de Visite Process . . . Stereoscopic Pictures.* The eighth edition appears to turn up much more frequently than the earlier ones; a copy was recently sold at auction for $50. A first edition has been priced at $225.

Burton, W. K.

Japanese Earthquake at Ai-Gi, 1891.

Published with 29 large photographs, of which just 11, which had been removed, sold for $90 at auction in 1972.

Bussey Bridge Disaster, 1887

This work was one of the earliest uses of photography to provide evidence. It includes four heliotypes showing the scene of a train wreck which resulted in the deaths of 23 persons. A copy has sold for $70.

Byron, Percy C.

Once Upon a City: New York from 1890 to 1910, 1958.

There is a foreword by Edward Steichen. Copies have sold at $30-40.

Caffin, Charles H.

Photography as a Fine Art, 1901.

A fine copy of the first edition has sold for $95; a second copy, with a weak hinge, has been offered at $50.

Camera Notes

The illustrated photographic journal published by the Camera Club of New York, a club established in 1896 by the merger of two earlier organizations. From 1897 to 1902 Alfred Stieglitz was the Chairman of its Publications Committee and served as both editor and manager. Under his direction *Camera Notes* became a pioneer publication in the field of photography, and many of its photogravure plates anticipated the extraordinary quality of the work which appeared later in *Camera Work,* also edited by Stieglitz. A single issue of this important journal is likely to be worth $100 at auction today, and any issue containing examples of the work of Steichen, Kasebier or Stieglitz himself, among other artists, may be worth well over $400—complete and in fine condition, of course.

Camera Work

The quarterly publication of the informal group of photographers who designated themselves Photo-Secessionists, founded by Alfred Stieglitz following his resignation as editor of *Camera Notes.* He remained its editor for the entire 50 issues which appeared between 1903 and 1917. *Camera Work* has been called itself a work of art, "one of the stellar achievements of American culture in this century" (Hilton Kramer, writing in *The New York Times*). It utilized the best available in paper and type faces, developed a distinctive style, and was most notable for the quality of its hand-pulled photogravures. Printed in editions of no more than 1,000 copies, *Camera Work* contained the work of leading photographers, the reproduction of which the photographers themselves had generally supervised. Stieglitz himself once suggested that the gravures could "in reality be considered original prints, having been made directly from the original negatives and printed in the spirit of the original picture and retaining all its quality." This journal also published articles by such leading innovative writers as G. Bernard Shaw, Maurice Maeterlinck and Gertrude Stein. There were also the reproductions of the work of controversial artists in media other than photography. Expensive to produce, *Camera Work* had to cease publication, finally, for lack of public support. Today a full run of all 50 issues is one of the treasures of photography. Such a run, lacking only a few plates, has sold at auction for $32,000. Single issues have sold at auction for well over $1,000. Issue No. 36, for October, 1911, with its 16 photogravures by Stieglitz and a halftone engraving of a Picasso drawing, has sold for $3,700 to 4,750. Some of the other most valuable issues include Nos. 14 ($800 or more), 22 ($500 or more), 30 ($800 up), 41 (more than $650), and the double issue, 42/43 (up to $1,600). Generally, to command such a price, all the original plates must still be present and in at least good condition.

Cameron, Julia Margaret

(Tennyson's) *Idylls of the King and Other Poems*, 1875.

Twelve photographs by Mrs. Cameron were used to illustrated a first volume of this Tennyson work, and later another 12 appeared in the second volume. In 1976 Volume II alone brought $4,250 at auction.

Alfred, Lord Tennyson and his Friends, 1893.

From negatives by J. M. and H. H. Cameron, 25 portraits and a frontispiece; a dealer has asked $2,000 for this work, which was published in a limited edition of 400 copies.

Capa, Robert

Death in the Making, 1938.

This is Capa's commentary on the Spanish Civil War.

Images of War, 1964.

With its 99 photographs, this may be worth $30.

Carbutt, John

The Early and Later History of Petroleum, 1873.

The text is by J. T. Henry, and there are 28 Woodburytypes by Carbutt. A dealer has asked $225.

Carroll, Lewis (C. L. Dodgson)

"Hiawatha's Photographing."

First published in *The Train* in December, 1857, and then again in *Phantasmagoria and Other Poems*, 1869, and then in 1883 in *Rhyme? and Reason?*, the three versions are all different. The first contains the following lines, a sample of the style:

Secondly, my Hiawatha
Made with cunning hand a mixture
Of the acid pyrro-gallic,
And of glacial-acetic,
And of alcohol and water—
This developed all the picture . . .

Alice's Adventures Under Ground, 1886.

A photo-zincographic copy from the original manuscript, but, however, lacking the photograph of Alice which appeared at the end of the original.

Cartier-Bresson, Henri
The Decisive Moment, 1952.
Critically acclaimed an important work; in folio size, worth $125–$175.
Carvalho, S. N.
Incidents of Travel and Adventure, 1859.
The story of Col. Fremont's last expedition, recounted by the "artist to the expedition," the daguerreotypist. A dealer has asked $90 for this edition; it was originally published in 1856.
Clifford, Charles
Vistas del Capricho, 1856.
An album containing 50 views of a palace in Spain near Guadalajara.
Voyages en Espagne, 1858.
The 400 photographs contained in this work include both calotypes and albumen prints.
Coburn, Alvin Langdon
London, 1909.
This volume contains 20 photogravures. There is also another book of the same title, by G. K. Chesterton, produced in 1914 but with only 10 photogravures. The 1909 edition has sold at auction for $2,400. The 1914 edition has been variously priced by dealers at $125–$400.
New York, 1910.
This London publication has brought $1,900 at auction.
The Door in the Wall, 1911.
Men of Mark, 1913.
More Men of Mark, 1922.
With their tipped-in, hand-pulled photogravures, the *Men of Mark* books may be worth $300 or more.
Cole, Henry Hardy
The Architecture of Ancient Delhi . . ., 1872.
An archaeological survey of the North Western Provinces of India, published by the Arundel Society with photographs by Shepherd.
Coyle, T.
(Scott's) *The Lady of the Lake*, 1863.
An edition which contained photographs by Coyle.
Crofutt, George A.
Crofutt's New Overland and Pacific Coast Guide, 1879.
Croucher, John H.
Plain Directions for Obtaining Photographic Pictures by the Calotype and Energiatype . . . Hints on the Daguerreotype, 1853.
An English manual printed in the United States, which also appeared in two later editions, in 1855 and 1860.
Crystallotype, The, 1855
One of the first American books to be illustrated with actual photographs, published by Putnam and consisting of an illustrated account of the 1853 Crystal Palace Fair at New York. This may be one of the great treasures of the photographic world, since as of this writing there is *no known copy*.
Curtis, Edward S.
Harriman Alaska Expedition, 1901.
Volumes I and II only of a set of 14 volumes, but complete in themselves, with 45 gravures from photographs by Curtis. A dealer asks $250.
The North American Indian, 1907–30.
Produced under the patronage of J. Pierpont Morgan; 20 volumes of text accom-

panied by as many elephant folios, each with at least 36 photogravures, a total of 722. This work represents the results of Curtis' lifetime project of photographing the Indians of Western America and Alaska as they had lived before their traditions were altered by contact with the white man. Published serially, the edition was to be limited to 500, but it is thought that fewer than 300 copies were actually produced. The complete work has sold at auction for $60,000. The individual plates, printed on imported Holland paper, Japan vellum, or tissue, offered separately command from $50 to $600 to $800, the most desired including some exceedingly handsome portraits. A single portfolio is sometimes offered as a unit.

Daguerre, Louis J. M.
Historique et description des procedes du Daguerreotype et du diorama, 1839.
This is the earliest booklet providing instructions for making a daguerreotype, with scale drawings of the camera and other equipment necessary. Within five months this important manual had gone into no fewer than 30 editions in many languages and many countries. In England it appeared under the title *History and Practice of Photogenic Drawing on the True Principles of the Daguerreotype,* translated by J. S. Memes and published in London in 1839. A copy of this work was recently sold at auction for $700. (See also **Mapes,** for the first American edition.)

Daguerreian Journal
According to Beaumont Newhall, the first journal in the world to be exclusively devoted to photography. A fortnightly, it was established in 1850 by S. D. Humphrey of New York. After briefly suspending publication between January and April of 1852, it continued thereafter as *Humphrey's Journal* (q.v.), until July, 1870.

The Daguerreotype
A short-lived journal which was founded in 1847 and dealt with matters of interest in the fields of literature and science as well as photography.

Daily Graphic
The issue of March 4, 1880, in which there appeared the first halftone to be published in any newspaper—a view of New York City's "shantytown" photographed by H. J. Newton.

Darwin, Charles
The Expression of the Emotions in Man and Animals, 1872.
Containing heliotypes from photographs by O. G. Rejlander, this was the first book to be illustrated with heliotypes. A good copy might be worth more than $200, the amount at which a first edition recently sold at auction.

Davies, G. Christopher
Norfolk Broads . . . , 1883.
With 12 photogravures anticipating the work of P. H. Emerson; $950 from a dealer.

Dellenbaugh, Frederick S.
A Canyon Voyage, the Narrative of the Second Powell Expedition . . . in the Years 1871 and 1872, 1908.

Demeny, Georges
Les Origines du Cinematographie, 1909.

Disderi, Andre A. A.
Renseignements Photographiques Indispensable a Tous, 1855.
L'art de la photographie, 1862.
A handbook of photography which includes instructions for posing different kinds of sitters; translated into English in 1864.

Dixon, John Ross

A collection of 124 carbon prints made by Dixon for the Society for Photographing the Relics of Old London, published in 1874; an important first use of photography to document a need for preservation.

Dixon, Joseph K.

The Vanishing Race: The Last Great Indian Council, 1913.

Containing 80 photogravures of Indian Life; recently sold for $75.

Downey, W. and D.

The Cabinet Portrait Gallery, 1890–93.

The first series: the subjects are the members of European royalty, famous authors, statesmen, etc. A work in four volumes, the *Gallery* has been priced at $250 by one dealer.

DuCamp, Maxime

Egypte, Nubie, Palestine et Syrie, 1851.

With over 125 of his photographs, issued in installments beginning in the month of September and published in book form in 1852 in Paris, this may be the first travel book to be published containing actual photographs. There is a London edition, also published in 1852.

Duchenne de Boulogne, Guillaume B. A.

Album Photographies Pathologiques, 1862.

Emerson, Peter Henry

Life and Landscape on the Norfolk Broads, 1886.

Prepared in collaboration with T. F. Goodall, this is the first of a series of six albums presenting an honest view of the life of the East Anglian peasant through the combination of photography and text. *Life and Landscape* appeared in a limited edition of 850 copies, with 40 original platinotypes by Emerson. Today a single one of those plates may be worth about $550 to around $1,000.

Pictures of Life in Field and Fen, 1887.

With 20 photogravures by Emerson, each signed in the negative; folio size; unbound as issued. The first edition, which was limited to 550 copies, has brought $1,600 at auction.

Pictures of East Anglian Life, 1888.

Containing 32 photogravures signed by Emerson in the plate, only 575 copies were issued. The individual plates are worth $100–$300 each.

(Walton and Cotton's) *The Compleat Angler,* 1888.

Twenty-seven of the photogravures are by Emerson. This edition was issued in two volumes and limited to 500 copies, of which one may now be worth $1,200 from a dealer.

Naturalistic Photography, 1889.

In this landmark book Emerson declared his view of the proper function of photography as the servant of realism, recommending the use of a view camera using plates of a whole size, and attacking the then-prevalent practice of retouching. A first-edition copy has sold at auction for $170.

Wild Life on a Tidal Water, 1890.

A portfolio of 30 photogravures, all but one by Emerson, which has been sold at auction for $1,300.

The Death of Naturalistic Photography, 1890.

This is the pamphlet, issued with a black border, repudiating Emerson's previous statements. At the time of its publication Emerson withdrew from circulation the remaining copies of his earlier work, *Naturalistic Photography.*

Marsh Leaves, 1895.
Containing 16 photogravures by Emerson in a limited edition of 300 copies, this final book by Emerson has been called "the most exquisite of them all." It has brought $2,500 at auction.

Ernst, Max
Mr. Knife/Miss Fork, 1931.
With a text by Rene Crevel, published by the Black Sun Press of Paris; the frontispiece alone, if signed, may be worth $800, and single photographs from this work have been valued at up to $400.

Estabrooke, Edward
The Ferrotype and How to Make It, 1872.
A copy should still have its two tinted ferrotype mounted inside the covers. This manual has sold at auction for $160.

Evans, Walker
Let Us Now Praise Famous Men, 1941.
Prepared in collaboration with James Agee.
Portfolio, 1971.
Published in a limited edition of 100 copies with 14 signed prints; each of the signed prints may be worth $300 or more.

Excursions Daguerriennes, 1840–44
A serial publication containing travel views issued by the publisher N. P. Lerebours in Paris. Lerebours had commissioned a number of daguerreotypists to travel abroad, some to the Middle East and Egypt, to secure pictures and send them back for publication, apparently the first time such a project had been launched.

Fardon, G. R.
San Francisco Album . . . Public Buildings . . . , 1856.

Fenton, Roger
The Crimean War, 1854–55.
A series of five portfolios illustrated with photographs including the work of Fenton and of James Robertson.
The Conway in the Stereoscope, 1860.
Illustrated with 20 "photostereographs" by Fenton; a first-edition copy has sold at auction for $230, although dealers have priced copies as low as $100.

Frapie, Frank R. and Walter E. Woodbury
Photographic Amusements, 1931.
This is the tenth edition with a last chapter on the avant-garde photography of the 1920s, worth possibly $30.

Frith, Francis
Photo-pictures from the Lands of the Bible, n.d.
Egypt and Palestine Photographed and Described, c. 1857.
Egypt, c. 1862.
A set of three albums separately published, as follows: *Egypt, Nubia and Ethiopia Illustrated*, 100 mounted stereographs with text, for which $150 had been paid at auction; *Lower Egypt and Ethiopia*, with 37 folio-size photographs, $300; and *Upper Egypt and Ethiopia*, also 37 photographs, $500.
The Gossiping Photographer at Hastings, 1864.
(The Queen's) *Bible*, 1862.
Popularly called the Queen's, this edition of the *Bible* was issued in a limited edition of 170 copies.

Fountains Abbey (1870–75).
Both photographed and printed by F. Frith, this work contains 20 examples of his photography; now worth $200.
(Longfellow's) *Hyperion*, 1865.
$100.

Gardner, Alexander
Photographic Sketch Book of the War, 1866.
Rare; a two-volume work consisting of a comprehensive photographic record of the Civil War years, 1861–65, containing 100 mounted photographs by Gardner and members of his staff, each print accompanied by text and bearing the name of the photographer. A superlative copy was sold at auction in 1977 for $17,000. Other copies might be worth closer to $2,500.

Gardner, James
Report on Niagara Falls Reservation, 1879, 1880.
Gardner was the director of a survey of the Reservation; the report published at Albany contains ten heliotypes by George Barker and is valued at $80.

Genthe, Arnold
Impressions of Old New Orleans, 1926.
Valued at over $50.
As I Remember London, 1937.
Again, over $50.
Walt Whitman in Camden, 1938.
With two photogravures inside and one on the cover, this limited edition from Haddon Craftsmen has sold for $125.

Gernsheim, Helmut
New Photo Vision (1942).
This is Gernsheim's first book and is illustrated with his own photographs. Now rare, it may be worth around $40.
Lewis Carroll, Photographer, 1949.
A monograph of only 121 pages; the first edition is worth $40, the second $20.

Gilman and Mower
The Photographer's Guide, in which the Daguerrean Art Is Familiarly Explained, 1842.
A very early work on the daguerreotype, published at Lowell, Massachusetts.

Gleason, Herbert W.
Through the Year with Thoreau, 1917.
With 91 halftones from Gleason's photographs, a work which one dealer has priced at $90.

Gordon, M. M.
Home Life of Sir David Brewster, 1869.
With a portrait frontispiece of Sir David and two additional photographic reproductions, this rare work is now worth around $110.

Gouraud, Francois
Description of the Daguerreotype Process, 1840.
A publication, now very rare, describing the daguerreotype process, providing instructions for taking portraits and arranging the light so as to pose the "patient." Gouraud was Daguerre's emissary to the United States.

Gross, Harry
Antique and Classic Cameras (1965).
The first book on modern camera collecting, now scarce and worth possibly $35.

Guild, Jr., W. H.
The Central Park, 1864.
With a text by Fred B. Perkins. Few copies are known to exist, and a dealer has priced this work at $1,250.
Guillot, Laune Albin
Micrographie decorative, 1931.

Hardwich, T. F.
A Manual of Photographic Chemistry . . . , 1858.
Hawthorne, Nathaniel
Transformation; or, the Romance of Monte Beni, 1860.
This is the Tauchnitz edition. With 60 albumen prints, one in color, it may now be worth $150. However, in different editions by the same publisher there were different photographs, in varying numbers. Some of the other books have been priced by dealers at $100.
Hayden, Ferdinand V.
Sun Pictures of Rocky Mountain Scenery, 1870.
Views of the construction of the transcontinental railroad, with 30 photographs by A. J. Russell. In fine condition, a copy has sold at auction for $600 and, on another occasion, $900.
Haynes, F. J.
Yellowstone National Park, 1887.
An oblong folio album with 25 gravures printed in sepia or blue, worth $100.
Hearn, Charles W.
The Practical Printer: A Complete Manual of Photographic Printing, 1874.
Sold recently at auction for $50.
Hill, David O.
Contributions Towards the Further Development of Fine Art in Photography, 1862.
Hill, Levi L.
A Treatise on Daguerreotypes, 1850.
At the third printing this work was retitled *Photographic Researches*; a second edition was published in 1854.
A Treatise on Heliochromy, 1856.
Hill's own account of his controversial claim to having perfected a process for achieving natural color in the daguerreotype, worth around $150.
Hillard, E. B.
The Last Men of the Revolution, 1864.
With six small albumen prints, portraits of the last remaining veterans of the American Revolution, contained in a 64-page book, which may be the first example of a published photo-interview, antedating the Nadar interview of the chemist Chevreul by 12 years. A dealer has priced this at $300.
Himes, Charles F.
Leaf Prints: on Glimpses at Photography, 1868.
Published in Philadelphia, this work contained as frontispiece an original print of three leaves. A copy has been sold at auction for $120.
Hine, Lewis W.
The Pittsburgh Survey, 1908.
Men At Work, 1932.
A documentary on the construction of the Empire State Building.

Hittel, John S.

Yosemite: Its Wonders and Its Beauties, 1868.

The first guidebook to the Yosemite region, containing 20 original photographs reproduced from the Muybridge negatives.

Hogg, Jabez

Practical Manual of Photography, 1843.

Holmes, Oliver Wendell

Three articles by Holmes in the *Atlantic Monthly* as follows: "The Stereoscope and the Stereograph," March, 1859; "Sun Painting and Sun Sculpture," August, 1861; and "Doings of the Sunbeam," December 1863.

Soundings from the Atlantic, 1864.

About one-third of this book is devoted to photography, including the earlier material on the stereoscope and stereograph. Copies sell at auction for $50–$70.

Homes of American Statesmen, 1854

This work "by various writers" contains as mounted frontispiece a Whipple crystal-lotype labelled "Hancock House, Boston, an original sun print." One of the earliest American books to be illustrated with a photograph, any copy in good condition could be worth between $100 and $150. There is some evidence, from a Christmas inscription, that there was a first issue of this book which actually appeared in 1853, and this issue, since it apparently antedated Warren's book (q.v.), has been priced at $300.

Hoppe, E. O.

The Book of Fair Women (1922).

With 32 tipped-in photogravures, in a limited edition of 500 copies, worth possibly as much as $500.

Taken from Life, 1922.

A good copy may be worth $125.

Romantic America . . . , 1927.

Now scarce, this is worth up to $50.

Houseworth, Thomas and Co.

Books illustrated by Houseworth as well as the Houseworth illustrated catalogues are of interest to collectors because of their subject—the American West—and the photographers represented. For example, the 1869 catalogue offers a selection of the mammoth-plate photographs of various western scenes, many of Yellowstone, drawn from the work of Weed, Watkins, and Muybridge. A good copy of *Sun Pictures of the Yo Semite Valley* (1874) with 44 mounted albumen prints has been priced by a dealer at $4,500. Most of the plates have been reduced from the mammoth photographs by C. L. Weed made a decade earlier.

Howitt, William and Mary

Ruined Abbeys and Castles of Great Britain and Ireland, 1862.

The 27 photographs used as illustrations include the work of Francis Bedford, Roger Fenton and others; a good copy is worth about $100.

Humphrey, Samuel D.

A System of Photography, 1849.

American Hand Book of the Daguerreotype, 1853.

This work went into numerous editions, and any early edition may be worth around $100.

Practical Manual of the Collodion Process.

We know that there was a second edition published in 1856; a copy of the third edition, published in 1857, has sold at auction for $95.

Humphrey's Journal of Photography

Founded as *The Daguerreian Journal* in 1850 by Samuel D. Humphrey, the title was changed to *Humphrey's Journal of Photography and the Heliographic Arts and Sciences*, with volume 14, after publication had been briefly suspended betwen January and March, 1852. After absorbing the *American Journal of Photography* in 1867, this journal itself ceased publication in July, 1870.

Hunt, Robert
A Popular Treatise on the Art of Photography, 1841.
Researches on Light, 1844.
A dealer has asked $225 for an author's presentation copy of the second edition (1854).
Manual of Photography, 1851.
This is the second edition, for which a dealer has asked $150. Other editions command about the same price.

Hutchings, James Mason
Scenes of Wonder and Curiosity in California, 1861.

Illustrated London News
With the issue of October, 1912, this British periodical was the first to establish a regular rotogravure section.

International Photography Yearbook
The British counterpart to *U.S. Camera*, an individual issue may be worth around $15.

Jackson, Clarence S.
Picturemaker of the Old West, William H. Jackson, 1947.
One dealer asks $80 for the first edition of this biography, which contains about 400 illustrations from photographs.

Jackson, William Henry
Yellowstone's Scenic Wonders, 1871.
One of two presentation volumes, the second issued in 1873 under a different title, *Photographs of the Yellowstone National Park . . .* , with 41 folio-size photographs. The latter has brought $5,750 at auction in New York. However, other Jackson collections of photo-views have brought, to date, only about $100. These include his *Rocky Mountain Scenery* (c. 1885) with 12 full-page Albertypes.

Journal of the Franklin Institute
The issue of April, 1839, contains the first technical account of a photographic process (the calotype) to be published in the United States. It also includes some description of the daguerreotype, yet the exact process remained secret for another five months. A copy of this issue has sold at auction for $100.

Journal of the Photographic Society of London
The world's most enduring publication in the field of photography. It was founded in 1853, and the first volume appeared the following year. After 1859 it was titled *The Photographic Journal*. In 1865 it became a weekly, and it now appears under the title of *The British Journal*.

Kertesz, Andre
Enfants, 1933.
King, Clarence
Three Lakes: Marian, Lall and Jan and How They Were Named, 1870.
Illustrated with photographs by Timothy H. O'Sullivan.
King, Thomas Starr
A Vacation in the Sierras . . . , 1862.
The White Hills, 1866.

Kneeland, Samuel
The Wonders of the Yosemite Valley, and of California, 1871.
Containing ten original mounted photographs, some believed to be by Muybridge.
Kodakery
"A journal for amateur photographers" which began publication in September, 1913, and continued until 1932. Issued by the Eastman Kodak Company of Rochester, New York, this publication is now a valuable source of information on popular styles in photography and on types of equipment—including cameras—used in the past. A complete run may be worth $100. A second series began in 1943 and runs to the present.
Kouwenhoven, John A.
The Columbia Historical Portrait of New York, 1953.
A fine copy which is still in its dust jacket might be worth around $50.
Krausz, Sigmund
Street Types of Chicago . . . , 1892.
Street Types of Great American Cities, 1896.
Although the subjects were generally posed, the photographs do show authentic street personalities, including types which have disappeared, such as the beer man, the scissors grinder, and the match-boy.

Lumiere. See *La Lumiere.*
Land of the Free
A collection of photographs published in 1938, most from the files of the Farm Security Administration, with a commentary by Archibald MacLeish.
Lange, Dorothea
An American Exodus: A Record of Human Erosion, 1939.
A study of the displaced American tenant farmer, written in collaboration with Paul Taylor. In dust jacket, this may be worth up to $80.
Langlois, Jean Charles
Souvenirs de la Guerre de Crimee, 1855.
Lea, M. Carey
A Manual of Photography . . . , 1868.
LeGray, Gustave
A Practical Treatise on Photography, 1850.
This is a translation from the French first edition published in the same year; the French title is *Traite pratique de photographie sur papier et sur verre.*
Lerebours, N. P.
A Treatise on Photography . . . Appertaining to the Daguerreotype, 1843.
This is the first edition of this manual in English, translated from the French by J. Egerton and published in London.
LeSecq, Henri
Amiens: Recueil de Photographies, 1852.
Paris Photographique, 1852.
Life
A weekly periodical issued between November, 1936, and December, 1972. The first issue contained a lead picture-story and cover by Margaret Bourke-White on a Montana mining town. Founded by the publishing tycoon Henry Luce to provide a "show book of the world," *Life* gave employment to some of the most capable documentary photographers of the twentieth century and established new high standards for realistic photography. The earliest issues may be worth $5 each.

Litchfield, R. B.
Tom Wedgwood . . . , 1903.
Now rare, a book on the man who dabbled in photography 25 years before Niepce's experiments. A copy is worth around $40.

Look
A picture magazine founded by Gardner and John Cowles; the first issue appeared in January, 1937. *Look* helped initiate a journalistic approach which specialized more in photographic essays than in the straight reporting of the news.

La Lumiere
A French photographic journal, the source of a great deal of information on the early days of the daguerreotype, published from 1851 until 1870.

Maddox, Richard Leach
In the September, 1871, issue of the *British Journal of Photography*, an article by Leach described his new dry-plate process.

Magic Buff
A technical photographic manual which, in its November, 1850, issue, carried the announcement by Levi L. Hill that he had succeeded in producing a daguerreotype in natural color.

Man Ray
Champs delicieux: album de photographes, 1922.
A collection of Man Ray's innovative "rayographs."

Mapes, J. J., Editor
A Full Description of the Daguerreotype Process . . . , *Extracted from the American Repository*, 1840.
Apparently this was the only separate edition of Daguerre's original manual to be published in the United States.

Marcy, L. J.
The Sciopticon Manual, 1877.
Explaining lantern projection and describing the apparatus which was required.

Maxwell, Marius
Stalking Big Game with a Camera in Equatorial Africa, 1924.
With 113 plates from photographs taken by the author—published in limited edition—a signed copy could be worth up to $300.

Mayhew, Henry
London Labour and the London Poor, 1851.
Containing woodcuts copied from daguerreotypes made by Richard Beard and thus very likely the earliest social documentary based on photographs. A dealer asks $300 for the three-volume first edition.

Mechanics Magazine
For the year 1839, issues dated between February 9 and December 14 containing articles on photography.

Miller, Francis T., Editor
A Photographic History of the Civil War, 1911.
A ten-volume work consisting of an outstanding collection of wartime photographs including the work of Mathew B. Brady's crew of photographers and Alexander Gardner, published by E. B. Eaton from the contents of the Ordway-Rand collection. A dealer has asked $135 for a set in close-to-mint condition. There is also the 1907 publication, *Original Photographs*, with 211 halftones of superior quality, sometimes available at $35.

Moholy-Nagy, Laszlo
Malerei, Photographie, Film, 1925.

This book helped initiate the era of modern scientific photography. It was first published in English in a revised edition in 1928 under the title *The New Vision*. (Benedetta's) *The Street Markets of London*, 1936. Illustrated with Moholy-Nagy's photographs and with a foreword by him; the 64 halftone plates are printed in sepia. This book is an early example of modern photo-reportage, and a dealer may want $225 for it.

Morgan, Barbara
Martha Graham, Sixteen Dances in Photographs, 1941.
An autographed copy has brought $60.

Muir, John
My First Summer in the Sierra, 1911.
With 12 photographic illustrations by Herbert Gleason, this book is worth around $50.

Muybridge, Eadweard
The Pacific Coast of Central America and Mexico . . . , 1876.
Illustrated by Muybridge, this work was apparently issued in a very small edition, and it is possible that *each* volume was different.
Photographic Studies of Central America, 1877.
The Horse in Motion, 1882.
By J. D. B. Stillman, with the plates by Muybridge, a first edition of this innovative work commands around $150 or more.
Animal Locomotion, 1887.
A monumental work, in eleven volumes, containing 781 collotype plates from photographs by Muybridge made in the course of his experiments on animals in action. A single portfolio (99 plates) has brought $1,000 at auction, a single plate, $200.
Animals in Motion, 1899.
This is the reprint of *Animal Locomotion*, and it also is a much sought-after work, with third and even fourth impressions commanding over $100.

Nadar (G. F. Tournachon)
The September 5, 1886, issue of *Le Journal Illustre* contains what might be the world's first photo-interview, combining the answers to questions posed by Nadar (pere) with a series of photographs taken at the same time by the son. The subject of this first interview was the aged but lively chemist M. E. Chevreul.

Nares, Captain Sir G. S.
Narrative of a Voyage to the Polar Sea, 1878.
In two volumes, illustrated with six Woodburytypes, this is the account of the British voyage begun in 1876. A dealer may ask $200.

Natkin, Marcel
Photographing the Nude, 1937.
Only 38 pages but with 22 illustrations—eight by Man Ray. This pamphlet is worth $50.

New York Daily Graphic. See *Daily Graphic*.

Niepce, Isidore
Historique de la decouverte improprement nomme daguerreotype, 1841.

Nordhoff, Charles
California: A Book for Travellers and Settlers, 1873.

Notman, William
Portraits of British Americans, 1865.
Published in Montreal, this work has five mounted photographs and, if in good condition, it may be worth over $50.

The Canadian Handbook and Tourist's Guide, 1866.

If all ten photographs by Notman are still present, a copy, even one somewhat foxed, might be worth $125.

Oakley, R. B.

The Pagoda of Hallibeed (Mysore), 1859.

There should be 56 photographic views still present.

Ogawa, K.

A Photographic Album of the Japan-China War (1905).

As a leading Japanese photographer, Ogawa has been compared with Mathew B. Brady of the United States. A dealer has priced this folio of wartime collotypes by the Japanese master of the collotype at $250.

Ogle, Thomas

Our English Lakes, Mountains and Waterfalls, 1864.

The text is by William Wordsworth and the photographs by Ogle. A copy bound in leather has been priced at $100.

Old Glasgow. See Annan, Thomas.

O'Sullivan, T. H. and W. Bell

Photographs—of the United States—West of the 100th Meridian (*Seasons of 1871, 1872, & 1873*), n.d.

Philadelphia Photographer. See **Wilson, Edward L.**

Photograms of the Year

Published in London beginning in 1903, "a pictorial and literary record of the artistic photographic work of the year." The word "photogram," derived from the Greek, was invented by the editor in the belief, apparently, that it was a more accurate term than "photography."

Photographic Art Journal

This was a monthly journal edited by H. H. Snelling beginning in January 1851. In 1854 the name was changed to *The Photographic and Fine Art Journal*. Its first issue contained the announcement that Levi L. Hill had succeeded in producing an image in natural color on the daguerreotype plate. And in April, 1853 it became the first American journal to employ photographs for illustration by publishing one of Whipple's crystallotypes. Among the especially interesting articles to appear in the *Journal* was an illustrated account of the Anthony "factory" —shop or studio—for the processing of daguerreotype plates at Daguerreville, New York, which appeared in the July, 1854 issue. The first announcement of the invention of the ambrotype appeared in its pages, in December, 1854. The *Journal* ceased publication in 1860. Volume 1, No. 1 has sold at auction for $130.

Photographic Journal. See *Journal of the Photographic Society of London*.

Photographic News

A London weekly published between 1858 and 1908 and then incorporated into *The Amateur Photographer*. This was the first independent British journal devoted to photography. Its issue of October 22, 1858, contained information on Fox Talbot's new process of "photoglyphic engraving," and the November 12th issue contained a single example. Nine scattered volumes have brought $300 at auction.

Photographic Notes

Begun as a monthly, with its first issue appearing in January, 1856, it had become a fortnightly by September of the same year. The editor was Thomas Sutton. The last issue appeared, in London, in December, 1867.

Photographic Times

This publication began in London as a fortnightly in 1861. At the end of four years the title was appropriated by the Scovill Manufacturing Company of Waterbury, Connecticut, for its own journal, the full title for which was *The Photographic Times and American Photographer.*

Piot, Eugene

Italie Monumentale, 1851.

This seems to have been the first French book to appear illustrated with photographs.

Plumbe's Popular Magazine

An American journal of photography published irregularly between 1846 and 1847 by the Plumbe National Daguerrian Gallery founded by John Plumbe, Jr.

Pouncy, John

Dorsetshire Photographically Illustrated, 1857.

Published in four parts, in two oblong folios, with 39 and 40 plates respectively, this may have been the first English publication to be illustrated with photolithographic views.

Price, Lake

Manual of Photographic Manipulation, 1858.

According to Gernsheim, this was the first manual published which offered aesthetic as well as technical advice to the photographer. A copy has sold at auction for $160.

Queen's Bible, 1862. See **Frith, Francis.**

Rejlander, Oscar G. See **Darwin, Charles.**

Reports of the Juries

A four-volume publication issued in 1851 reporting on the London Crystal Palace Exhibition and containing 155 calotypes printed by Henneman and Malone.

Riis, Jacob A.

How the Other Half Lives, 1890.

The illustrated first edition may be worth $60.

The London first edition (1891) has been priced at $75.

The Children of the Poor, 1892.

Battle with the Slum, 1902.

With its 92 halftones and the frontispiece gravure of Theodore Roosevelt, this may be worth $50.

Robinson, Henry Peach

Pictorial Effect in Photography, 1869.

This was a highly successful handbook by the ultimate master of combination printing.

Art and Practice of Silver Printing, 1881.

Written in collaboration with W. Abney, contains an original photograph mounted as frontispiece. The London first edition along with a copy of the American first has brought $90 at auction.

Picture Making by Photography, 1884.

Recently a copy of the second edition was priced by a dealer at $90.

The Studio and What to Do in It, 1891.

A rare first-edition copy has sold at $75.

The Photographic Studio, 1905.

Root, Marcus A.
The Camera and the Pencil; or the Heliographic Art, 1864.
Even a poor copy sells for $100.

Russell, Andrew J.
The Great West Illustrated, 1869.
Rare.The result of an ambitious private project undertaken for the Union Pacific Railroad, apparently it was never offered for general sale to the public. It contains 50 photographs of Imperial size.
Sun Pictures of Rocky Mountain Scenery, 1870.
With a text by F. V. Hayden, it contains 30 albumen prints, each mounted, which are sometimes offered separately at $50 apiece. The photographs are reduced copies of the plates in the preceding item. One dealer asks $1,350 for this book, which was one of the most popular ever to be issued showing western scenes.

Ryder, James F.
Voightlander and I in Pursuit of Shadow Catching, 1902.
Recently sold at auction for $85, this was an important source of some of the material used by Robert Taft in writing *Photography and the American Scene* (1938).

Saint-Victor, Niepce de
Recherces photographiques, 1855.
Traite pratique de gravure heliographique sur acier et sur verre, 1856.

Smith, Theophilos
Sheffield and its Neighborhood, 1865.
This brief work contains only 132 pages but there are 16 original photographs, each about 3½ by 4 inches. If the binding is in good condition it may be worth $100.

Smyth, C. Piazzi
Teneriffe, an Astronomer's Experiment, 1858.
With its 19 albumen stereograph photographs, this was the first book published with stereo illustrations; possibly worth $50.

Snelling, Henry Hunt
The History and Practice of the Art of Photography, 1849.
This is believed to be the first American book to cover the subject of photography in its many varied aspects, dealing primarily with the daguerreotype and yet providing some information on the production of the paper negative. A second edition appeared in 1850, a third in 1851, and a fourth in 1853.
A Dictionary of the Photographic Art, 1854.
An illustrated encyclopedia of photographic terms.
A Guide to the Whole Art of Photography, 1858.

Soule, John P.
The Wonders of Yosemite Valley and of California, 1872.
With its original photographs, a copy may be worth $150.

Steichen, Edward
The First Picture Book, 1930.
A copy in hardcover may be worth $125, even without the dust jacket.
(Thoreau's) *Walden,* 1936.
From the Limited Editions Club, signed by Steichen; now worth over $100. (There is also, among the many other editions, the more rare Boston Bibliophile edition of 1909 with photographs by H. W. Gleason, worth about $150.)
The Picture Garden Book and Gardener's Assistant, 1942.

The text is by Richard Pratt and the color photography by Steichen. This may be a "sleeper" among Steichen's works, worth possibly $50.

A Life in Photography, 1963.

With the color plates, which were not in the remaindered copies, worth $25.

Stereoscopic Magazine

Published from July, 1858 to February, 1865, illustrated with stereoscopic photographs.

Stieglitz, Alfred. See *American Photographer, Camera Notes,* and *Camera Work.*

Stieglitz Memorial Portfolio, 1864–1946, 1947

Folio, 62 pages and with 18 screen reproductions, limited to 1500 copies. The *Portfolio* is now worth $400.

Stillman. See **Muybridge, Eadweard.**

Stirling, William

Annals of the Artists of Spain, 1845.

Rare. Published in a limited edition of only 25 copies, and containing 66 calotypes furnished by Fox Talbot, the *Annals* is honored as the first art book illustrated with photographs.

Stone, Benjamin

Sir Benjamin Stone's Pictures (1906).

A two-volume record of English folkways, containing numerous country views, for which a dealer may ask $200.

Strand, Paul

Photographs of Mexico, 1940.

Time in New England, 1950.

Edited by Nancy Newhall; at auction this has brought $90, signed, $220.

Sun Artists, 1889-91

Photogravures representing "the artistic position in photography"; an English series, worth about $1,500 if complete.

Sutton, Thomas

A Dictionary of Photography, 1858.

Possibly the first dictionary of photography published in London and worth about $200.

Taft, Robert

Photography and the American Scene, 1938.

This book has recently brought $70.

Talbot, W. H. Fox

Some Account of the Art of Photogenic Drawing, 1839.

Extremely rare. A privately published brochure which, according to Helmut Gernsheim, was "the world's first separate publication on photography."

The Pencil of Nature, 1844-46

Extremely rare. One of the most important works in the history of photography. A first edition of 200 copies containing just five prints on chloride paper was later expanded to six installments with a total of 24 prints. Fox Talbot describes his discovery of the calotype process and provides illustrations from his own photographs. He explains to the possibly skeptical reader that "the plates in the present work are impressed by the agency of light alone, without any aid whatever from the artist's pencil. They are the sun pictures themselves, and not, as some persons have imagined, engravings in imitation." The 24 prints include still-lifes, landscapes, architectural vews, and views of statues, and there are some photographs of engravings. There are also the "photographic drawings" of botanical specimens and of lace. There are no portraits. It is believed that no more than a dozen copies of *The Pencil of Nature* exist today. In 1971 a copy sold at auction for $6,500; it is now worth $50,000.

Sun Pictures of Scotland, 1845.

Contains 23 calotypes by Talbot. A copy with the usual faded prints brought $3,000 in 1972 at auction in London.

Taunt, Henry W.

A New Map of the River Thames, 1886.

This is the scarce fifth edition, with its frontispiece photograph of Taunt with his wife, with the camera, on their houseboat. A copy believed to have been Taunt's own copy was sold at auction for $95. However, one dealer has offered a copy of the third edition (c. 1878) for $225. Taunt's book may be the first guidebook to be illustrated with photographs.

Tennyson, Alfred

The Idylls of the King. See **Cameron, Julia Margaret.**

Thomson, John

Antiquities of Cambodia, 1867.

This is the first of Thomson's photographic essays. It contains 16 albumen prints "taken on the spot." A copy has sold at auction for $6,400, to the surprise of the auction house, which had estimated that it might bring no more than $2,000.

Illustrations of China and Its People, 1873–74.

Four volumes, with 200 photographs; a major work which appeared in just one edition. A dealer asks $3,500.

The People of India, 1868–75.

Published in eight volumes and containing over 450 photographs by 14 photographers—including Thomson—this is, according to Helmut Gernsheim, the first large-scale ethnological work to be undertaken with photography.

Street Life in London, 1877–78.

Prepared in collaboration with A. Smith, this work was issued in six parts and contained 36 Woodburytypes. Each of these, only 4½ by 3½ inches, still mounted on the original card and with titles and borders in red ink, may now be worth $250. *Street Life* may be the earliest example of social documentation with photography.

Tissandier, Gaston

History and Handbook of Photography, 1877.

The translation from the French edited by J. Thomson, may be worth around $80.

Towler, J.

The Silver Sunbeam, 1864.

"A practical and theoretical textbook of photography," Towler's manual went into at least nine editions. It was also widely translated, and for around 20 years it remained an important handbook both for the amateur and the professional photographer. It is still available today, in facsimile.

Tripe, Captain L.

Photographic Views in Madura, 1858.

In four parts (volumes), of folio size, with large mounted photographs by the government photographer at Madras; a dealer asks $6,000.

291

Named after the Fifth Avenue address of the Little Galleries, this Photo-Secessionist publication appeared in a total of 12 issues in 1915 and 1916. The first nine, including two double issues, offered as one lot, brought $3,500 at auction, and a complete set sold for $5,800.

Ulmann, Doris

A Portrait Gallery of American Editors, 1925.

One of the 375 copies published by William Rudge, containing 43 gravures, all in fine condition, has been offered for around $300.

Roll, Jordan, Roll, 1933.

With a text by Julia Peterkin; may be worth over $35.

Handicrafts of the Southern Highlands, 1937.

With 58 gravures by Ulmann, published by the Russell Sage Foundation, a very good copy might sell for $60. This provides an example of the fine photography which can sometimes be found in an unexpected source.

United States Magazine and Democratic Review

The issue of November, 1839 contains an important early article titled "The Daguerreotype."

U.S. Camera

An American publication, edited by Tom J. Maloney, begun in 1938. This annual contains important reports on current photographic trends and examples of the work of various eminent photographers. Among the photographers whose work appeared in some of the early issues were Bourke-White, Genthe, Hine, Morgan, and Steichen. The 1948 issue published prints by Jacob Riis which lent new stature to the work of this turn-of-the-century photographer. A full run of the first 25 issues has sold at auction for over $200. An individual early issue may possibly be worth $10.

Vacquerie, Auguste and Charles Hugo

Victor Hugo Album, 1854.

Vogel, Hermann

Handbook of the Practice and Art of Photography . . . , 1871.

This is the translation by Edward Moelling, adapting the work to American use.

Chemistry of Light and Photography, 1875.

The first American edition, with its mounted Woodburytype from Rutherford's original negative showing the moon, has brought $55 at auction.

Wall, Edward J.

Dictionary of Photography, 1889.

Walton, Izaak and Charles Cotton

The Compleat Angler, 1888.

The Lea and Dove edition, with 54 photogravures, of which 27 are by P. H. Emerson, in two volumes. A copy signed by the editor, R. B. Marston, is worth up to $2,000.

Warren, John C.

Remarks on Some Fossil Impressions . . . Connecticut River, 1854.

Only 54 pages but containing a single inserted folding salt print; thus, the first scientific American book illustrated with a photograph. It was published the same year as *Homes of American Statesmen* (q.v.), and recently sold at auction for $200.

Watkins, Carleton E.

Yosemite Book, 1868.

The report of the California State Geological Survey under Josiah D. Whitney, containing 50 of the photographs made for the Survey by Watkins. The first edition was limited to 250 copies. Separated from the book, the individual albumen prints, just over 8 by 6 inches, on the original card mount, have brought $150 and more at auction.

Bentley's Hand-Book of the Pacific Coast, 1884.

An edition containing 31 Watkins New Boudoir Series cabinet photos, 5 by 8 inches. One dealer asks $3,000.

Weed, C. L.

Sun Pictures in Yosemite, 1874.

Most of the plates have been reduced from photographs believed to have been made by Weed.

Weegee (Arthur Fellig)

Naked City, 1945.

A dealer asks $60; for an inscribed copy, $75.

Weegee's People, 1946.

From a dealer, $25.

Weston, Edward

Photography, 1934.

An early pamphlet containing an important statement of Weston's credo as a photographer.

California and the West, 1940.

With its 96 photographs in good condition, even a somewhat worn copy may be worth $70.

(Whitman's) *Leaves of Grass*, 1942.

Published by the Limited Editions Club in two volumes with slipcase, signed by Weston; a copy today may be worth $375.

Whittock, N.

Photogenic Drawing Made Easy: A Manual of Photography, n.d.

Although not dated, this work was probably published in 1839 and if so would be the world's first manual of photography. Daguerre's work appears to have been unknown to this author, who confines himself to describing the calotype process devised by Fox Talbot.

Williams, James Leon

The Home and Haunts of Shakespeare, 1892.

A limited edition of 300 sets with five portfolios; the plates include 45 folio-size photogravures (another copy, for 1894, has 30). This collection has sold at auction for $1,100.

Wilson, Edward L., Editor

Philadelphia Photographer

Established in 1864 as a publication of the Philadelphia Society. After *Humphrey's Journal* ceased publication in 1870, this journal became the country's leading photographic magazine. Volumes I through XXV were published under the original name. In 1888, however, the name was changed to *Wilson's Photographic Magazine*, and it continued through Volume LI in 1914, when it merged with *Camera*. A defective copy of Volume 8 (Nos. 85-96) missing some photographs has sold at auction for $200.

Wilson's Quarter Century in Photography, 1887.

In good condition, this would bring around $85 from a dealer.

Wright, Richard

12 Million Black Voices, 1941.

Containing more than 80 photogravures from the collection of the Farm Security Administration; a good copy brings $40.

Selected Bibliography

Ackerman, Carl W. *George Eastman.* Boston, 1930.

Braive, Michel F. *The Photography: A Social History.* New York, 1966.

Buckland, Gail. *Reality Recorded, Early Documentary Photography.* Greenwich, Connecticut, 1974.

Burgess, N. G. *The Photograph Manual; a Practical Treatise . . . Carte de Visite Process, and the Method of Taking Stereoscope Pictures . . .* (8th edition). New York, 1862.

Camera Work: A Critical Anthology. Edited with introduction by Jonathan Green. Aperture, Millerton, New York, 1973.

Darrah, William Culp. *Stereo Views: A History of Stereographs in America and their Collection.* Gettysburg, Pennsylvania, 1964.

Estabrooke, Edward M. *The Ferrotype and How to Make It* (facsimile of the 1872 edition with a new introduction by Eugene Ostroff). Hastings-on-Hudson, New York, 1972.

Feininger, Andreas. *The Complete Photographer.* Englewood Cliffs, New Jersey, 1971.

Gernsheim, Helmut, in collaboration with Alison Gernsheim. *The History of Photography, From the Earliest Use of the Camera Obscura up to 1914.* London, 1955.

————. *A Concise History of Photography.* New York, 1965.

————. *The Recording Eye—A Hundred Years of Great Events as Seen by the Camera, 1839–1939,* New York, 1960.

Gilbert, George. *Collecting Photographica/The Image and Equipment of the First Hundred Years of Photography.* New York, 1976.

Greenhill, Ralph. *Early Photography in Canada.* Toronto, 1965.

Hill, Levi L. *A Treatise on Daguerreotypes; the Whole Art Made Easy . . .* Parts 1 and 2, with Part 3 by W. McCartney, Jr. Lexington, New York, 1950.

Howarth-Loomes, B. E. C. *Victorian Photography: An Introduction for Collectors and Connoisseurs.* New York, 1974.

Jenkins, Harold F. *Two Points of View—The History of the Parlor Stereoscope.* Elmira, New York, 1957.

Jones, Bernard E., Editor. *Encyclopedia of Photography* (facsimile of the 1911 edition with a new introduction by Peter C. Bunnell and Robert Sobieszek, and new picture portfolio). New York, 1974.

Jussim, Estelle. *Visual Communication and the Graphic Arts/Photographic Technologies in the Nineteenth Century.* New York and London, 1974.

Lea, M. Carey. *A Manual of Photography* (2nd edition revised). Philadelphia, 1871.

Lewis, Steven, with James McQuaid and David Tait. *Photography/Source & Resource.* (Turnip Press) State College, Pennsylvania, 1973.

Lyons, Nathan, Editor. *Photographers on Photography.* Englewood Cliffs, New Jersey, 1966.

Mathews, O. *Early Photographs and Early Photographers.* London, 1973.

Morgan, Willard D., Editor. *The Encyclopedia of Photography,* New York, 1949.

Naef, Weston J., in collaboration with James N. Wood, with an essay by Therese Thau Heymar. *Era of Exploration: The Rise of Landscape Photography in the American West, 1860–1885.* Boston, 1975.

Newhall, Beaumont. *The Daguerreotype in America.* New York, 1968.

———. *The History of Photography.* New York, 1949.

——— with Nancy Newhall, Editors. *Masters of Photography.* New York, 1958.

Pollack, Peter. *The Picture History of Photography—from the Earliest Beginning to the Present Day.* New York, 1958.

Rinhart, Floyd and Marion. *American Daguerreian Art.* New York, 1967.

———. *American Miniature Case Art.* New York and London, 1969.

Rodger, H. J. *Twenty-three Years under a Sky-Light.* Hartford, 1873.

Root, M. A. *The Camera and the Pencil; or the Heliographic Art . . .* Philadelphia, 1864.

Rudisill, Richard. *Mirror Image.* Albuquerque, New Mexico, 1971.

Shafran, Alexander. *Restoration and Photographic Copying . . .* New York, 1967.

Snelling, Henry H. *The History and Practice of the Art of Photography* (4th edition revised). New York, 1853.

Swedlund, Charles. *Photography: A Handbook of History, Materials, and Processes.* New York, 1974.

Taft, Robert. *Photography and the American Scene: A Social History, 1839–1889.* New York, 1938.

Time-Life Library of Photography. New York, v.d.

Tissandier, Gaston. *A History and Handbook of Photography.* (Scovill) New York, 1877.

Towler, J., M.D. *The Silver Sunbeam* (reprint of the 1864 edition with an introduction by Beaumont Newhall). Hastings-on-Hudson, New York, 1969.

Tucker, Anne, Editor. *The Woman's Eye.* New York, 1973.

Waldack, Charles, with Peter Neff, Jr. *Treatise of Photography on Collodion . . .* Cincinnati, 1857

Welling, William. *Collectors Guide to Nineteenth Century Photographs.* New York and London, 1976.

Index

This index does not include the listings on pages 17-21, 22-27, 30-77, 79-90, and 234-258 or the Glossary on pages 91-176.